T0301737

Navigating the New Political Economy in Southeast Asia

Perspectives from Japan, Taiwan and the Region

Series on Regional Dynamics of the Indo-Pacific

Print ISSN: 2811-0471
Online ISSN: 2811-048X

Series Editors: Alan Hao Yang *(National Chengchi University, Taiwan)*
Masahiro Matsumura *(St. Andrew's University, Japan)*

Published:

SERIES ON REGIONAL DYNAMICS OF THE INDO-PACIFIC VOLUME 1

Navigating the New Political Economy in Southeast Asia

Perspectives from Japan, Taiwan and the Region

Alan Hao Yang

National Chengchi University, Taiwan

Masahiro Matsumura

St. Andrew's University, Japan

World Scientific

NEW JERSEY · LONDON · SINGAPORE · BEIJING · SHANGHAI · HONG KONG · TAIPEI · CHENNAI · TOKYO

Published by

World Scientific Publishing Co. Pte. Ltd.

5 Toh Tuck Link, Singapore 596224

USA office: 27 Warren Street, Suite 401-402, Hackensack, NJ 07601

UK office: 57 Shelton Street, Covent Garden, London WC2H 9HE

Library of Congress Cataloging-in-Publication Data
Names: Yang, Alan Hao, editor. | Matsumura, Masahiro, 1963–   editor.
Title: Navigating the new political economy in Southeast Asia : perspectives from Japan,
    Taiwan and the region / Alan Hao Yang, National Chengchi University, Taiwan,
    Masahiro Matsumura, St. Andrew's University, Japan.
Description: New Jersey : World Scientific, [2023] | Series: Series on regional dynamics of
    the Indo-Pacific ; Vol. 1 | Includes bibliographical references and index.
Identifiers: LCCN 2022040079 | ISBN 9789811265693 (hardcover) |
    ISBN 9789811265709 (ebook) | ISBN 9789811265716 (ebook other)
Subjects: LCSH: Southeast Asia--Economic conditions. | Southeast Asia--Economic integration. |
    Regionalism--Southeast Asia. | Southeast Asia--Foreign economic relations.
Classification: LCC HC441 .N38 2023 | DDC 330.959--dc23/eng/20221130
LC record available at https://lccn.loc.gov/2022040079

British Library Cataloguing-in-Publication Data
A catalogue record for this book is available from the British Library.

For any available supplementary material, please visit
https://www.worldscientific.com/worldscibooks/10.1142/13124#t=suppl

Desk Editors: Sanjay Varadharajan/Kura Sunaina/Thaheera Althaf

Typeset by Stallion Press
Email: enquiries@stallionpress.com

Printed in Singapore

About the Editors

Alan Hao Yang is the Executive Director of Taiwan-Asia Exchange Foundation (TAEF). He also serves as the Executive Director of the Center for Southeast Asian Studies (CSEAS) and the Director of Chinese Language Center (CLC) at National Chengchi University, Taiwan. He teaches at the Graduate Institute of East Asian Studies (GIEAS) as a distinguished professor of Southeast Asia studies, offering courses related to regionalism and Sino-Southeast Asian relations. Dr. Yang engages in track II diplomacy in the Asia-Pacific. Dr. Yang has been nominated as a senior fellow of George HW Bush Foundation for US-China Relations in the United States since 2021 and a non-resident fellow of China Desk of the Reconnaissance Research in Kuwait since the July of 2021. His research interests cover ASEAN regionalism, disaster governance, border politics, and resistance politics in Southeast Asia. Dr. Yang has published more than 100 publications in English and Chinese, focusing on China-ASEAN relations, international relations of Southeast Asia, security governance and disaster preparedness as well as the international political economy in the Asia-Pacific in international refereed journals, such as *Pacific Affairs, Pacific Review, Politics and Governance, Issues & Studies, Journal of Asian Public Policy,* and *Journal of Human Values*. His latest co-edited book is *When East Asia Meets Southeast Asia: Presence and Connectedness in Transformation Revisited* published by World Scientific Publishing in 2022.

Masahiro Matsumura is Professor of International Politics at St. Andrew's University (Momoyama Gakuin Daigaku) in Osaka and a non-resident

Senior Research Fellow of the Research Institute for Peace and Security in Tokyo. He specializes in national security studies with his academic training in international political economy and development. Dr. Matsumura received his LLB. from Kwansei Gakuin University in 1986, M.A. in political science from Ohio University in 1987, and Ph.D. in government and politics from the University of Maryland at College Park in 1992. He experienced visiting fellowships at Harvard University, Brookings Institution, Heritage Foundation, Cato Institute, NDU Institute for National Strategic Studies, and NCCU Institute of International Relations. Among his extensive publications, Dr. Matsumura's articles in English appear in journals, such as *Survival, Defense Analysis, Issues & Studies, International Journal of China Studies, International Journal of Korean Unification Studies, Austral,* and *Jebat,* as well as many op-eds in *Project Syndicate, Japan Times, Taipei Times, and Nikkei Asia,* among others. His recent co-edited books include *Defense Policy And Strategy Development: Coordination Between Japan and Taiwan* by World Scientific Publishing.

About the Contributors

Akio Egawa is a Professor of development economics and international political economy at St. Andrew's University (Momoyama Gakuin Daigaku). He holds a master's degree from the SOAS University of London. He worked as a government officer in Cabinet Office of Government of Japan until 2014 and dealt with coordinating international and bilateral economic consultations, writing annual report on world economy, and coordinating official development assistance.

Ivy Kwek is a Malaysian researcher who works on geopolitical and regional security issues in Asia Pacific, with a particular focus on Southeast Asia. She was a recipient of the Taiwan Fellowship 2021 and spent a year as a Visiting Fellow at the Institute of International Relations, National Chengchi University. Prior to that, she served as a policy aide to the Deputy Defence Minister of Malaysia (2018–2020) and has had extensive experience working with think tanks and international organizations. She is currently the Fellow (China) for the International Crisis Group.

Jeremy Huai-Che Chiang holds an M.Phil. in international relations and politics from the University of Cambridge and a B.A in diplomacy from National Chengchi University. His research interests focus on the politics and political economy of East Asia. He is the author of *The Origins of Modern Philippine Politics* (in Chinese; Rive Gauche Publishing House) and co-author of *Understanding the Economy of Southeast Asia Through Maps* (in Chinese; Business Weekly Publications) and has also published research articles in journals, such as the *International Journal of Taiwan Studies*.

Karl Chee Leong Lee is a Senior Lecturer at the Institute of China Studies (ICS), Faculty of Arts and Social Sciences, University of Malaya, and Expert Advisor to Market Research Future. He is a specialist on Taiwan's soft power and quasi-state relations with Southeast Asia.

Mark Bryan Manantan is the Director of Cybersecurity and Critical Technologies at the Pacific Forum in Honolulu, Hawaii. At the Forum, he currently leads the US Technology and Security partnerships with Japan, Australia, Taiwan, and South Korea as well as the Digital ASEAN Initiative that focuses on cyber-capacity building, artificial intelligence, foreign interference, and space diplomacy. He is also the host of Pacific Forum's official podcast, the Indo-Pacific Current.

Roger Chi-feng Liu is an Associate Professor of international politics with the Department of Social Sciences at FLAME University, where he also serves as the chair of the Center for South and Southeast Asia Studies (CSSAS). Professor Liu earned his Ph.D. in political science from the University of South Carolina, and his research areas span political geography, geopolitics, armed conflicts, great power politics, India in the Indo-Pacific, and the politics of China. He is also the recipient of 2021's Taiwan Studies Project in India, a national research project funded by the Ministry of Education of Taiwan to promote studies in social sciences and humanities between Taiwan and foreign countries.

Ruei-Lin Yu is currently an Associate Professor and the Director of Graduate Institute of Strategy Study at the NDU, ROC (Taiwan). He is leading the highest military research and study institute in Taiwan and is also responsible for teaching high-level cadres from several different countries with domestic high-rank (O5-O6) officers. His study field includes international relations, international law of the sea, national security, social theories, and PLA studies.

Sadamasa Oue is a retired Lieutenant General (LTG) of the Japan Air Self-Defense Force (JASDF) and currently serves as a Consulting Senior Fellow and the Group Head of the International Security Order, Institute of Geoeconomics. His military career includes being Commandant of the

Air Staff College and Commander of the Northern Air Defense Command and he retired in August 2017 as Commander of Air Materiel Command. LTG Oue earned his Master of Public Administration from the J. F. Kennedy School of Government, Harvard University, in 1997 and Master of National Security Strategy from the National War College, National Defense University of the U.S.A. in 2002. Between July 2019 and June 2021, he served as a Senior Fellow at the Harvard Asia Center.

Yoshiaki Ozawa is a Professor of accounting, with a focus on auditing, at Osaka's St. Andrew's University (Momoyama Gakuin Daigaku). He received his master's in professional accounting from Martin J. Whitman School of Management at Syracuse University and Ph.D. in accounting from the Kwansei Gakuin University.

Acknowledgment

This book is a joint project, led by Professor Masahiro Matsumura and Professor Alan Hao Yang, between St. Andrew's University in Japan and National Chengchi University in Taiwan. A joint research team of St. Andrew's University and National Chengchi University has organized four workshops, both in-person and online format, presenting the findings of all team members. The manuscript has been sent, reviewed, and accepted by World Scientific Publishing, an international publisher based in Singapore. The editors on behalf of all chapter authors would like to express their gratitude to both St. Andrew's University and the Institute of International Relations at National Chengchi University for the kind endorsement and support to publish this collective effort. In particular, without the long-term generosity of St. Andrew's University, this intellectual product may not have been realized.

This publication is a product of the collaborative project (21REN283) at Japan's St. Andrew's University (Momoyama Gakuin Daigaku) Research Institute. The project consists of St. Andrew's Japanese members (Masahiro Matsumura, Akio Egawa, Yoshiaki Ozawa, Sadamasa Oue), Taiwanese members (Alan Hao Yang, Rosa Sun, and Linjun Wu), and non-members. The chapters by these members are results of the project.

Contents

Chapter 1

Introduction: Delineating Driving Forces for New Political Economy in Greater Southeast Asia

Masahiro Matsumura and Alan Hao Yang

Introduction

Southeast Asia is embedded in the regional context of the Indo-Pacific, and the dynamics of its political economy have long been structured by the overlapping power struggles of the Indo-Pacific (Doyle and Rumley 2019; Ciorciari and Tsutsui 2021). The strategic currents of the Indo-Pacific are changing rapidly, mainly affected by three structural determinants, which further trigger the changing faces of political economy in Southeast Asia. In recent years, the first structural determinant is the strategic competition between the United States and China, which is also a major power struggle at the structural level of the international system (Shambaugh 2020). Beijing's long-term wrestling with Washington reflects the challenge imposed by a revisionist power, China, against the *status quo* Hegemon, the United States. From the bilateral trade fiction to the trade and technology war focused on espionage, the bilateral tension has been even escalated to geopolitical rivalry.

Since 2013, after Xi Jinping took power and initiated the Belt and Road Initiative (BRI), China has moved westward along its ancient Silk Road through Central Asia to the European continent. By connecting these countries via investment and infrastructure projects, China has looped regional countries in need of its economic presence and assistance (Lampton *et al.* 2020), and then challenged the global leadership of the United States. The rising influence of China's economy has become more and more comprehensive in its neighboring countries, particularly Southeast Asia (Strangio 2020). After 2017 when U.S. President Donald Trump took office, Washington's China policy changed, leading to the U.S.–China trade war and strategic competition. With the start of Joe Biden's Presidency in 2021, the U.S. has been maintaining the competitive stance against China. The tension between the U.S. and China has also caused political-economic changes in the Indo-Pacific region, compelling regional countries to take either side as well as the reorientation of supply chains, etc., which in turn impacted Southeast Asia (Lin, Bonny *et al.* 2021; Stromseth 2021).

The second structural determinant is the continuous strengthening of multilateralism or international cooperation in the Indo-Pacific. This is consequent on U.S. initiatives in multilateralism and emerging international strategic arrangements in countering with the confrontation with China, such as Quadrilateral Security Dialogue (QUAD) or Australia U.K., and U.S., new security partnership (AUKUS). On the other hand, to defend their respective national interests, Japan, India, and Australia have also stood up to take active middle-power diplomacy in responding to the changing dynamics caused by U.S.–China rivalry (Ciorciari and Tsutsui 2021; Malhotra 2022), shouldering some responsibility in stabilizing the Indo-Pacific region. Their regional strategies and policies have been advocated by Southeast Asian countries in recent years that facilitate the growth of the regional stability.

The third structural determinant has happened more recently. That is, Russia's sudden invasion of Ukraine in February 2022 will cause a profound impact on the world politics and the Indo-Pacific region under the condition of the weakening influence of the United States in Indo-Pacific security. Without clear and immediate impact on Southeast Asia so far, Indo-Pacific countries have been highly concerned about the resultant uncertainty of peace and stability and, more specifically, with possible intensification of China's aggressive behavior in the South China Sea and with the present danger of its aggression against Taiwan.

The impact of these three determinants on Southeast Asia should not be overlooked. First of all, amid the U.S.–China rivalry, most of the significantly inferior-in-power Southeast Asian countries have been forced to take a side at the expense of national interests. Consequently, hedging strategy is the only choice for ASEAN and its members, yet without guaranteeing strategic certainty. Second, Japan, India, and Australia will booster their collaboration with ASEAN and its member countries, involving a good potential to benefit them. Third, most ASEAN countries during the Ukraine war, at least up to September 2022, did not condemn Russia or impose sanction against it, except Singapore. A new post-war geopolitical configuration may dilute ASEAN and its members' international influence.

In addition to the aforementioned three structural factors, there are also three constant factors worth mentioning for the stable development of Southeast Asia.

First, for a steadily growing Southeast Asia, Japan's role as a regional stabilizer and reliable partner has been crucial for decades (Kaplan and Mushakoji 1976). Since its providing of reparations to Southeast Asian countries in the post war era, Japan began to implement its heart-to-heart diplomacy following the Fukuda Doctrine in 1977. Japan's ideas, systems, and even its role as the thought leader have been valued by Southeast Asian countries. For example, four chapters included in this book on infrastructure development (by Akio Egawa), Japanese capitalism and accounting systems (by Masahiro Matsumura and Yoshiaki Ozawa), technology-led and knowledge-based economy (by Akio Egawa), and data governance (by Mark Bryan Manantan) can be regarded as important examples and features of Southeast Asian trust toward Japan.

In addition, almost every Japanese prime minister has launched his signature Asian strategy in general or Southeast Asia policy in particular. More recently, the "Free and Open Indo-Pacific" vision of Prime Minister Abe in his second term and the subsequent polices had aimed at continuing Japan's Official Development Aid as the policy tool to facilitate his flagship foreign policy toward ASEAN and the Indo-Pacific region that even reached out to the farthest east of Africa. Now Abe's vision and policy has charted an important regional architecture for the confluence of the Indian and Pacific Oceans. Notably, Japan hopes to contribute to the urgent needs of human security and development of the region, which has an important impact on the political and economic development of the Southeast Asian Community and the ASEAN countries.

It is worth noting that, in addition to the overall regional strategy for ASEAN and the regional community, Japan's influence and assistance to respective countries in Southeast Asia are of strategic importance. For example, Japan has actively hoped to provide high-quality infrastructure since the implementation of the New Tokyo Strategy in the Mekong Subregion or even earlier. The strategy enables Southeast Asian countries with urgent needs to obtain quality infrastructure, thereby enabling more stable national development. In addition, at a time when Indonesia is about to carry out its capital relocation plan, the support of Japan, whether from the government or the private sector, is imperative for planning and thus the Jokowi administration in holding on power. In fact, Japan has been an important partner of Southeast Asia for more than 50 years. No matter in the past, present, or the near future, Japan becomes more and more engaged to facilitate the ASEAN integration and its members to weather the great power rivalry.

Second, Taiwan has never been absent from taking part in the political economy of Southeast Asia. Although Taiwan has not established formal diplomatic ties with ASEAN countries, the Taiwanese government, private sector, and civil society organizations have been actively developing collaborations with major Southeast Asian countries since the 1980s in particular with the advancement of the "Go South Policy" in the 1990s (Yang 2018). Since then, Taiwan's informal ties with most Southeast Asian countries as well as the regional production networks have been strengthened. Under the current leadership of President Tsai Ing-wen, Taiwan launched its New Southbound Policy (NSP) since 2016, taking a comprehensive approach to more proactive and active participation in regional networks. Taiwan is not only reinvigorating its presence in Southeast Asia but also working very hard to take innovative initiatives to strengthen its contribution to the region by sharing its "warm power".[1] Taiwan's approach to collaboration covers a wider range of issue-areas, making it a multifaceted institutional partnership. A chapter of this book addresses the connection and contribution of Taiwan's NSP in response to the human values highlighted by the United Nations Sustainable Development Goals (UNSDGs) unpacking this island country's practice in engaging itself in political economy of Southeast Asia.

Third, ASEAN continues to play an important role as an institutional platform and regional community (Acharya 2021). Particularly, ASEAN did not make it clear whether to support the U.S. Indo-Pacific strategy or

---

[1] Warm power here refers to the sharing of warmth in terms of resources and experiences for governance through the government-led NSP since 2016, which distinguishes the NSP approach from other major power's Southeast Asia Policies (Yang and Chen 2019; Olivier 2021).

to resist China's BRI, but responded to the regional policies of the great powers with a vague "outlook," which may not be regarded as formal or concrete for some policymakers or national leaders, nor meaningful. But for ASEAN, this is already a clear presentation of the consensus among its members, and it is also the collective stance among ASEAN countries to flexibly navigate in the great power struggles for decades. In addition to responding to hedging risks among major powers, ASEAN must also take a continuing lead to respond to the ongoing non-traditional security threats, that is, the COVID-19 Pandemic. ASEAN must consolidate the centrality and unity to ensure the stability of the region and national interests of its members. As being hit by the COVID-19 Pandemic, ASEAN has charted a comprehensive recovery framework in 2020 to call upon collaboration among its members in key policy dimensions (Yang 2022).

In order to review the above-mentioned changes and trends, this book will explore important issues in Southeast Asia from the perspective of political economy.

Navigating in Political Economy: A Regional Nexus

The mainstream academic discussion on political economy highlights the relationship between politics and economy within specific framework of national development. However, with the intensifying globalization and regional integration, the diversification of cross-border movement and the multifaceted exchanges among societies, the essence and configuration of political economy have also become more intricate. In particular, the simultaneous emergence of various transnational forces and border-crossing connectivity has, in effect, loosened the limit of national boundary and penetrated the state-centric governance, reshaping the configuration of domestic political economy. In this regard, emerging agendas in social, cultural, and development-related issue-areas have gradually become new facets of political economy where traditionally strategic, geopolitical, and regional security scholars can be articulated and bridged through new dialogues. This book will unpack the making of political economy in Southeast Asia, with an introduction addressing the importance of this book from the perspective of the International Relations (IR) discipline, and the actors involved. Then it will delineate the driving forces for New Political Economy in Southeast Asia.

It is important to highlight our understanding that the discussion on Southeast Asia cannot be contextualized in power vacuums, given that Southeast Asia is right located in the international system of East Asia and the Indo-Pacific that is ridden with power political confrontation and cooperation between China and the United States. Moreover, it coexists with the concern and profound exchanges between neighboring India and Russia in the north, while enjoying the close political and economic ties with Australia in the southern hemisphere. With the U.S.–China rivalry becoming more global, European countries, especially the NATO members, have shown great interests in engaging Southeast Asia in a wider Indo-Pacific region. From the perspective of this increasingly intricate power politics, Southeast Asia is becoming more and more important. Nevertheless, an exclusive emphasis on the bilateral relationship between individual major power and Southeast Asia will only lead to a relatively fragmented analysis and understanding of the regional dynamics. Instead, this book focuses on the overall regional setting and its dynamics. It begins by outlining the three forces that affect the regional political and economic dynamics, and further lays out the two parts of the book, geopolitical and security factors, and alternative issue-areas of cooperation, inclusive of economic and non-traditional security cooperation. The third section finally provides some regional account by using Malaysia for a critical case study to demonstrate that ASEAN countries face and respond to domestic political changes and international dynamics.

Regarding the three critical factors mentioned earlier, first of all, from the perspective of international relations, the new political economy of Southeast Asia is the main driver that causes the changes in this region. The direction of the changes is extremely important, because the nesting regionalism centered on Southeast Asia is the focus of multiple subregional overlaps, and the driving force from Southeast Asia to East Asia, and even further to the entire Indo-Pacific and the world, which cannot be ignored. This is not only the focus of negotiation and compromise among political leaders and policymakers but also the key to actively think about how to maintain and promote mega-regional stability and prosperity in the policy community and think tank circles. More importantly, from the academic perspective of Asian scholars, it is necessary and impelling to put forward regional and local perspectives on this issue. The discussion formed through brainstorming of regional intellectuals will help to present the regional dynamics of Southeast Asia, forming a pulse for the future of the Indo-Pacific region.

Furthermore, studying the emerging new political economy is not limited to the state level of analysis. This is because not only major powers, international organizations, and regional communities play key roles but also more micro social actors, NGOs, and stakeholders. It is worth noting that in addition to traditional powers and international organizations, the economic strategies of Japan, South Korea, and Taiwan also deserve attention. In particular, Taiwan's NSP has received international attention because its agenda is integrated into human values, responding to ASEAN's people-centered community development agenda and needs.

An Even More Intricate Regional Context

It is true that the security dynamics in the Indo-Pacific region is quite tense due to power political struggle, and might be even worse in the future due to the unilateral aggressive attempt of the Chinese hegemonic aspirant. In addition to the COVID-19 pandemic as non-traditional security threat, the regional arms race among major powers has also led to various uncertainties in traditional military security. In particular, China has rapidly built up its extensive missile arsenals, while engaged in active research and development of hardly trackable hypersonic missiles that might disable the existing air defenses. This move has been taken when international focus is directed on U.S.–Russia relations in arms control.

Notably, the current dynamics in Southeast Asia and in a broader Indo-Pacific region are much more complicated than those in the first decade of this century. Today the global U.S.–China rivalry is taking place and the nascent multipolar international system after the post-Cold War period is undergoing drastic changes. ASEAN countries, in particular, progressed from the early non-aligned movement to the ASEAN-led regional community-building process, while having been ensured with regionwide national resilience under the aegis of the ASEAN institution. This means that ASEAN has provided them with an institutional buffer against pressure to choose sides between the competing great powers. With the regional dynamics increasingly becoming intricate, the tasks ahead of ASEAN are more challenging, just as the neighboring powers and regional stakeholders.

Furthermore, as the great power struggle continues to heat up, ASEAN must strengthen its internal unity and strategize its importance in the Indo-Pacific context. Hence, *ASEAN Centrality* should not be merely rhetorical; instead, a reinforcement of it needs to match the importance of this regional community. Against the backdrop, there are as three important elements that will propel further development and consolidation of the ASEAN community in the near future. First, the ASEAN as institution must be highly needed by its member states. It is not an "either/or" option but a precondition for national survival and regional autonomy. How can ASEAN offer a clear sense of security for its well-being as the umbrella or architecture of peace and stability for its members in the event of a crisis? What kind of institutional buffer crafted by ASEAN can increase the flexibility and resilience for ASEAN member states?

Second, ASEAN must also ensure its driver's seat is not being undermined or replaced by great powers. In this regard, *ASEAN Centrality* is the key.

Third, how can ASEAN clearly chart a bright future and bring its members to work together for overcoming the pandemic, great power rivalry, and other challenges?

These three elements mentioned above are crucial to the continuous success of ASEAN as recognized by major powers and international community. At this critical moment, it is the right time to review and reboot ASEAN collaboration in the Indo-Pacific dynamics.

New Political Economy in the Making

The new political economy in Southeast Asia should highlight the complex regional issues. This book will unpack three underlying factors that keep shaping the configuration of the new political economy in Southeast Asia. These factors influence and restrain each other, and at the same time, they also jointly shape the current intricate regional dynamics of cooperation and conflict. These three factors are, first of all, traditional geopolitical security factors, including the rivalry between the United States and China as well as the competition and cooperation among Indo-Pacific powers, such as India. The second is the continuous advancement of multifaceted cooperation, including economic and trade, development, and non-traditional security. Moreover, East Asian powers' regional strategy toward Southeast Asia, such as Japan's Indo-Pacific policy as well as Taiwan's people-centered NSP, is of specific importance and has been highlighted among policy communities and academia in the Indo-Pacific. Finally, this book also presents the insights from the ASEAN region, that is, Malaysia in particular, which has been an important leading state and voice for the Islamic world, and Thailand has also undergone changes of government; the latter is a land power, and the future political situation is still unclear after the coup of 2014.

The abovementioned first two factors follow an outside-in approach in which ASEAN and its member states play an active role in international relations, to some extent, being ignored, while the third factor clearly represents their passive role. The third factor is related to internal dynamics. The two chapters deal with Thailand and Malaysia as cases studies highlight the voices of Southeast Asia, and the regional and national choices that directly influence the new political economy of Southeast Asia.

(Re-)Envisaging the Importance of ASEAN in Indo-Pacific Region

The development of the ASEAN itself is essential for strategic autonomy or the so-called regional and national resilience of Southeast Asia. On the one hand, the ASEAN, on behalf of the ASEAN Community as well as its member states, had to respond to the new structure of the U.S.–China rivalry, especially Trump's Indo-Pacific Strategy (IPS) by facilitating a consensus on the Indo-Pacific Outlook. ASEAN countries have faced China's economic offensives and inducements, especially the BRI and pandemic/vaccine diplomacy. This requires the ASEAN countries to be united on common grounds for further collaboration in responding to such an external influence. However, internal issues such as Myanmar's uncertain democracy after the military coup of 2021 and the long-term unsolved South China Sea disputes may undermine the solidarity of regional community and weaken the institutional ASEAN.

So far, there are two guiding ASEAN documents in effect that is based on consensus regarding the future (short term to mid-term) direction of its development, namely, *The ASEAN Outlook on the Indo-Pacific (AOIP)* and *the ASEAN Comprehensive Recovery Framework: Implementation Plan (ACRF)*. The strategic meaning and importance of these two documents are worthy of scrutiny.

ASEAN outlook on the Indo-Pacific

The concept of Indo-Pacific is not unfamiliar to the ASEAN. In 2013, the Indonesian Foreign Minister, Marty Natalegawa, shared the strategic vision of linking up two oceans, namely, the Pacific and Indian Oceans to his ASEAN counterparts, and argued that in the political and economic domain, the Indo-Pacific refers to an area encompassing some of the most dynamic economies in the world. The Indo-Pacific should be highlighted both geo-economically and geopolitically. That is, the Indo-Pacific region is the engine for global economic growth.[2] Natalegawa once suggested that the ASEAN should advance the Treaty of Amity and Cooperation in Southeast Asian (TAC) to the Indo-Pacific Treaty of Friendship and Cooperation.[3]

Then in 2017, Thailand, a land power, also reminded ASEAN members to recognize "the Indo-Pacific" as not just a geographic concept but also a geopolitical one.[4] This view immediately gained support from Indonesia. It is worth noting that only after *ASEAN's Indo-Pacific Outlook* was adopted in mid-2019 that the ASEAN countries reached such a consensus. Through the *AOIP* document, ASEAN expressed its united tone and position over the Indo-Pacific strategies and policies practiced by external major powers narrating their own interests and interpretations on the Indo-Pacific geopolitical and geo-economic settings. ASEAN presents therewith its own stance on the concept, its regional strategic interests, and the future direction of cooperation and competition.

Among the key features included in the *AOIP* document, the "existing," "inclusivity," and "ASEAN Centrality," and "complement" are the key words and concerns. First, "existing" means ASEAN will not reject or embrace any major powers' Indo-Pacific regional initiatives, while inclusivity too echoes this statement. Moreover, ASEAN Centrality is to highlight and prioritize ASEAN as the key driver of the Indo-Pacific dynamics while it has established the institutional platform for regional interaction and cooperation. The *AIPO* not only serves as the strategic reference of ASEAN Way to its member states, but calls upon external major powers to respect *ASEAN Centrality*. Last but not the least, it is important to pinpoint the term "complement" as the *AOIP* highlights its purpose for complementing the existing mechanisms, rather than creating

---

[2] https://www.thejakartapost.com/news/2013/05/20/an-indonesian-perspective-indo-pacific.html.

[3] https://thediplomat.com/2013/05/an-indo-pacific-treaty-an-idea-whose-time-has-come/.

[4] https://asean2019.go.th/en/news/%E0%B8%A3%E0%B8%B2%E0%B8%A2%E0%B8%87%E0%B8%B2%E0%B8%99-%E0%B9%81%E0%B8%99%E0%B8%A7%E0%B8%84%E0%B8%B4%E0%B8%94%E0%B8%AD%E0%B8%B4%E0%B8%99%E0%B9%82%E0%B8%94-%E0%B9%81%E0%B8%9B%E0%B8%8B%E0%B8%B4/.

new ones. This echoes the previous concepts, that is, the ASEAN has its own rules and regulations, and all regional initiatives intended to cover ASEAN should respect its own ASEAN norms as well as positively recognize it in the driver's seat of regional integration.

This document represents the strategic development of ASEAN responses to contending Indo-Pacific power configuration with three features. First, it aims to strongly embrace the Indo-Pacific concept and helps promote a favorable environment for regional peace, stability, and prosperity, responding to common challenges and maintaining a rule-based regional order.

Second, it strengthens the ASEAN community building process and further facilitates the existing ASEAN-led mechanisms, such as the East Asia Summit (EAS), as an inclusive regional architecture amid power struggle in the Indo-Pacific countries.

Third, it aims to implement intra-ASEAN cooperation of existing issues and explore other priority areas of its integration, including economic and trade, maritime cooperation, connectivity, the UNSDGs, and other emerging issues with specific interests among stakeholders.

U.S. Secretary of State Antony Blinken traveled to Jakarta in the mid of December 2021 on a 48-hour visit for the purpose of enhancing U.S.–Indonesia collaboration and strategizing President Biden's policy aimed for the Indo-Pacific, involving the following three strategic meanings.

First, democracy has indeed become the key word for the United States to actively work with Southeast Asia and strengthen its ties with the Indo-Pacific region. With common challenges ahead, democracies with shared values need to work together and support each other to jointly cope with common crises in the Indo-Pacific region.

Second, the COVID-19 pandemic has attracted significant attention amid the challenges. With the United States suffering the surge of omicron, the key issue of Blinken's visit probably centered on collaboration in pandemic control. However, his remark showed a wider range of concerns of President Biden, especially related to the Indo-Pacific policy that tracks the threats to human rights, climate emergency as well as the COVID-19 pandemic crises. Blinken's call for cooperation on human rights issues is, of course, in response to the ideological challenge of Chinese authoritarianism eroding the free and democratic order in the region. Also, Biden regards climate change as a key issue for international cooperation. Of course, while effective collaboration against the pandemic is still on priority, plans for resilient recovery also need to be considered simultaneously.

Third, of course, the concrete mission of Blinken's trip was to express support for Indonesia for its G20 chairmanship and to reiterate U.S. commitment to the *ASEAN Centrality*. It echoed the U.S. position in adhering the rules-based international order and, in particular, addressing its importance to the geopolitical and geo-economic order in the Indo-Pacific region. The U.S. engagement and commitment to *ASEAN Centrality* calls on all stakeholders to respect ASEAN as the architecture of regional cooperation, so that the ASEAN Comprehensive Recovery framework may be central to enhance collaboration in the Indo-Pacific region.

Finally, it is worth noting that the United States and Indonesia agreed to build a 2+2 dialogue mechanism to strengthen exchanges and discussions between senior defense and foreign officials. What's more, the two countries signed an MOU to strengthen cooperation in maritime security, marine resources, conservation, fisheries, and freedom of navigation to 2026.

The abovementioned areas are also of strategic interests of another Asian democracy, India. New Delhi has actively implemented Prime Minister Modi's Act East Policy, through the seven pillars of the Indo-Pacific Ocean Initiative (IPOI). As the U.S.–Indonesia maritime cooperation and India's IPOI continue to advance, Blinken's visit strongly showed the key importance of "democracy" as well as the framing role of "maritime," in understanding the strategic dynamics of the future Indo-Pacific region.

U.S.–Indonesia Maritime Cooperation	India's Indo-Pacific Ocean Initiatives
• Maritime security	• Capacity building and resource sharing
• Marine resources	• Disaster risk reduction and management
• Conservation	• Maritime ecology
• Fisheries and	• Maritime resources
• Freedom of navigation	• Maritime security
	• Science, technology, and academic

A more active U.S. presence through its trade and investment as well as security engagement will be expected in the Indo-Pacific region, especially in the post pandemic era. U.S.–Indonesia cooperation would encourage regional democracies, too. Therefore, a more solid tone and joint ASEAN efforts will be directed to enhance implementation of the ASEAN Comprehensive Recovery Framework (ACRF).

Taiwan, as a maritime democracy, a responsible stakeholder, and the facilitator of good governance in the Indo-Pacific, will be important to the making of the robust supply chain (not just in terms of providing semiconductor chips). Taiwan needs to earnestly implement the New Southbound Policy to contribute to post-pandemic recovery and to restore the socioeconomic resilience in the region. Taiwan's multifaceted engagement through the NSP will facilitate a more resilient regional collaboration for the emerging Indo-Pacific configuration in 2022.

Summary of the Book

This book is aimed at providing its readers with the toolbox of navigating the regional dynamics of political economy in greater Southeast Asia with specific focus on exploring key factors determining the shifting dynamics. There are 12 chapters in this book. In addition to the introductory and conclusion chapters, this edited volume is divided into three parts featured with three key factors determining the political economy of Southeast Asia, that is, geopolitical and security factors, alternative field of regional cooperation, and the regional considerations of Southeast Asian countries, such as Thailand and Malaysia. More importantly, it is the joint research efforts of policy discussion and timely assessment of COVID-19 recovery plans in Southeast Asia, in comparison with other academic titles. The authors are professors, policy practitioners from the fields of international relations and political economy, as well as military specialists and young policy practitioners with innovative insights.

It is also worth noting that the authors of this book are from international academic communities from leading universities and institutions of Japan, Taiwan, India, the Philippines, and Malaysia, etc. This edited volume, as the joint efforts of international collaboration, is the research outcome of three high-quality workshops coorganized by Japan's St. Andrew's University and Taiwan's National Chengchi University, after rigorous academic publishing procedures. Special thanks go to both the Universities for the endorsement of the workshops and copyediting efforts.

The first part addresses the important factors of geopolitics and security, consisting of four chapters. Akio Egawa's chapter highlights the competition and cooperation in infrastructure development in the Greater Mekong subregion, which has been in the heart of Southeast Asia development for more than 60 years among the long-term geopolitical competition and cooperation among China, Japan, and the United States. The second chapter is written by a former Japanese Lieutenant General (Japan Air Self-Defense Force (Ret.) Sadamasa Oue addressing the relationship between port facilities and Chinese military projections. Oue unpacks the heated debates over the roles and strategic purpose of port facilities in the BRI projects. The third chapter is a comparison between two sets of strategic triangles between the United States, China and Taiwan, and the Philippines, the United States and China, written by Ruei-Lin Yu, a Professor at the National Defense University in Taiwan. Dynamic changes over two decades have been observed and analyzed. The last chapter is an analysis of the strategic cooperation between India and Vietnam by Roger Liu, a Taiwanese scholar who teaches in India.

To sum up, the first part discusses political security factors that affect the regional political and economic development from a strategic point of view. It includes the macro-structure of the U.S.–China competition and cooperation, as well as the roles of key extra-regional powers, such as two major powers as India and Japan and the middle power, Taiwan. Also the analysis captures the situation in which rising ASEAN countries, such as Vietnam and the Philippines are influenced by great power politics. Certainly, conflict potential may be a latent subject matter among the respective four chapters. But the geopolitical and security factors do not necessarily lead to great power armed conflicts. What will happen remains to be seen because rivalry and cooperation coexists concurrently in the regional context of Southeast Asia. The chapters in this part remind readers that the national development and foreign policy of respective countries in Southeast Asia should not be comprehended in power vacuum. Instead, in order to better understand the current regional dynamics and the future trends, readers must carefully incorporate the impact and influence of the structural factors of great power politics at the same time.

The second part also includes four chapters featured with alternative issue-areas of regional cooperation and, furthermore, the development of individual country's national flagship policies beyond political security. The first chapter, written by Akio Egawa, focuses on how Southeast Asian countries work with an extra-regional power (i.e., Japan) to build a technology-led, knowledge-based economy. The second chapter, co-authored by Masahiro Matsumura and Yoshiaki Ozawa, discusses the characteristics of Japanese Capitalism and its impact on East Asia. This chapter is a rare one devoted to reveal the Japanese accounting system and its implication to East Asian neighbors. The chapter portrays an innovative perspective from a young Filipino talent, Mark Byrant Manantan, a Senior Research Fellow in Cybersecurity and Critical Technology at Pacific Forum based in Hawaii, of examining data governance in Japan and Southeast Asia, especially for cyber security, which is extremely important in the data free flow at a regional level. Matsumura and Ozawa's chapter utilize the traditional accounting system as the means of influence, while Manantan's chapter accounts for the data free flow in terms of trust-based coalition building process. Both provide in-depth analysis of policy content of Japan in leading regional configuration in Southeast Asia. Last but not least, Yang and Chiang's chapter demonstrates the detailed evaluation of Taiwan's New Southbound Policy since 2016. This chapter aims at reviewing how Taiwan, an extra-regional middle power, incorporates human values into its foreign policy practice, in line with the regional people-centered integration agenda, and strengthens the connection with Southeast Asia.

This part shows the common characteristics of people-centered practice as a soft appeal compared to hard cooperation[5] in the field of political security. These chapters also show that in addition to the sensitive security field and the struggles among major powers, other people-centered and development-oriented appeals for regional political economy is pragmatic in intensive cooperation among stakeholders.

The third part covers two chapters on Malaysia's national profile and one conclusion chapter by the editors, all of which help shape a regional narrative. Ivy Kwek's chapter explains the new policy response of Malaysia facing the regional dynamics in great Southeast Asia and changing national political climate, while Chee Leong Lee's chapter discusses the outbreak of COVID-19 pandemic and its impacts on Malaysia. In particular, the two chapters on Malaysia are written by Malaysian think tank experts and young scholars, and also provide innovative observations and assessments on political economic currents of the country and the region. Then the concluding chapter outlines possible implications of

---

[5]The soft appeal here refers to development-oriented collaboration initiatives ranging from economic, education, medical, and publication as well as regional agriculture while the hard cooperation emphasizes on cooperation on political and security issues.

ACRF and its regional implementation for better understanding the region's emerging political and economic dynamics. The analysis in this chapter also timely corresponds to possible issue areas and future direction of cooperation between the ACRF and the regional strategies of other regional stakeholders, namely, Taiwan's New Southbound Policy, India's Act East Policy, and the United States' Indo-Pacific Strategy of 2022. Furthermore, the prospect for regional dynamics in Southeast Asia, as embedded in the Indo-Pacific region, will be wrapped up, while priority issue-areas for regional cooperation will also be highlighted.

References

Acharya, Amitav. 2021. *ASEAN and Regional Order: Revisiting Security Community in Southeast Asia*. London and New York: Routledge.

Ciorciari John D. and Kiyoteru Tsutsui. 2021. *The Courteous Power: Japan and Southeast Asia in the Indo-Pacific Era*. Ann Arbor: University of Michigan Press.

Doyle, Timothy and Dennis Rumley. 2019. *The Rise and Return of the Indo-Pacific*. Oxford: Oxford University Press.

Kaplan, Morton A., and Kinhide Mushakoji. 1976. *Japan, America, and the Future World Order*. New York: The Free Press.

Lampton, David M., Selina Ho, and Cheng-Chwee Kuik. 2020. *Rivers of Iron: Railroads and Chinese Power in Southeast Asia*. Oakland: University of California Press.

Lin, Bonny *et al.* 2021. *Regional Responses to U.S.–China Competition in the Indo-Pacific: Study Overview and Conclusions*. Santa Monica: Rand Corporation.

Malhotra, Aditi. 2022. *India in the Indo-Pacific: Understanding India's Security Orientation towards Southeast and East Asia*. Berlin: Verlag Barbara Budrich.

Olivier, Jeremy. 2021. "New Southbound Policy Offers New Prospects for 2022." *Taiwan Business Topic*. December 27, 2021: https://topics.amcham.com. tw/2021/12/new-southbound-policy-prospects-2022/.

Shambaugh, David. 2020. *Where Great Powers Meet: America and China in Southeast Asia*. Oxford: Oxford University Press.

Strangio, Sebastian. 2020. *In the Dragon's Shadow: Southeast Asia in the Chinese Century*. New Haven: Yale University Press.

Stromseth, Jonathan R. 2021. *Rivalry and Response: Assessing Great Power Dynamics in Southeast Asia*. Washington, DC: Brookings Institution Press.

Yang, Alan. H. 2018. Unpacking Taiwan's Presence in Southeast Asia: The International Socialization of the New Southbound Policy. *Issues & Studies* 54 (1): 1840003–1840033.

Yang, Alan H. 2022. "From Supply Chain to Survival Chain? Strategizing ASEAN–Taiwan Collaboration in the Post-Pandemic Recovery." *AEI Insights*, 8: 87–100.

Yang, Alan H. and Ding-liang Chen. 2019. The Yushan Forum and Taiwan's Warm Power. Foreign Policy Research Institute, October 18, 2019. https://www.fpri.org/article/2019/10/the-yushan-forum-and-taiwans-warm-power/.

Part I
Geopolitical Security Factors

Chapter 2

Competition and Collaboration in Infrastructure Development: The Case of the Greater Mekong Subregion

Akio Egawa

Introduction

The ASEAN countries have taken steps toward becoming a single large economic zone. The establishment of the ASEAN Economic Community (AEC) incentivizes multinational manufacturing companies to reallocate their production networks throughout the ASEAN region. Cambodia, Laos, Myanmar, Thailand, Vietnam, and China's Yunnan Province and Guangxi Zhuang Autonomous Region — collectively referred to as the Greater Mekong Subregion (GMS) — have the potential to develop increased overland mutual accessibility and to take advantage of ASEAN economic integration.

Against this backdrop, infrastructure development is now an urgent task for the GMS. The Asian Development Bank (ADB) has already presented its vision concerning the development of key subregional infrastructure, the building blocks of which are the relevant infrastructure projects of the individual GMS countries and Japan's participation in them, especially in the form of financial and technical assistance. However, China has recently begun to play a more active role in regional infrastructure development. Apparently, China is not only trying to connect its part of the GMS with other countries on its borders but is also cooperating with infrastructure development projects in the Indo-Chinese countries.

Chinese companies, with their strong bargaining power and cost advantages, have the capacity to win almost all the contracts for infrastructure development projects in the GMS against Japanese and other competitors. Despite their apparent zero-sum competition, however, collaboration between the Chinese and Japanese governments and companies has been observed at the project level in the late 2010s. This chapter will present a case study on Japan–China collaboration in Thailand, focusing on the Thai government's policy stance on infrastructure development.

I will examine Japanese and Chinese infrastructure development strategies in the GMS, using major projects in Thailand to illustrate how China is attempting to replace the existing international cooperation frameworks.

Infrastructure Development in the GMS

The significance of improved connectivity

For almost a quarter of a century, GMS countries have sought to strengthen their intra-regional logistics networks, or "connectivity." Connectivity in this context is defined as working toward "a seamlessly and comprehensively connected and integrated ASEAN that will promote competitiveness, inclusiveness, and a greater sense of Community" (ASEAN Secretariat 2016). There are three aspects to connectivity: physical connectivity (or the development of infrastructure linking ASEAN countries, such as roads, railways, seaports, airports, energy supply networks, and information and communication technology infrastructure), institutional connectivity (or the removal of internal rules and regulations that hamper free movement of goods, money, and people through the realization of a multilateral agreement, and the establishment of the AEC), and people-to-people connectivity (or the freer movement of skilled workers, tourists, etc., across borders within the region).

Multinationals play a key role in enhancing connectivity through the ASEAN-wide reallocation of their production networks, involving the specialization of production processes that increase their business profits and concentration. Also, countries that are recipients of investment can expect significant trickle-downs to the whole manufacturing sector and subsequently to the service sector. With increased regional connectivity,

ASEAN can expect more rapid growth and development in which border areas, especially the Mekong River Basin, will play a primary engine role. Given the ongoing regional transformation, Thailand, with its status as the region's upper middle-income country, risks falling into the "middle-income trap" in relation to international production networks. Thailand's labor-intensive industrial structure needs to transition to a capital- and then a technology- or knowledge-intensive one (ADB 2011). This is "Thailand-Plus-One," or the business strategy of Japanese multinational companies that locate their subsidiaries and affiliates in Thailand and its surrounding countries to increase production efficiency. More specifically, Thailand's increased connectivity prospects will surely attract overseas investment in infrastructure building in the pursuit of profits through agglomeration and the diversification of industries and production processes. Thus, investing in Thailand and then in the entire GMS is increasingly becoming the optimal strategic choice, particularly since a comprehensive approach to the elimination of trade barriers is being adopted to improve institutional connectivity. Japanese companies have also moved to lower-income countries in the subregion, such as Cambodia, Laos, Myanmar, and Vietnam (CLMV), and increased their investment in labor-intensive industries.

The implementation of infrastructure development projects is the key to the creation of an on-land seamless economic zone and to attracting global investment. However, some areas have experienced delays or challenges. The ADB's (2018a) assessment of the progress of road construction is positive, with three major economic corridors being constructed at a sufficient pace, while the bank recognizes that there have been delays in certain railway development projects and the construction of special economic zones (SEZs) along the borders. Such delays should be avoided, considering the ADB's (2017, pp. 42–44) estimate that another US$1.92 trillion-worth of domestic infrastructure (transportation, electricity, information and communication, water supply, and irrigation) will be needed in Southeast Asia (excluding Singapore, Brunei, and Indonesia) over the period 2016–2030. This is equivalent to US$128 billion per year, or 6% of these countries' gross domestic product (GDP). The increasing demand for infrastructure that connects these countries will add to this amount. As any one ASEAN country cannot meet such a huge infrastructure demand, international financial cooperation with other economies and international institutions is playing an important role in addressing the problems of infrastructure development in the GMS.

Major players in international cooperation frameworks: The ADB and Japan

International cooperation in the development of the GMS has accelerated since the early 1990s when the ADB launched its cooperation framework for the construction of three major economic corridors in the subregion, known as the Greater Mekong Subregion Economic Cooperation Program. Recent efforts by the ADB include the convening of annual Mekong–Japan Summit Meetings, which in 2011 saw the adoption of the GMS Strategic Framework 2012–2022 (ADB 2012). This framework asked summit participants to prioritize the linking of three economic corridors and the connection of their main domestic roads with those corridors in order to create more efficient logistics networks (ADB 2018a). In 2018, summit participants assessed the progress of the Strategic Framework and agreed to prioritize a list of infrastructure investment projects over the next 5 years known as the Hanoi Action Plan (ADB 2018a, 2018b).

As inward FDI increases, the GMS countries face a growing need for the development of domestic infrastructure that can enhance the GMS-wide reallocation of industries and production processes, or the Thailand-Plus-One strategy. Historically, Japanese official development assistance (ODA) has played a primary role in infrastructure development in the GMS. Japan placed the ADB's initiative at the core of its economic cooperation with the GMS because it trusted the ability of the ADB to handle the difficult task of coordinating the GMS economies and the multiple international cooperation frameworks and initiatives (Ito 2017). In addition, the ADB's frameworks are compatible with the Thailand-Plus-One strategy, which requires the networking of the main locations of production throughout the subregion with three economic corridors in order to achieve improved business efficiency. During the Mekong–Japan Summit Meeting in 2015, the Japanese pledged to invest ¥750 billion of ODA in the GMS over the following 3 years.

China's Belt and Road Initiative (BRI) for the GMS

Nowadays, it is China, rather than Japan, that seems to be playing a leading role in the development of physical connectivity in the subregion. Beijing's Belt and Road Initiative (BRI), which aims to connect

China with Europe via the subregion, emerged independently of existing Indochina-China development frameworks. The difference between the main infrastructure development objectives of the BRI and those of the ADB and Japanese initiatives adds another coordination process to GMS development. Even so, the BRI's focus on cooperation in infrastructure development has been compatible with that of the ADB so far, especially in relation to road networks. China's infrastructure cooperation in the subregion includes the development of the North-South Economic Corridor (overland logistics routes from Kunming in China through Vientiane to Bangkok via north-eastern Thailand, and through eastern Myanmar to Bangkok via western Thailand), a new economic corridor which connects the Guangxi Zhuang Autonomous Region in China with Ho Chi Minh City via Hanoi, a river route from Kunming down the Mekong River to Ho Chi Minh City in Vietnam, and railways connecting Singapore, Kuala Lumpur, Bangkok, and Vientiane.

China is also playing a leading role in coordinating the existing frameworks for improving connectivity within the GMS. At the GMS Ministerial Meeting in September 2017 China proposed that the GMS countries should adjust various multilateral initiatives and frameworks for the subregion's infrastructure development, including the ADB's frameworks, China's BRI, and the LMC (the Lancang–Mekong Cooperation, a cooperation framework including Thailand, Laos, Cambodia, Myanmar, and Vietnam that China proposed in 2016), and pledged government loans of more than US$10 billion. In 2019, China hosted the second BRI Forum for International Cooperation. Forty countries and international organizations, including the ADB, took part, and the forum reached a consensus on promoting connectivity.

Both the Thailand-Plus-One strategy and the BRI have their own objectives for infrastructure development in the GMS, but they are mutually complementary. For example, Japan and China are collaborating in Thailand's infrastructure development projects. In these circumstances, the following questions arise: (1) Why has Chinese assistance become more influential than Japanese ODA? (2) How have recipient countries, in this case Thailand, responded so far to increased assistance from China through the BRI? (3) How can we explain the collaboration between Japan and China in Thailand's infrastructure development projects? These questions will be addressed in the following sections.

The China Factor in Subregional Infrastructure Development: Local Responses

The background

The main factors driving China's increasing influence in GMS infrastructure development are as follows.

(1) *The conclusion of the Regional Comprehensive Economic Partnership agreement* (*RCEP*): By improving physical access to GMS countries, RCEP will facilitate overland exports of Chinese products to the ASEAN states. As their main objectives are different, the existing international frameworks and rules for the development of the GMS may not serve China's national interests. China has indeed introduced a new framework and a new financial resource — the BRI and the Asian Infrastructure Investment Bank (AIIB) — seemingly in competition with the existing international cooperation frameworks led by the ADB. China now has more scope to select projects, operating organizations, funding, and so on, for its own cooperation projects. This may be interpreted as a move by China toward Morse and Keohane's (2014) "state-led competitive regime creation," which occurs when the dissatisfied government "creates a new institution or establishes a new informal form of multilateral cooperation to challenge the existing institutional *status quo*" (Morse and Keohane 2014, p. 392).

(2) *Limitations on Japan's ODA disbursements*: Japan has faced difficulty in disbursing ODA to upper middle-income countries like Thailand due to the rules of the Development Assistance Committee of the Organization for Economic Cooperation and Development (OECD/ DAC). In addition, the basic principles of Japanese economic cooperation policy were changed by the replacement of the Official Development Assistance Charter with the new Development Cooperation Charter in 2015. The new charter states that "ODA, as the core of various activities that contribute to development, will serve as a catalyst for mobilizing a wide range of resources in cooperation with various funds and actors" (Ministry of Foreign Affairs of Japan 2015). Together with the need for fiscal consolidation and the limitations imposed by OECD/DAC rules, the main source of financing from Japan for infrastructure development projects

(or economic cooperation as a whole) is no longer ODA but private-sector investment and government-related financial institutions. That is, Japanese private companies "sell" infrastructure to the recipient countries with support from the Japanese government in the form of export credits and information and negotiations with the recipient government. Even though Japan is continuing to support GMS development, GMS countries recognize that Japan has reduced the level of its assistance, which makes Japan less influential in the subregion than it was in the past.

(3) *Increasing demand for infrastructure development*: Infrastructure development under the BRI is attractive to GMS countries because it has the potential to narrow the gap between infrastructure demand and supply. China offers additional financial resources for infrastructure development to those offered by the ADB and Japan. Besides, the participation of Chinese companies that have greater bargaining power than Japanese ones in BRI projects result in domestic public expenditure savings. In turn, GMS countries are becoming more eager to claim that their domestic infrastructure development projects are BRI-related and to negotiate with the Chinese government for financial assistance. Below, one example of an infrastructure development project in Thailand is used to illustrate this situation.

Thailand's need for greater connectivity

While it has cooperated with its neighbors in infrastructure development projects that physically connect their borders, Thailand has further increased connectivity by establishing domestic schemes for SEZs in border areas. This approach, reinforcing production networks throughout the GMS with Thailand at the core, seems to be compatible with the private sector's Thailand-Plus-One strategy.

One of Thailand's border-area projects is the Cluster Policy which motivates neighboring prefectures to form "clusters" and encourages new investment in a few selected manufacturing sectors through greater tax incentives and other privileges. As most clusters include border prefectures, this may contribute to improved GMS connectivity. Another project is the development of 10 border SEZs in which new private investors in both the manufacturing and services sectors which are aiming to operate their businesses in Thailand and a plus-one country will receive greater tax incentives. These projects are in line with the policy recommendations contained in the Master Plan on ASEAN Connectivity 2025 and are considered to have the potential to improve connectivity and further strengthen local industries. However, neither measure has been well-utilized by the private sector; only 59 project registrations have been received for just 3 border SEZs. The border cities should be well connected with Bangkok or other industrial areas to facilitate the reallocation of the private manufacturing sector's production networks, but the central government has not played a primary role in developing logistic networks. Instead, it opted to provide limited financial support for local governments' own infrastructure development projects.

The Thai government is more eager to develop road and railway networks between Bangkok and industrialized areas near the capital, known as the Eastern Economic Corridor (EEC), where heavy industry has been concentrated since the 1980s. The EEC development project is aimed at upgrading Thailand's industrial structure in those areas, supported by an efficient logistics network throughout the country via Bangkok. As Thailand becomes an upper middle-income country, increasing the level of sophistication of its manufacturing sectors and developing a service sector-led economy will also be necessary for economic development. The Thai government launched the Thailand 4.0 initiative in 2016 as a policy guideline for the promotion of 10 new industries (including next-generation automotive production, aviation, robotics, and smart electronics) which were to be fostered within the EEC. The EEC development includes infrastructure development with seven prioritized sites (Ministry of Industry of Thailand 2017). These include a high-speed airport rail link, U-Tapao Airport and aircraft maintenance, three commercial seaports, double track railways, and a highway and motorway to Bangkok. It should be noted that whereas the ADB urges GMS countries to develop infrastructure that connects efficiently between industrial areas and economic corridors in each country, EEC development focuses on the networks centered on Bangkok and does not seem to directly connect the EEC with the eastern prefectures on the border with Cambodia.

Thailand's EEC infrastructure development projects and the BRI

The EEC development projects are, in principle, not consistent with the BRI, because they are not aimed at connecting the area with China.

However, the Thai government has begun to regard the airport link high-speed railway construction project in the EEC and the high-speed intercity railway development project between Bangkok and Nong Khai (on the border with Laos) as part of the BRI. There is justification for considering the high-speed intercity railway development as part of the BRI as it will connect Bangkok and Vientiane via Nong Khai.

Why, then, has the Thai government begun to regard the airport link high-speed railway project as a part of the BRI? One possible reason is fear of the middle-income trap. The Thai government recognizes the need to accelerate domestic infrastructure development by creating an efficient logistics network. Thailand has adopted a public–private partnership (PPP) approach for each of the EEC infrastructure development projects to avoid a surge in the public debt outstanding over a short period of time. So in order to speed up the implementation of a number of infrastructure development projects within the region, the government needs to facilitate the procurement of a significant amount of capital with funding costs to private investors as low as possible. The Thai government is characterizing the EEC projects as part of the BRI to receive low-cost BRI financing from China, the only player that can possibly satisfy such requirements.

Japan–China Competition and Cooperation in Subregional Infrastructure Development

On account of their strong bargaining power, Chinese companies are likely to win almost all the bidding processes for infrastructure development projects in the GMS. In a situation where only economic gains matter, Chinese companies are unlikely to collaborate with their Japanese counterparts whose bids are weaker. The Chinese government would be willing to finance those projects, but the Japanese government would not, on account of the basic principle of development effectiveness contained in the new charter.

For the EEC infrastructure projects, however, Japan is still playing just as important a role as China. China had refused to hold a Japan–China summit meeting for many years due to the political tension that arose between the two countries in the early 2010s, but the meetings were resumed in 2018 and the leaders discussed economic cooperation. In October 2018, China, Japan, and Thailand agreed on a cooperation effort to develop new cities in the EEC through cofinancing.

Below, I try to explain why and how collaboration between China and Japan occurs in infrastructure development projects in the region, using the case of Thailand as an example.

Japan and China in the international political economy

The current Chinese regime may be thinking of the BRI in terms of international and domestic political gains rather than economic gains. Although it is impossible to measure the political gains for China involved in the BRI, it may be assumed that China is willing to accept the participation of Japanese companies in BRI projects if this could avoid criticism of the BRI and address its existing problems.

One important criticism is that excessive dependence on Chinese money in many of the countries targeted by the BRI will allow China to exercise hegemony in the area. Moreover, it has been claimed that China has tried to deprive recipients of the right to operate the infrastructure as collateral and has driven them into indebtedness through onerous financing conditions. Hurley *et al.* (2018) have estimated the degree of risk involved in BRI lending pipelines and point out that economically small countries near to China tend to have a higher risk of indebtedness with China on account of BRI projects. However, excessive financial dependence on China is partly due to inaccurate estimates of costs and the risks involved in the infrastructure design, or the recipient government's imprudent choices. Moreover, since the inception of the BRI, it has become clear that China is attempting to establish hegemony over Asia, Europe, and Africa. Even so, if it can make an effective response to this type of criticism, China could reap political gains. However, this criticism does not result in China having an urgent need to collaborate with Japan.

On the other hand, China needs to deal with skepticism regarding the likely success of the BRI. Once a project is regarded as part of the BRI, the recipient country can access concessionary funding from Chinese governmental institutions or the AIIB. Potential recipients who have an urgent domestic need for improved infrastructure would tend to prioritize negotiation with the Chinese government at the expense of close examination of a project that might be unprofitable. If it does not take any countermeasures, China may find itself short of BRI resources. There is also skepticism about China's ability to complete multiple infrastructure projects simultaneously in a short period of time using its own financial resources alone. Baltensperger and Dadush (2019) argue these points and point out that the BRI needs a clear objective, adequate resources, selectivity, a workable implementation plan, due diligence, and clear communication, suggesting that the involvement of multilateral lenders could help with this.

Regardless of these concerns, China can neither stop nor slow down the progress of the BRI because it is an important part of its domestic political agenda. In these circumstances, cooperation with the Japanese government provides a potential opportunity for China. Stricter examination of projects and the acceleration of infrastructure development through cofinancing would be more firmly guaranteed, together with the positive side effect that China could mitigate the first type of criticism of the BRI described above. The BRI would also become more popular domestically as Beijing could tell the Chinese public that it is helping Japan's stagnant economy by welcoming its participation in the BRI. In turn, collaboration with China would expand profit-making opportunities for Japanese multinationals. They would also have more opportunity to serve their own interests in the design of the infrastructure.

For Thailand, collaboration between Japan and China would reduce competitive pressure in the bidding process, resulting in a possible increase in the total cost of the project. However, a prior consultation process between the two countries on the infrastructure development could reduce the risk or the costs involved in coordinating similar projects proposed by the two countries individually. Besides, Thailand, needing to take steps as soon as possible to avoid the middle-income trap, needs to construct as many projects as possible. Therefore, the current administration is likely to accept collaboration between China and Japan and proceed with the implementation of PPP projects in the EEC.

Japan–China rapprochement under U.S.–China rivalry

What happens in practice may not be that China opts to accept Japan's request for collaboration, but that China has no choice but to accept it. One possible reason for this is a worsening of economic relations between China and the United States since late 2017, especially after the occurrence of their so-called trade war. The "game" between Japan and China relating to the possibility of collaboration in the provision of GMS infrastructure development should then be analyzed differently, as part of a trilateral political and economic relationship.

Here, the trilateral relationship is explained in terms of the following game. Assume that there are one sheep and two wolves in the ranch. The sheep wants to eat as much grass as possible, knowing that there is only one sheep (itself) and two wolves (wolves A and B) in the same ranch. The wolves want to eat sheep, but if one of two wolves (say, wolf A) eats the sheep, it will lose a fight against wolf B because it will be too heavy to escape. Then, wolf B will kill wolf A and take the sheep from wolf A's stomach (or *vice versa*). Each wolf will opt to leave the sheep alone if it realizes that eating the sheep would cause it to be killed by the other wolf. Wolves do not communicate and collude with each other. Then, the equilibrium in this game is that the wolves never eat the sheep, because wolf A, knowing that it would definitely be killed by wolf B if it ate the sheep, will choose not to eat it (or *vice versa*).

Then, we substitute the sheep, wolf A, and wolf B with Japan, China, and the United States, respectively. If Japan (sheep), by far the smallest of the three, offers bilateral cooperation only to either China or the United States, it would not be able to control the result of the negotiations. This would be as if Japan and only one of the other two giant countries were in the ranch. Therefore, Japan should offer cooperation to both countries at the same time. As long as the United States and China, because of their trade war, cannot join together against Japan, these two wolves have no choice but to increase their economic activities with Japan and, via good economic relations with Japan, the emerging Southeast Asian markets. As a result, the wolves will never reject Japan's offer for fear of becoming isolated in the Asian region and because they do not want to see Japan win over their opponent. This situation is illustrated in Figure 1.

Japan requested special treatment from the United States and China individually and independently but simultaneously. The United States accepted Japan's September 2018 request that it would not trigger safeguard provisions for Japanese automotive products. This could work to further strengthen Japan's bargaining power against China. In this situation, if China had refused Japan's offer of collaboration on infrastructure development in third countries, China would not only have become isolated from the trilateral economic relationship, but the refusal would also have triggered joint action by the United States and Japan against the BRI, or even action against the competitive regime created by the Chinese government. Therefore, China not only accepted the offer but also stepped up and compromised with Japan ("October 2018" in Figure 1). Besides, even

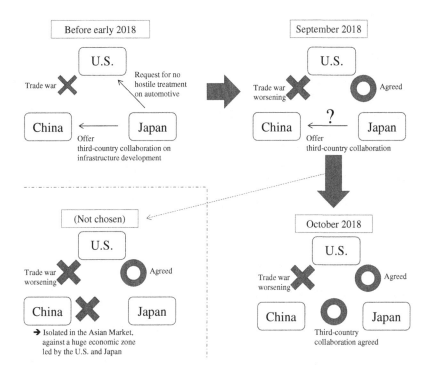

Figure 1: Illustration of the Game of Competition or Collaboration among Three Countries

though China may reduce its economic gains by accepting Japan's offer, it could gain a more apparent benefit in international politics by countering the criticism directed at it. By collaborating with Japan, China gives the world, including the United States, persuasive evidence that it intends to use BRI infrastructure facilities for peaceful purposes, and that it shares risks with the host countries appropriately. Note that if wolf A ate the sheep but was not killed, only injured, by wolf B, the loss for wolf A would be smaller than its gain from eating the sheep. In a real-world three-country game, the sheep (Japan) would be eaten if Japan's request would result in too big a hit to the opponent's national interests.

Thailand's BRI-related infrastructure development projects will be implemented in cooperation with China after China's political influence on Thailand is reduced. Other projects, such as the EEC infrastructure development projects, will be implemented through Japan–China collaboration, as long as the trade war between the United States and China lasts. If a PPP approach is adopted, Thailand would also enjoy the benefits of increased transparency and openness in the bidding and construction processes. In practice, however, Japan gave up participation in the airport link high-speed railway construction project, mainly because the Thai government refused the Japanese companies' request that the Thai side should bear the risks involved in the initial losses in its operation. Appropriate risk sharing between the government and the infrastructure-operating companies is essential for the success of PPP projects, and this risk should be borne by the Thai side (Engel *et al.* 2014). This implies that good governance in the recipient countries is another factor in the success of collaboration.

Conclusion

As the GMS has attracted attention in relation to regional investment for the reallocation of production processes, overcoming bottlenecks in physical connectivity is now at the top of the policy agenda. In this chapter, it has been shown that the creation of economic corridors has an increasingly positive impact on regional economic development, particularly if there are complementary policy efforts aimed at building other underdeveloped infrastructure.

It is clear that there are three reasons why the BRI is significantly affecting infrastructure development in the GMS. One is China's attempt to create a subregional competitiveness regime, the second is Thailand's urgent need for infrastructure development to avoid a middle-income trap, and the third is Japan's increasing difficulties in disbursing its ODA in the subregion.

With Japan's ODA power declining, China has become an alternative provider of economic assistance. This may indeed lead to a syllogistic conclusion that, without effective countermeasures, most subregional infrastructure development will be carried out by China in the foreseeable future. However, this study has highlighted the political-economic structure of Japan–China collaboration at the project level, whereby the two countries are collaborating in a limited but significant manner within the overall structure of bilateral strategic competition. This analysis has clarified that, as the U.S.–China trade war worsens, China has no choice but to accept closer collaboration with Japan in GMS development projects and to allow Japan more favorable conditions. Japan's participation in BRI projects would be welcomed by the GMS countries because it will accelerate good quality infrastructure construction. China may also welcome Japan's participation in the BRI projects because this could be used to ease worldwide concerns about the BRI.

This study is intended to make the case for a possible transformation of human values at both the macro- and local levels through the interplay of great-power geo-economic competition and the international economic order. That is, a local approach to policy framework and practice has metamorphosed to accommodate a mixture of competition and collaboration between Japan and China. Besides, given that Japanese and Chinese values are drastically different in terms of their approach to development, China's attempt to replace the existing international cooperation frameworks may further accelerate the transformation of local human values. The magnitude of China's influence under evolving international political and economic conditions remains to be seen. Given the nature of the positive-sum game in aid and development, the transformation of local human values does not directly reflect international conditions but is complicated by local responses. The analysis in this chapter will hopefully serve as a catalyst for further inquiry into the transformation of local human values in international contexts.

References

Asian Development Bank (ADB). 2011. *ASIA 2050: Realizing the Asian Century*. Manila: ADB.

ADB. 2012. *The Greater Mekong Subregion Economic Cooperation Program Strategic Framework 2012–2022*. Manila: ADB.

ADB. 2017. *Meeting Asia's Infrastructure Needs*. Manila: ADB.

ADB. 2018a. *The GMS Ha Noi Action Plan 2018–2022*. Manila: ADB.

ADB. 2018b. *GMS Economic Cooperation Program: Regional Investment Framework 2022*. Manila: ADB.

ASEAN Secretariat. 2016. *Master Plan on ASEAN Connectivity 2025*. Jakarta: ASEAN.

Baltensperger, Michael, and Uri Dadush. 2019. The Belt and Road Turns Five. Bruegel Policy Contribution, Issue no.1. Retrieved from http://bruegel.org/wp-content/uploads/2019/01/PC-01_2019_.pdf (accessed January 11, 2019).

Engel, Eduardo, Ronald D. Fischer, and Alexander Galetovic. 2014. *The Economics of Public–Private Partnerships*. Cambridge: Cambridge University Press.

Hurley, John, Scott Morris, and Gailyn Portelance. 2018. Examining the Debt Implications of the Belt and Road Initiative from a Policy Perspective. CGD Policy Paper, 121. Center for Global Development, March 4.

Ito, T. 2017. Regional Economic Exchanges. In *Thai-koku Keizai Gaikyou (2016–2017)*, edited by Japanese Chamber of Commerce in Bangkok, 638–650.

Ministry of Foreign Affairs of Japan. 2015. *Development Cooperation Charter* (Cabinet Decision). Retrieved from https://www.mofa.go.jp/policy/oda/page_000138.html (accessed January 22, 2020).

Ministry of Industry of Thailand. 2017. *Eastern Economic Corridor Development Project: Driving Forward...*. Presentation material dated March 23, 2017.

Morse, Julia C. and Robert O. Keohane. 2014. Contested Multilateralism. *The Review of International Organizations* 9(4): 385–412.

Chapter 3

BRI Port Facility Projects and China's Military Intentions: A Japanese Perspective

Sadamasa Oue

Introduction

For the last 5 years, China has sold the "One Belt One Road" initiative, now renamed the Belt and Road Initiative (BRI), as a major facilitator of economic development and prosperity in states that are recipients of Chinese investment. While the Silk Road Economic Belt (One Belt), over-land portion of the BRI, seems to be proceeding relatively well, the 21st Century Maritime Silk Road (One Road), maritime portion of the BRI, is experiencing major setbacks, as demonstrated by the extensive interna-tional criticism it has received, especially from recipient states and foreign research bodies. Many of the BRI projects, both on land and at sea, such as the construction of railroads and port facilities, appear to lack economic viability and profitability. Critics suggest the BRI is just a mask designed to conceal China's grand strategy to become the primary sea power in the Indo-Pacific region, with significant overseas ports.

In 2005, the world was alarmed by China's String of Pearls strategy. This "string" of military bases and diplomatic ties stretches from the Middle East to southern China, and its most conspicuous "pearl" is a new naval base under construction at the Pakistani port of Gwadar.

Additionally, since 2008, the People's Liberation Army Navy (PLAN) has modernized its maritime military strategy and equipment and expanded its activities and area of operations to include anti-piracy operations around the Gulf of Aden. A *Washington Times* article of 2005 further suggested that China is primarily aiming to serve its national security interests by strategically altering the operating environment of the militaries of the United States and its allies; it is not acting in the common interests of the investor and investees.[1]

To cope with the expansion of China's economic and military power, Japan and the United States had to adopt a coherent policy and strategy. On the one hand, both countries have pursued the Free and Open Indo-Pacific (FOIP) vision in the security domain, while on the other hand, they have been divided in the economic domain — for example, over the Trans-Pacific Partnership (TPP) arrangement. This trilateral dynamism in the Indo-Pacific region is not yet functioning well and its future remains to be seen. It is, however, worthwhile to analyze how these policies are being implemented by the three countries, so that critical elements of a coherent policy and strategy can be identified and put into practice. For this purpose, this chapter will analyze relevant developments in the three countries up to the end of November 2018 when Japan's new policy toward China emerged.

I will first analyze the relationship between the BRI and the String of Pearls strategy by examining the maritime military impact of China's investments in port facilities across the Indo-Pacific region. The discussion will center on China's employment of the BRI as a bandwagoning strategy that mobilizes domestic and foreign resources to win favor with the investees. Then, I will investigate the objectives and agenda of the FOIP which serves as the counterstrategy of Japan and the United States. Lastly, given the uncertainty of strategic interaction, I will present a policy proposal for FOIP planning and implementation that would enable Japan to limit China's military-strategic ambitions and rectify its predatory behavior.

---

[1] "China Builds Up Strategic Sea Lanes," *Washington Times*, January 17, 2005. https://www.washingtontimes.com/news/2005/jan/17/20050117-115550-1929r/ (accessed September 25, 2018).

Overview and Analysis of BRI Maritime Investment

The BRI as a key doctrine for realizing the Chinese Dream

Since 1978 when Deng Xiaoping launched the policy of reform and opening-up, China has developed into the world's second-largest economy. Taking full advantage of China's impressive success in enhancing its national power, in both economic and military terms, Xi Jinping declared the "Dream of the Rejuvenation of the Chinese Nation" in November 2012 when he became general secretary of the Chinese Communist Party (CCP). Xi's Chinese Dream has two goals. First, that China should become a "moderately well-off society" by the time of the CCP's centennial in 2021, and second, by the time of the centennial of the People's Republic of China (PRC) in 2049, China should be transformed into a fully developed nation.[2] The 18th National Congress of the CCP (hereinafter, Party Congress) adopted both the BRI as a basic foreign economic policy line and the Chinese Dream as a basic political construct. The 19th Party Congress in October 2017 amended the Party Constitution to include the terms of the BRI in its general provisions, thus politically endorsing the initiative.

It is important to know how Xi came up with the idea of the BRI as a key means of realizing his Chinese Dream as well as a guiding principle for the CCP. In 2010, just prior to Xi's election as general secretary, a book entitled *The China Dream: Great Power Thinking & Strategic Posture in the Post-American Era* was published in Beijing and became a bestseller (Liu 2015). The author, Senior Colonel Liu Mingfu, was at the time a professor at the Chinese National Defense University. From a Sinocentric position and based on Chinese values, Liu proposed a strategy and certain policy measures capable of making China the most powerful state in world politics in the 21st century. More specifically, he emphasized achievement of the Chinese Dream by 2049 within a DIME (diplomacy, information, military, and economic power) framework, with advanced technologies serving as the pivot. To what extent Xi was influenced by this book is difficult to prove, but one can assume that he was inspired by its popular aspirations.

---

[2]Robert Lawrence Kuhn, "Xi Jinping's Chinese Dream," *New York Times*, June 4, 2013. https://www.nytimes.com/2013/06/05/opinion/global/xi-jinpings-chinese-dream.html (accessed September 25, 2018).

The BRI, originally termed One Belt One Road, is an initiative proposed by President Xi Jinping in a series of speeches delivered in late 2013. In March 2015, the document *Vision and Actions on Jointly Building Belt and Road* was issued jointly by China's National Development and Reform Commission, the Ministry of Foreign Affairs, and the Ministry of Commerce.[3] This document presents a vision of China-led and China-centered trade and investment for growth and development over the Eurasian land mass and across the Indo-Pacific. It proposes key projects focused on infrastructure building, particularly port facilities.

Many of the BRI projects were, and still are, investments undertaken by Chinese state-owned companies (SOCs) well before the announcement of the BRI, or no more than blueprints for several multinational economic corridors and maritime passages. It was Xi Jinping who transformed these existing projects and combined them with new ideas to form a basic guideline for the PRC's global investment. Now, China seems to have committed itself to this national ambition, pouring in resources of all kinds, including those mobilized by its newly established Asia Infrastructure Investment Bank (AIIB). BRI investment is estimated to amount to US$1 trillion, meaning that it imposes a significant financial burden on the PRC government. Faced with slowing economic growth and a confrontation with the United States over trade, the future of Xi Jinping and the CCP regime are heavily dependent on the success of the BRI.

Criticism of BRI port projects

In 2018, the Washington-based think tank C4ADS published a detailed analysis of BRI port projects entitled, *Harbored Ambitions: How China's Port Investments Are Strategically Reshaping the Indo-Pacific* (Thorne and Spevack 2018), which identifies their predatory nature and contradicts China's self-righteous characterization of the investments. The study also offers a critical vantage point from which to analyze the relationship between China's pledge to promote economic development and

---

[3] *Vision and Actions on Jointly Building Belt and Road*, China.org.cn, accessed September 25, 2018. http://www.china.org.cn/chinese/2015-09/15/content_36591064.htm.

its growing military presence in the Indo-Pacific, thereby revealing its real political objectives. The analysis concludes:

China is neither pursuing geopolitical advantages merely as an aftermath to regional development nor pursuing regional military hegemony. Rather, Beijing is molding the Indo-Pacific to ensure its national security interests are adequately protected through the development of commercial ports that can facilitate long-range military patrols and investments that can generate political goodwill or — when necessary — coercive power (Thorne and Spevack 2018, p. 11).

This conclusion, however, offers no straightforward judgment as to whether BRI port investments affect the international *status quo*. Neither does it discount China's ability to use gunboat diplomacy to build a regional military hegemony, including the visits of its aircraft carrier *Liaoning* to Hambantota, Gwadar, or the Djibouti naval base. Yet, the C4ADS study issues a clear warning that China's security strategy utilizes infrastructure investments to generate political influence, stealthily expand its military presence, and create an environment that would give Beijing strategic advantages. How can we be sure that China's port investments respect the investee states' development interests and maintenance of the regional *status quo* in the Indo-Pacific? The world should carefully monitor China's port investments and curtail their military influence.

Another report by Parker and Chefitz (2018) analyzes China's maritime investments in the Indo-Pacific region from a U.S. security strategy perspective. The report's executive summary concludes thus,

Over the past decade, China has extended hundreds of billions of dollars in loans to countries that often can't afford to repay them. Through a process the authors have termed "debtbook diplomacy," China has begun to leverage this accumulated debt to achieve its strategic aims.

Three primary strategic goals the authors believe China could target with this technique are: filling out a "String of Pearls" to solve its "Malacca Dilemma" and project power across vital South Asian trading routes; undermining and fracturing the U.S.-led regional coalition contesting Beijing's South China Sea (SCS) claims; and enabling the People's Liberation Army Navy (PLAN) to push through the "Second Island Chain" into the blue-water Pacific (Parker and Chefitz 2018, p. 1).

The Harvard-sponsored report presents accurate and detailed findings and observations that suggest that the unclear objectives of China's BRI port projects are likely to challenge the United States militarily. More specifically, the report has led to wider use and understanding of the term "debtbook diplomacy" within the policy community in the United States and internationally. Vice President Mike Pence referred to it in a speech delivered on October 4, 2018, articulating a new American policy toward China.

Both of the above reports provide facts upon which we can build our analysis of the unexplored security implications of the BRI port projects and how they could affect Japan's security policy.

Deteriorating environment surrounding the BRI

Recently, the BRI has experienced challenges which are centered on its port projects. Various reports, including the ones cited above, have generated harsh criticism of China, thus aggravating the international environment surrounding the BRI. The governments of many indebted countries have changed their attitude toward the initiative. For example, Prime Minister Imran Kahn of Pakistan raised questions about the China–Pakistan Economic Corridor (CPEC) and promised to review the Gwadar port project in order to avoid a financial crisis. After his return to power, Prime Minister Mahathir Mohamad of Malaysia warned of the risk of "a new colonialism" being pursued by China. The BRI has also faced similar criticism in Sri Lanka, Myanmar, and the Maldives.

With its economic growth slowing, China is finding it increasingly difficult to finance BRI projects, while unprofitable projects have suffered from non-performing loans (Matsumura 2018). Moreover, China was confronted by the Trump administration in the United States concerning its hegemonic aspirations centered on the trade war. The centerpiece of the U.S. policy is correction of export/import imbalances, including China's unilaterally favorable rules and customs. The mutual imposition of more tariffs will impact China's economy and the outcome of this trade dispute is yet to be determined. Furthermore, the AIIB, despite its stated objectives, has made a very limited financial contribution to BRI projects and has failed to mobilize international funds.

In spite of increasing criticism of the BRI port projects, Xi Jinping seemed to be determined to continue to promote the BRI as a whole. In his remarks at the fifth anniversary roundtable discussion in August 2018,

Xi proudly listed the achievements of the BRI and the international support it had garnered. He also dismissed criticism of the initiative, characterizing the BRI as "an important measure to promote global cooperation in healthy economic developments."

However, this unusual rebuttal of criticism from China's top leader could be proof of his apprehension concerning growing resistance to the BRI. China has undertaken several practical improvements to the BRI aimed at getting it back on its feet — for example, by introducing some overdue risk management measures, both at the basic planning and project implementation levels. Now, BRI port projects need to be scrutinized in the light of their geostrategic implications as well as their relationship with the Chinese military presence in the Indo-Pacific region.

Evolution of China's Maritime Military Strategy and Activities

China's core interests and the Malacca dilemma

The Chinese Dream must be buttressed by military as well as economic measures. While the BRI performs the economic role in the Indo-Pacific region, the Chinese armed forces play the military part, with focus on the protection of China's core national interests, including its territorial integrity and sea lines of communication (SLOC). And the Chinese Dream will not be achieved until the PRC reunifies Taiwan with China, either peacefully or by force.

As early as 2005, at the Third Session of the 10th National People's Congress, China enacted its Anti-Secession Law, which forms the legal basis for preventing Taiwan from declaring independence or for taking back the island, if necessary (Easton 2017). In 2003, the then president of the PRC, Hu Jintao, expressed concerns about a situation since referred to as the Malacca Dilemma: that the U.S. Navy would be able to close the Malacca Strait, a choke point in China's vital SLOC, to deter China from using force against Taiwan (Storey 2006). China's military strategy has been formulated to cope with this risk that jeopardizes one of China's core interests, Taiwan, which is also integral to the Chinese Dream.

For more than two decades, China has consistently and significantly increased its military spending, involving huge arms buildups in the pursuit of enhanced air and sea power focused on Anti Access/Area Denial (A2AD) in the East and South China Seas. This buildup followed the adoption of the Three-Stage Development Strategy in which maritime military strategy plays a central role. According to the *China Security Report 2016*, published by Japan's National Institute for Defense Studies (NIDS 2016), the PLAN has changed its basic concept three times as China's military policy has evolved from coastal defense via near seas defense to open seas protection. In other words, the PLAN has been steadily transformed from a brown-water navy to a full-fledged blue-water navy. In addition, the *NIDS China Military Strategy*, published in May 2015, speculates that the wording change from "defense" to "protection" may reflect China's intention to emphasize the cooperative nature of PLAN offshore activities such as escorting merchant vessels threatened by piracy in the Gulf of Aden.

As for future modernization of the military, in his remarks to the 19th Party Congress in October 2017, General Secretary Xi Jinping proclaimed that the goals of mechanization and the application of IT had come a long way, and that strategic capabilities would see a big improvement by the year 2020. He also mentioned that by 2035 the modernization of China's national defense and its armed forces would be completed, and that by the mid-21st century, the people's armed forces would be fully transformed into a world-class force. These goals are said to be ahead of the target of the third stage of the Three-Stage Development Strategy and suggest further acceleration of military power buildup as China's power grows.[4]

Although President Xi has not referred specifically to the Malacca Dilemma, he has referred to steadfast progress with a military strategy designed to achieve the unification of China by keeping to the present maritime strategy. In accordance with the abovementioned strategies, China has also expanded PLAN operations and activities, on which this chapter will focus.

The expansion of Chinese maritime military operations

Although China insists on the defensive nature of its military buildup, we can assume that the PLA will prepare for contingency operations.

---

[4]"Nippon no Bouei 2018" [Defense of Japan 2018], Ministry of Defense. http://www.mod.go.jp/e/publ/w_paper/pdf/2018/DOJ2018_1-2-3_web.pdf Japan (accessed October 15, 2018).

Therefore, it is useful to know how neighboring countries such as Japan understand the PLA's goals.

Japan's 2018 Defense Whitepaper articulates the military objectives of the PLAN and the PLA Air Force (PLAAF) as follows. Their first objective is to intercept operations by adversaries in waters and airspace as far as possible from China in order to defend Chinese territory, territorial waters, and territorial airspace. The second objective is to develop military capabilities to deter and prevent Taiwan independence. The third is to weaken the control of other countries and to strengthen China's claim to Taiwan through various surveillance activities and use of force, at sea and in airspace surrounding the island over which China claims sovereignty. The fourth is to acquire, maintain, and protect China's rights and interests, such as those in relation to oil and gas. The fifth is to defend its SLOC, as if it is to expand its global economy, China will need to protect its sea lanes, including its oil transportation routes from the Middle East.[5]

The Whitepaper also points to China's remarkable progress in securing overseas bases and logistical support facilities in distant regions. The PLAN can play a role in shoring up the BRI through SLOC protection. In return, BRI-related port infrastructure will enhance China's military activities in the Indo-Pacific region. China's Whitepaper on Asia-Pacific Security Cooperation of 2017 acknowledges that "security and development are closely linked and mutually complementary," in that one facilitates the other (State Council, People's Republic of China 2017). Indeed, it is difficult, if not impossible, to draw a neat and clear line between the power that allows a country to open and maintain trade routes and the clout that builds an empire. Capabilities are easy to measure — for example, military bases and civilian port facilities. Intent is harder to discern. While the relationship between strategic military objectives and the BRI port projects will be discussed in the next section, dual usage of port infrastructure for military and civilian purposes should be recognized as critical to understanding the nature of the BRI. The Maldives provides a clear example. Since 2014 China has assisted the country in building the interisland Friendship Bridge, an apartment complex on an artificial island, and a resort development. In August 2017, three Chinese submarines

---

[5] *Ibid.*

docked at a Maldivian port, caused an angry reaction from India whose coast lies less than 500 km from the Maldives' northernmost atoll.[6]

Given China's military objective of expanding PLAN operations and the utility of civil port facilities, it will be increasingly necessary to assess PLAN offshore activities.

The increase in PLAN offshore activities

While the PLAN has significantly intensified its drills, exercises, patrols, and other military activities in the East and South China Seas, it has also expanded its operations into the Western Pacific and the Indian Ocean. Since 2008, the PLAN has periodically dispatched its ships to carry out exercises beyond the so-called first island chain, stretching from the Japanese archipelago via Taiwan to the Philippines. One example was the Maneuver 5 exercise of October 2013. The PLAN also sent a flotilla of four vessels to participate in the RIMPAC multinational naval exercises held by the U.S. Pacific Navy in waters near Hawaii in 2014. In the Indian Ocean, China dispatched two frigates and a supply ship to carry out anti-piracy operations in December 2008. And according to one high-ranking PLAN official, in 2009, China had already demonstrated its intention to seek logistics bases to support enduring maritime operations. Since then, the PLAN has continued its anti-piracy operations, and the 26th Flotilla has been on patrol with logistics support from a newly constructed naval base in Djibouti.

The PLAN also improved its operational capacity by undertaking bilateral military exercises, with, for example, Pakistan and the U.S. Navy. The PLAN has also dispatched naval assets for humanitarian assistance and disaster relief purposes. For example, a destroyer on anti-piracy duty helped with a non-combatant evacuation operation from Libya in February–March 2011. In March 2015, PLAN anti-piracy vessels again evacuated 255 people from 10 countries, including Japan, from Yemen, while in May that year, the PLAN conducted disaster relief activities in Sri Lanka after that country had suffered from flooding and landslides.

---

[6]"Maldives' New Leaders Confront a Chinese-Funded Building Binge," *Wall Street Journal*. https://www.wsj.com/articles/maldives-new-leaders-confront-a-chinese-funded-building-binge-1543401005 (accessed November 30, 2018).

Moreover, PLAN submarines have been conspicuously active in the Indian Ocean. In 2014, a Song-class submarine visited Colombo, Sri Lanka, for the first overseas port call by a Chinese submarine. In 2015 and 2016 respectively, Yuan-class and Shang-class submarines visited Karachi, Pakistan, and in 2017, Song-class and Yuan-class submarines showed up in Kota Kinabalu, Malaysia. Given the clandestine nature of submarine operations, these activities may have been paving the way for China to conduct full-scale underwater operations in the Indian Ocean while utilizing BRI-related ports.

In line with the three-stage maritime military strategy, the PLAN has expanded and increased its military operations and activities in the Indian and Pacific Oceans.

China's Veiled Military-Strategic Intentions and the BRI as an Instrument for Enhancing China's Maritime Posture

The BRI in the String of Pearls strategy

The *Harbored Ambitions* study examines 15 port projects and finds that 7 of them began in 2013 or later, while others were either restored or expanded after China announced the BRI (Thorne and Spevack 2018). All the 12 port projects which are in progress under the banner of the BRI are located in strategically important positions and suitable for dual use, although their actual functions and roles are not transparent. The January 2005 *Washington Times* article mentioned above was the first to raise the alarm about a String of Pearls made up of the Pakistani port of Gwadar, a port facility at Chittagong (Bangladesh), naval bases in Burma, and a military agreement with Cambodia. All these cases were examined in the C4ADS study, and given the date of this article, China was evidently harboring ambitions in this regard long before it unveiled the BRI. Beijing simply used the BRI to accelerate the formation of the String of Pearls.

The first official BRI policy document, *Vision and Actions on Jointly Building Belt and Road*, published in 2015, states that "the initiative will focus on ... jointly building smooth, secure, and efficient routes connecting major seaports along the Belt and Road." The stated aim of the BRI is to enhance economic development through infrastructure and energy connectivity. Many developing countries are indeed seriously in need of infrastructure, and the existing international development banks, such as the Asian Development Bank (ADB), cannot fulfil this need, primarily due to their rigorous financing criteria and conditions. This has given China a good opportunity to bring these developing countries into the BRI, using its funds, resources, and labor force, with its profit-seeking SOCs acting as the agent.

Also, the China-led AIIB commenced operations in January 2016 with a mission to promote the BRI. As it boasts on the homepage of its website,

> The Asian Infrastructure Investment Bank (AIIB) is a multilateral devel-opment bank with a mission to improve social and economic outcomes in Asia. Headquartered in Beijing, we began operations in January 2016 and have now grown to 87 approved members worldwide. By investing in sustainable infrastructure and other productive sectors in Asia and beyond, we will better connect people, services and markets that over time will impact the lives of billions and build a better future.[7]
>
> True, the BRI seems to have been largely accepted by the interna-tional community, but it is now facing impediments and setbacks as major investee states have postponed, suspended, or even cancelled their BRI projects.[8]

Clearly, the BRI has contributed to Beijing's String of Pearls strategy. First, it has dexterously transformed the "pearls" into infrastructure devel-opment initiatives. According to the source for the *Washington Times* article (an internal report entitled *Energy Futures in Asia*, prepared for Donald Rumsfeld when he was U.S. secretary of defense), "China is building strategic relationships along the sea lanes from the Middle East to the South China Sea in ways that suggest defensive and offensive posi-tioning to protect China's energy interests, but also to serve broad security objectives." This view squarely contradicts the officially announced BRI objectives which make no mention of China's geostrategic goals. On the contrary, Xi Jinping has emphasized that "we will not resort to outdated

---

[7]https://www.aiib.org/en/index.html (accessed September 25, 2018).
[8]For one example, see https://www.nikkei.com/article/DGKKZO36376070R11C18A 0FF1000/ (accessed October 5, 2018).

political maneuvering" and that "what we hope to achieve is a new model of win-win cooperation."[9]

By using the BRI to implement the String of Pearls, China has transformed the strategy from a limited, slow, and secretive process into a rapid and well-publicized project. The notorious case of debt diplomacy involving Sri Lanka provides a typical example of this process. Hambantota Port in Sri Lanka, in conjunction with the Colombo Port City Project (CPCP), is the BRI maritime initiative at the most advanced stage of construction. A feasibility study began in 2001 and in 2006, China and Sri Lanka signed an agreement on the port development. Construction of the first phase began in 2008 and upon the completion of the construction of the berths the opening ceremony took place in November 2010. The second phase of construction started in May 2011 and at the time of writing had yet to be completed. In September 2014, Xi Jinping visited Sri Lanka to celebrate the inauguration of the CPCP as a Maritime Silk Road project. In April 2016, the Sri Lankan Prime Minister, Ranil Wickramasinghe, visited China and the two countries signed an agreement on the Hambantota development project, including the resumption of the second phase of the port construction and the development of the industrial area, the dockyard, LNG plants, the airport, and highway. During his visit to Beijing, Prime Minister Wickramasinghe denied the possibility of Chinese military deployment to the port, saying that "China has never requested military bases in Sri Lanka." He said, "Our policy is to make Sri Lanka a hub of the Indian Ocean which will benefit both Silk Road and Made-in-India" (Arai 2017). After some bitter wrangling between the two sides, the state-owned China Merchants Port Holdings Co., Ltd. (CM Port) acquired a 90-year lease on the port and the adjacent 15,000-hectare special economic zone in exchange for China writing off Sri Lanka's US$1.12 billion debt. PLAN vessels have been careful to stay away from Hambantota, although they have made a brief call (or calls) at Colombo. How China is going to exercise its political influence over Sri Lanka and whether it will use the port for military purposes remains to be seen.

---

[9]"Full Text of President Xi's Speech at Opening of Belt and Road Forum," May 15, 2017. https://www.fmprc.gov.cn/mfa_eng/wjdt_665385/zyjh_665391/t1465819.shtml (accessed October 15, 2018).

Geostrategic Implications

Many military experts and analysts question China's use of economic aid through the BRI to pursue Beijing's grand strategy (Thorne and Spevack 2018, pp. 19–21) and refute official Chinese assertions that no military motivations are involved. Indeed, China has exercised restraint in the deployment of naval assets to Hambantota. This is in contrast to cases in the South China Sea and its first overseas military base and naval facility in Djibouti.

In February 2016, China announced the construction of its first overseas supply base in Djibouti. On August 1, 2017, the 90th anniversary of the PLA, an opening and deployment ceremony was held in Djibouti, attended by the vice commander of the PLAN and China's defense minister. Nine years had passed since China first dispatched PLAN vessels off the coast of Somalia.[10] The defense minister described the purpose of the base as being to provide "peace keeping as well as humanitarian assistance in Africa and West Asia," while the Xinhua News Agency suggested it was for military cooperation, naval exercises, and noncombatant evacuation operations.[11] One official Chinese website protested that the base did not represent a "China threat," given that the large U.S., Japanese, and French military bases in Djibouti were close to the Chinese base.[12] Japan also constructed its first overseas military base in Djibouti in 2011 to support the counter-piracy operations of the Japan Maritime Self-Defense Forces (JMSDF), which were undertaken at almost at the same time as China's. Certainly, there is no legitimate reason to criticize China alone.

The BRI is exerting a significant economic and strategic effect. China has taken advantage of this ambiguity, leveraging its economic power to achieve strategic objectives. China's "debtbook diplomacy" has turned out to be a very effective instrument for influencing authoritarian, often corrupt, governments to act in its favor. Even though they are aware of the

---

[10]"Chugoku Kaigun Ga Jibuti Ni Hatsu No Kaigunnkiti" [PLAN Opens the First Overseas Base], August 22, 2017. https://www.businessinsider.jp/post-102460 (accessed September 22, 2018).

[11]*Ibid.*

[12]"Hatsu No Kaigai Gunjikiti Ha Chugoku No Kyoui Ka?" [Is the First Overseas Base China Threat?]. http://japanese.china.org.cn/politics/txt/2017-07/13/content_41207268.htm (accessed October 10, 2018).

risks involved, many developing countries are vulnerable to Chinese offers of aid and investment rather than using the more regulated international development banks and the mechanisms of the OECD countries. In other words, China has succeeded in filling the vacuum left by the United States and other developed countries, most conspicuously in the field of aid and investment for infrastructure development. Therefore, the developed world will have to find alternative measures for aid and investment in order to compete with China and maintain the stability of the Indo-Pacific region.

Moreover, China has denied that it is using the BRI ports for military purposes, which is consistent with PLAN activities, at least until now. Nevertheless, as all of the ports are dual purpose, given host government approval, the PLAN would be able to dock at any of these assets. This is instrumental in achieving both naval supremacy *vis-à-vis* the United States in the Indo-Pacific and the Chinese Dream. True, China is working in the common interest when it engages in security activities in the Indian Ocean, such as countering piracy, evacuating civilians, and carrying out humanitarian assistance/disaster relief (HA/DR) operations. While PLAN cooperation in these areas should be welcomed, future PLAN deployments as well as any predatory unilateral moves on the part of China must be checked. For this purpose, the United States, its allies, and other likeminded states will have to jointly deploy overwhelming naval assets *vis-à-vis* PLAN so as to maintain maritime supremacy in the theater.

This chapter has analyzed the BRI port projects in the light of China's covert military objectives. To cope with China's well-crafted strategy, Japan and the United States have adopted the FOIP policy and strategy in both the economic and military domains. I will focus on that below.

Japan's Strategy and Policy Toward the BRI

The FOIP vs. the BRI

Prime Minister Shinzo Abe formally announced the FOIP in his keynote address of June 28, 2016, to the Sixth Tokyo International Conference on African Development (TICAD) held in Nairobi, Kenya. The address made it clear that the FOIP is centered on investment in the development of quality infrastructure and the building of resilient health systems that will lay the foundations for peace and stability under Japanese public–private partnership.[13] The FOIP is based on the principles of free trade and freedom of navigation, the rule of law, and the market economy. While the BRI has attracted criticism of various kinds, Japan's FOIP is endorsed by leaders across the Mekong River region of Southeast Asia. On October 9, 2018, the Tenth Mekong–Japan Summit Meeting was held in Tokyo, where the Tokyo Strategy 2018 for Mekong–Japan Cooperation together with its annexes was adopted.[14] This pact was bolstered by a promise of investment in "quality infrastructure," that is, infrastructure that is financially and environmentally sustainable. These moves are neither exclusive nor are they in opposition to the BRI. They are intended to be viable alternatives to the BRI as well as inclusive of it.

Japan has taken a leading role in the security aspect of the FOIP by promoting cooperation with the United States, Australia, and India — the so-called QUAD (Quadrilateral) states — and with the member states of the Association of Southeast Asian Nations (ASEAN). The QUAD was initiated as an informal strategic dialogue in 2007 by Prime Minister Abe. The four countries held security consultations on the margins of the Twelfth East Asia Summit in Manila on November 12, 2017, and reaffirmed the importance of the QUAD for the first time since 2007 (Shimodaira 2018). Leaders of all four countries, including President Donald Trump, agreed to revive the security pact given the rising tension in the South China Sea caused primarily by China's assertion of its territorial ambitions.

With strong leadership from Prime Minister Abe and the unanimous support of the United States, Australia, and India, the influence of the FOIP prevailed across the Indo-Pacific. Now, the FOIP, in which the Japan–U.S. alliance plays a central role, is buttressing the security and stability of the Asia-Pacific *vis-à-vis* China's increasing military presence and influence. However, Japan was dismayed when President Trump abruptly withdrew from the TPP during his first week in office.

---

[13]"Japan's Measures for Africa at TICAD VI: Quality and Empowerment," August 27, 2016. https://www.mofa.go.jp/files/000183835.pdf (accessed October 2, 2018).
[14]"The 10th Mekong–Japan Summit Meeting," October 9, 2018. https://www.mofa.go.jp/s_sa/sea1/page4e_000937.html (accessed October 12, 2018).

The U.S. factor

Japan and the United States prudently stayed outside of the BRI while joining forces to establish the TPP. Although it has not been admitted publicly, the TPP and the FOIP are inherently ripostes to the BRI. Prime Minister Abe announced on March 15, 2013, that Japan would begin negotiations for joining the TPP.[15] It was a critical as well as a difficult decision which was opposed by other factions within the ruling Liberal Democratic Party. But Abe gave priority to cooperation with the Obama administration in the creation of a new economic zone. He said,

> The significance of the TPP is not limited to the economic impact on our country. Japan is creating a new economic zone with our ally, the United States. Other countries who share the universal values of freedom, democracy, basic human rights, and the rule of law are joining. I firmly believe that creating new rules in the Asia-Pacific region with these countries is not only in Japan's national interests, but also certain to bring prosperity to the world.[16]

From the beginning of negotiations in March 2010 to February 4, 2016, when the TPP treaty was signed by the 12 participating countries, the process was led by the United States. The agreement was meant to reduce or eliminate tariffs on up to 18,000 agricultural and manufactured products, boosting trade, economic growth, and political ties between the 12 countries. Barack Obama and the other top leaders, including Prime Minister Abe, believed that this deal had the potential to bolster U.S. power and influence on the Asia-Pacific rim and balance a rising China.

Obama's successor believed otherwise, however, as withdrawal from the TPP was one of Trump's "America first" policies. He believed that it would deprive the United States of jobs and only benefit large U.S. multinational corporations. Although his argument may not have been totally wrong, there is a huge downside to Washington's withdrawal. For example, it meant the United States would lose the many benefits of free trade. Free trade in the Pacific will probably continue, but it will not be U.S.-led free trade. As one critic has written,

---

[15]Press Conference by Prime Minister Shinzo Abe, March 15, 2013. https://japan.kantei.go.jp/96_abe/statement/201303/15kaiken_e.html (accessed September 22, 2018).
[16]*Ibid.*

One of the biggest benefactors from TPP's ending is the superpower that didn't participate in the deal from the start — China. China now has the call on how regional trade is conducted … which also enhances financial and political ties with other countries. Regardless of the United States' stance, free trade will continue. But this time, the U.S. is no longer pulling the strings (Pham 2017).

So to meet the challenge from China, Japan, instead of the reluctant United States, took the lead in the negotiations for the conclusion of a new Comprehensive and Progressive Agreement for Trans-Pacific Partnership (CPTPP), or TPP-11 on account of the 11 signatories. Japan is still calling for the United States to return to the CPTPP, while at the same time exploring appropriate cooperation with China.

Formulating a New Policy for Japan

The impending issue

The BRI is a pillar of the Chinese Dream that exploits China's economic power, enhances its military presence, and expands its political influence. The United States, Japan, and most other developed countries are trying to counter China's predatory pursuit of this dream. The recipients of China's BRI investments are now burdened with China-sponsored, economically unviable projects and are mired in a debt trap, and this has attracted criticism both within those countries and abroad. However, there has been no serious armed conflict between China and a major power as a result. Neither has any major BRI project collapsed or any investee state gone bankrupt. Xi Jinping and other top Chinese leaders, both political and military, unanimously insist that the BRI is a win-win opportunity for all. As Xi Jinping has said, "Through the BRI, a peaceful, prosperous, open, innovative, and civilized road will be built."[17] Therefore, Japan, in tandem with the declining U.S. hegemon, must develop a new approach to entice — or if necessary force — China to match its words with deeds, no matter whether its intentions in promoting the BRI are malicious or

---

[17]"Work Together to Build the Silk Road Economic Belt and the 21st Century Maritime Silk Road," speech by Xi Jinping at the Opening Ceremony of the Belt and Road Forum for International Cooperation, May 14, 2017. http://www.xinhuanet.com/english/2017-05/14/c_136282982.htm (accessed September 16, 2018).

benevolent. Japan, the United States, and China have intensified their strategic interaction, both bilaterally and trilaterally, now most conspicuously in the form of bilateral trade negotiations that can potentially shape the geo-economic landscape of the Indo-Pacific region. Thus, as all the parties involved are approaching a critical juncture in their relations, they now have to seek solutions.

The U.S. approach

Under President Donald Trump, the United States clearly shifted its China policy from one of engagement to confrontation. The National Defense Strategy (NDS) saw China as "a strategic competitor using predatory economics to intimidate its neighbors while militarizing features in the South China Sea."[18] Vice President Mike Pence's remarks of October 4, 2018, touched on the BRI thus:

> In fact, China uses so-called "debt diplomacy" to expand its influence. Today, that country is offering hundreds of billions of dollars in infrastructure loans to governments from Asia to Africa to Europe and even Latin America. Yet the terms of those loans are opaque at best, and the benefits invariably flow overwhelmingly to Beijing.
>
> Just ask Sri Lanka, which took on massive debt to let Chinese state companies build a port of questionable commercial value. Two years ago, that country could no longer afford its payments, so Beijing pressured Sri Lanka to deliver the new port directly into Chinese hands. It may soon become a forward military base for China's growing blue-water navy (White House 2018).

Pence's remarks constituted a harsh, straightforward demand that China change its predatory behavior and relinquish its military ambitions. Under Trump, the United States adopted an unequivocal declaratory policy line involving long-term strategic competition with China, which would require the seamless integration of multiple elements of national power — diplomacy, information, economics, finance, intelligence, law

---

[18]"Summary of the 2018 National Defense Strategy of the United States of America," https://dod.defense.gov/Portals/1/Documents/pubs/2018-National-Defense-Strategy-Summary.pdf#search='US+national+defense+strategy' (accessed September 15, 2018).

enforcement, and the military (Department of Defense 2018). This was aimed at getting China to modify its BRI-related strategies and policies.

Japan should expect the bilateral trade negotiations to be similar to those between the United States and the Republic of Korea. Yet, given its limited power and influence in world politics, Japan will most likely assume that the United States will take the lead and continue to share values and principles with Japan, other likeminded countries, and the debt-burdened investee states. Ultimately the United States must leverage its soft power to mobilize support among the countries of the region for a policy designed to counter China.

The emerging Japanese approach

In contrast to the United States' confrontational line, Japan adopted a more cooperative stance toward China's BRI. For example, Prime Minister Abe's visit to Beijing in October 2018 to mark the 40th anniversary of the Japan–China Peace and Friendship Treaty moved bilateral relations away from competition toward cooperation.[19] The two countries signed 52 memorandums of understanding on issues including bilateral cooperation in the areas of innovation and intellectual property, Prime Minister Abe set four prerequisites for bilateral collaboration in aid and investment for other countries without referring to the BRI. These were that funding should be evaluated according to the criteria of: (1) openness, (2) transparency, (3) economic efficiency, and (4) healthy budgetary conditions of the recipient country.[20] In other words, Japan was trying to persuade China to voluntarily modify its basic approach to aid and investment without losing face. This soft approach carries the risk that Japan's rapprochement with China may undermine the U.S. strategy, but Japanese diplomats consulted in advance with the United States to avoid any possible misunderstandings. If Japan and the United States play "good cop, bad cop" roles in a coherent manner, they may be able to reorient the approach to BRI projects in such a way that they truly become win–win cooperation. At this point, China could make a decisive choice between a strategically cooperative or a competitive policy toward Japan and the

---

[19]"Japan, China Peace and Friendship Treaty Marks 40th Anniversary," *The Mainichi*, October 23, 2018. https://mainichi.jp/english/articles/20181023/p2a/00m/0na/003000c.
[20]For example, https://www.nikkei.com/article/DGKKZO35747260V20C18A9PP8000/ (accessed October 7, 2018).

United States. Choosing the latter would mean collision and confrontation with all the countries involved.

Prime Minister Abe's approach to China was a natural extension of the FOIP strategy, which had been quietly renamed the FOIP vision. While some observers see the FOIP as a strategy for countering China's BRI, Abe repeatedly emphasized that it is not intended to exclude China but to include it in the Indo-Pacific region, so that economic development can be achieved through free trade and infrastructure investment. The United States paid close attention to Japan's FOIP initiative, and Abe discussed it, along with the four criteria mentioned above, with President Trump at the Japan–U.S. summit meeting in November 2017. After that, Washington introduced the term "free and open Indo-Pacific," instead of "Asia Pacific, as a key concept in the *National Security Strategy* (NSS) of December 18, 2017." Moreover, Secretary of State Mike Pompeo announced that the United States would invest US$113 million in ASEAN countries at the Foreign Ministerial Meeting on August 3, 2018 (Watts 2018). The size of this investment was dwarfed by that of China, which cast doubt on U.S. policy commitment in the region. The FOIP is a viable alternative as well as an effective instrument for containing the BRI if it can supply more attractive development projects.

The Abe administration adopted more active policies in the security area, too. During the prime minister's visit to Beijing, Japan concluded the long-awaited agreement on maritime search and rescue cooperation with China. In September 2018, the Maritime Self Defense Force dispatched a submarine, a helicopter-carrier destroyer, and two destroyers to conduct bilateral live-fire exercises with the U.S. Navy in the South China Sea. After the exercise, the Japanese submarine docked in Vietnam, while the surface flotilla headed to the Philippines and Indonesia before conducting more war games with the British, Sri Lankan, and Indian navies. These moves were intended to send the message to China as well as to the United States that Japan is striving to be a regional balancer and a guardian of the rule of law.

Policy Recommendations for Japan

Based on the above analysis, Japan and the United States should pursue the following policies. First in the security realm, both countries have to maintain superior military strength in the maritime Indo-Pacific theater so that they can reassure allies and deter China. QUAD will be an effective framework for maritime military cooperation and capability enhancement. Japan and the United States need to support countries whose BRI ports are being used by the PLAN and, if necessary, warn China that it must keep its promises concerning non-military use. In this regard, China's reclamation and militarization activities in the South China Sea provide valuable lessons. It will be a test for China to prove whether it has covert hegemonic ambitions. At the same time, Japan and the United States should welcome cooperation with the PLAN in anti-piracy, HA/DR, and freedom of navigation activities. This interactive cooperation and transparency might be improved with respect to China's strategic goal.

In the economic and trade arena, Japan and the United States must align their policies toward China, particularly those designed to counter the BRI. The ongoing U.S.–China trade war and technological competition may or may not turn out to be a "new Cold War," but it is time for the three sides to come to the table to discuss and identify their respective roles in the Indo-Pacific region, roles that are sustainable and mutually acceptable. Although Japan and the United States should pursue this trilateral dialogue with China, they first have to discuss how they should each behave toward China, not their bilateral trade deficits. Japan will probably promote cooperation with China on a case-by-case basis in accordance with the criteria and principles on which the FOIP and the TPP are based.

The BRI does not yet constitute a frontal challenge to the rules-based liberal international order. As China cannot finance BRI projects on its own, Western countries can be complementary financial contributors, thereby exercising some form of benign control over projects from within. This will surely give these countries bargaining power. More specifically, Japan and the United States have to begin by more closely monitoring the ongoing BRI projects and finding viable ways to rescue the indebted countries. Clearly, we should start by making better use of the AIIB and other development banks or funds that provide a just and transparent alternative to the BRI.

The Possible China Response

True, it remains to be seen how the BRI port projects will pan out. There are four possible scenarios: termination, continuation, reinforcement, and adaptation. The BRI plays a central role in the achievement of the Chinese

Dream as formally stipulated in the Chinese Communist Party Constitution. This makes it impossible for Xi Jinping to terminate the projects. Yet, continuation on the present course is likely to be difficult, because of China's slowing economic growth, worsening financial situation, and closer scrutiny by concerned critics. However, if Japan, the United States, and other democratic countries are unwilling to offer viable alternatives to BRI projects, China may be able to appease heavily indebted investee states with limited but favorable rescheduling. Beijing may reinforce the BRI if Xi judges that a new Cold War against the United States is unavoidable and if he is determined to challenge Washington for global hegemony. In fact, many developing countries in the Middle East, Eastern Europe, and the Mediterranean are interested in BRI projects, so the attractions of the Chinese offer should not be underestimated. In this sense, a U.S.–China trade war would have a critical impact on the BRI's future, too. If China cannot afford all-out confrontation with the United States, it must opt for adaptation of the BRI.

The Way Forward

To make the BRI a win–win game, therefore, China must be a responsible investor and avoid driving its development projects into bankruptcy. Japan would reciprocate and welcome China's new strategy by cooperating with it. The United States would respond in a similar way. As Mike Pence said,

> We want a constructive relationship with Beijing where our prosperity and security grow together, not apart. While Beijing has been moving further away from this vision, China's rulers can still change course and return to the spirit of reform and opening that characterize the beginning of this relationship decades ago....
>
> ...Today, America is reaching out our hand to China. And we hope that soon, Beijing will reach back with deeds, not words, and with renewed respect for America. But be assured: we will not relent until our relationship with China is grounded in fairness, reciprocity, and respect for our sovereignty (White House 2018).

The above analysis has hopefully made it clear that, assuming China is a rational actor, a successful Japanese–U.S. policy for countering the BRI will surely compel Beijing to follow the adaptation scenario, particularly as China's power position has been weakened considerably through the trade war with the United States. But this assumption may or may not be correct.

Finally, timing is everything. Given the COVID-19 pandemic and an impending global recession/depression, it remains to be seen who has the upper hand in negotiating a better long-term security arrangement in the Pacific. The current global health and economic crises should once again force nations to realize we are all in this together. Cooperation, compromise, and strong bilateral relationships with allies should once again determine a more secure and prosperous world.

References

Arai, Etsuyo. 2017. Baransu Gaiko To Chugoku Kaiki De Yureru Sri Lanka [Oscillating Sri Lanka between Balanced Diplomacy and Back to China]. *Aji-ken World Trend* 2017 (2): 44–51.

Belt and Road Forum for International Cooperation. 2015. *Full Text: Vision and Actions on Jointly Building Belt and Road.* http://www.beltandroadforum. org/english/n100/2017/0410/c22-45.html.

Department of Defense. 2018. *Summary of the 2018 National Defense Strategy of the United States of America.* https://dod.defense.gov/Portals/1/Documents/ pubs/2018-National-Defense-Strategy-Summary.pdf#search='US+national+ defense+strategy.

Easton, Ian. 2017. *The Chinese Invasion Threat: Taiwan's Defense and American Strategy in Asia.* California: Amazon Digital Services.

Liu, Mingfu. 2015. *The China Dream: Great Power Thinking & Strategic Posture in the Post-American Era (English Version).* Cn Times Books.

Matsumura, Masahiro. 2019. A Realist Approach to Japan's Free and Open Indo-pacific Strategy vs. China's Belt and Road Initiative: A Propaganda Rivalry. *International Journal of China Studies* 10 (2): 131–155.

Ministry of Defense, Japan. 2018. *Nippon no Bouei 2018* [Defense of Japan 2018]. http://www.mod.go.jp/e/publ/w_paper/pdf/2018/DOJ2018_1-2-3_ web.pdf.

NIDS (National Institute for Defense Studies). 2016. *China Security Report 2016.* http://www.nids.mod.go.jp/publication/chinareport/pdf/china_report_ EN_web_2016_A01.pdf.

Parker, Sam and Gabrielle Chefitz. 2018. *Debtbook Diplomacy: China's Strategic Leveraging of Its Newfound Economic Influence and the Consequences for U.S. Foreign Policy.* Cambridge, MA: Harvard Kennedy School Belfer

Center. https://www.belfercenter.org/sites/default/files/files/publication/ Debtbook%20Diplomacy%20PDF.pdf#search='Debtbook+Diplomacy.

Pham, Peter. 2017. *Why Did Donald Trump Kill This Big Free Trade Deal?* https://www.forbes.com/sites/peterpham/2017/12/29/why-did-donald-trump-kill-this-big-free-trade-deal/#4e0879694e62 (accessed September 20, 2018).

Shimodaira, Takuya. 2018. *Maritime Security in the Indo-Pacific and the Way Forward for Maritime Cooperation: QUAD-ASEAN Partnership.* Briefing memo. http://www.nids.mod.go.jp/english/publication/briefing/pdf/ 2018/briefing_e201806.pdf (accessed August 12, 2018).

State Council, Peoples Republic of China. 2017. *Full Text: China's Policies on Asia-Pacific Security Cooperation.* http://english.www.gov.cn/archive/ white_paper/2017/01/11/content_281475539078636.htm.

Storey, Ian. 2006. China's "Malacca Dilemma." *China Brief* 6(8), accessed October 18, 2018, https://jamestown.org/program/chinas-malacca-dilemma/.

Thorne, Devin and Ben Spevack. 2018. *Harbored Ambitions: How China's Port Investments Are Strategically Reshaping the Indo-Pacific.* Washington, DC: C4ADS. https://static1.squarespace.com/static/566ef8b4d8af107232d5358a/ t/5ad5e20ef950b777a94b55c3/1523966489456/Harbored+Ambitions.pdf.

Watts, Jake Maxwell. 2018. Pompeo Pitches U.S. Investment to Leery Southeast Asian Countries. *Wall Street Journal.* August 3. https://jp.wsj.com/articles/SB1 04107040748798633041045843870031229269826982 (accessed September 15, 2018).

White House. 2018. Remarks by Vice President Pence on the Administration's Policy Toward China. October 4. https://www.whitehouse.gov/briefings-statements/remarks-vice-president-pence-administrations-policy-toward-china/.

Chapter 4

The Political-Economic Dependent Triangle Variation of Philippines– China–U.S. and Taiwan–China–U.S. Relations from 2000 to 2018

Ruei-Lin Yu

Introduction

In discussions of international relations in the 21st century, mention of the political structures of the United States and China — the G2 — seems to be unavoidable. Countries located on strategic frontiers, such as those of East Asia, struggle to choose sides between these two big powers. In this chapter, I take as the objects of my research the Philippines and the Republic of China (ROC, Taiwan), two states that are caught in this situation. Although unlike the Philippines, Taiwan is limited by the complex issue of its relations with China and its unclear international status, it is still faced with the same dilemma: whether its national interests are best served by dependence on the United States or on China.

The strategic triangle is a simple and dynamic theory that is often used as a tool in strategic analysis of relations involving three actors, in order to predict which strategy would be best for an actor to adopt through a process of rational decision making. Since the concept of game theory was first introduced into the strategic triangle by Dittmer (1987, p. 34), it has been widely used to predict how three actors will interact.

However, when one of these three actors is a great deal less powerful than the other two, the least powerful actor will inevitably have fewer policy choices at its disposal than the other two big powers. In this regard, Wu (2017) has proposed a different kind of strategic triangle relationship when a small power is caught between two opposing big powers. Wu uses East Asian countries as examples to explain his theory, and this is what I shall introduce in this chapter.

Whether growing interdependence improves the chances of peace is arguable, but both neorealists and neoliberals agree that excessive dependence will limit a country's policy options. The neorealist Waltz (1979, pp. 157–158) mentions that "dependent parties conform their behavior to the preferences of those they depend on." Keohane and Nye (2012, p. 9), who are neoliberals, also argue that "less dependent actors can often use the interdependent relationship as a source of power in bargaining over an issue and perhaps to affect other issues." This chapter will combine the theory of interdependence with the strategic triangle to present a framework for analyzing strategic decision-making. I will argue that small nations try to attain the position of a pivot in their economic and political relations with both major powers, but before they reach that position, small nations use political and economic tools to leverage their relationships. In other words, if a state is too economically reliant on one major country, it will try to balance that by relying on another major country politically. In the following sections, the examples of the Philippines and Taiwan will be used to examine individual political and economic dependency on the United States and China from 2000 to 2018. This will enable us to understand the strategic choices faced by a small power in relation to two big powers.

The Dependent Triangle

Wu (2017) argues that a small power caught between two big powers (in this case Taiwan caught between China and the United States) has five available choices: to partner with China (bandwagon with China, balance against United States), to become a hedging partner of China (bandwagon with China, hedge against the United States), to act as a pivot (remain noncommittal and tilt between the two), become a hedging partner of the United States (bandwagon with the United States, hedge against China), and to partner with the United States (bandwagon with the United States,

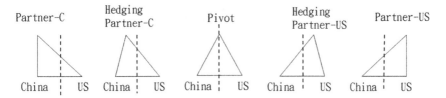

Figure 1: The Available Choices of Lesser Powers

Source: Wu (2017), pp. 204–205.

balance against China) (see Figure 1). A partner is fully allied with one great power and distanced from the other. A hedging partner is committed to one camp but engaged positively with the other camp. A pivot holds itself at equal distance from both camps, typically tilting between the two if that will reap benefits.

When the small power's political utterances favor both of the big powers, it is in a pivot position; if it is friendlier to one side than the other, it is in the position of a hedging partner; if it is friendly toward one side but hostile to the other, it is a partner of one of the powers.

There is another issue to be discussed here. That is, as far as the power relationship of unequal dependence is concerned, a strategic triangle consisting of small and powerful countries is not an equal relationship. When a small, highly vulnerable country is excessively dependent on one more powerful country, the more powerful country will be able to manipulate the power it gains from this unequal, dependent relationship to make demands on the small country. When a small country loses the space it needs to exercise its policy autonomy, its situation is described as being one of overdependence (see Figure 2).

In view of each country's development model, domestic political factors, stakeholders, other external actors, and complex changes in the international political and economic environment make it difficult to determine the threshold of excessive dependence either qualitatively or quantitatively. However, by means of this analytical framework, it is possible to discern some warning signs to which national policy makers should pay attention. That is to say, when a weaker country does not have the internal support it needs to become a partner of one of the powerful countries, or the target big power has not provided substantial guarantees of its willingness to enter a partnership with the smaller country, the small country has not reached the point of no return.

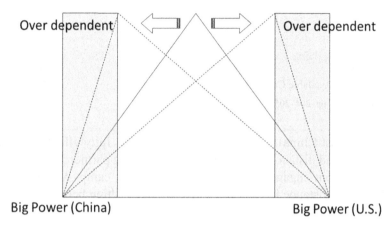

Figure 2:   The Concept of Overdependence

In the political dependence part of my discussion, I will mainly use qualitative methods to clarify the level of dependence. For the economic dependence part, quantitative methods (that is, statistics on the trade relationship between two countries) will be used to demonstrate the degree of dependence.

The Philippines, the United States, and China: A Politically Dependent Triangle

The Republic of the Philippines is the United States' oldest treaty ally in Asia. On July 4, 1946, full independence was granted to the Philippines by the United States. On account of the need for Washington to maintain its military deployment in the Asia-Pacific region after World War II, the Philippines retained an important strategic position for the United States. In 1951, the two countries signed a joint defense treaty, and since then, the Philippines has regarded the United States as its military ally and protector. Although there was serious anti-American sentiment in the 1980s which caused the U.S. troop withdrawal from the Philippines in 1992, the two countries have maintained their military alliance.

President Gloria M. Arroyo's presidential pronouncement, entitled "The Eight Realities of Philippine Foreign Policy," delivered after her election in 2001, contained some bold diplomatic gambits, such as the need to balance the major powers (the United States, Japan, and China) to ensure national security. After the 9/11 terrorist attacks in the United States, President Arroyo declared her full support for Washington's war on terror. She offered American forces access to the country's airspace and allowed U.S. Special Forces to conduct training operations with the Armed Forces of the Philippines (AFP). Subsequently, the Philippines became one of the principal recipients of American security assistance and an important front in the U.S. military's expanded counterterrorism operations against al-Qaeda in Southeast Asia (De Castro 2014, p. 8).

On the other side, cooperative diplomacy was the cornerstone of Arroyo's policy toward China. The tempo of high-level China–Philippine exchanges and consultations accelerated between 2002 and 2006. The Philippine secretaries of agriculture, tourism, foreign affairs, and the interior, and the speaker of the House of Representatives all visited China in 2003, while the secretary of defense went there in 2004 and the foreign secretary and the chief justice in 2005 (Medeiros *et al.* 2008, p. 111). In January 2007, when Premier Wen Jiabao of China visited Manila, President Arroyo declared that Sino-Philippine relations were experiencing a "golden age of partnership" as the two countries upgraded bilateral cooperation and launched more dialogues on political, defense, and sociocultural affairs. During Wen's short visit, he signed 15 agreements with Arroyo to accelerate the two countries' economic and cultural relations, including trade deals worth billions of dollars (De Castro 2007). Basically, President Arroyo used the U.S.-led campaign against terrorism and China's economic emergence to engage these two major powers in a delicate "equi-balancing game" (De Castro 2014, p. 9).

Since 2010, China has taken a more assertive approach to the South China Sea by including it among what the Chinese call "core national interests." The responses to this from Southeast Asian states were varied, but regional concerns about China increased rapidly. Despite the improved relationship between China and the Southeast Asian states over the past two decades, regional attitudes toward China quickly turned negative (Cho and Park 2013, p. 69). President Benigno Simeon Aquino III won the 2010 presidential election with 42% of the votes cast, the largest margin of victory since the Philippines adopted a multi-party system in 1987. After taking over the reins of government, President Aquino discarded the policies of his predecessor, including her diplomatic strategy of "equi-balancing" and tilted the balance in favor of the country's long-time strategic ally — the United States. This policy shift had a two-pronged consequence: it strengthened the Philippine–U.S. alliance while straining Philippine–China bilateral relations (De Castro 2014, p. 6).

Responding to China's rise, Manila chose to pursue a policy of leveraging its international relationships by seeking to regionalize the South China Sea dispute through the Association of Southeast Asian Nations (ASEAN) and by developing closer defense cooperation with the United States (Medeiros et al. 2008, p. 98). Furthermore, Aquino also instituted arbitral proceedings against China (the South China Sea Arbitration) in 2013 which worsened relations between the two countries. Manila's goal was to obtain a ruling that the features claimed by China in the South China Sea do not qualify as islands and therefore cannot generate an exclusive economic zone (EEZ) or a continental shelf under the United Nations Convention on the Law of the Sea (UNCLOS) and that as a result, those areas should belong to the Philippines. The South China Sea Arbitration Award, issued on July 12, 2016, was totally in the Philippines' favor. This ruling, that China firmly refuses to accept, brought relations between China and the Philippines to freezing point.

On May 9, 2016, Rodrigo Roa Duterte won the Philippine presidential election with 39% of the votes. In an effort to slow down the deterioration in Sino-Philippine relations, Duterte led a more than 200-strong delegation to China in October 2016. During this visit, he announced the Philippines' separation from the United States, in both military and economic terms. President Xi Jinping of China called the visit a "milestone" in Philippine–China ties (Blanchard 2016). Although on his return from this trip, Duterte clarified that the Philippines would not cut diplomatic ties with the United States, in addition to making friendly remarks about China, he also made various unfriendly remarks about the United States which undermined U.S.–Philippine relations. This behavior does not fit with that of a "hedging partner of China (bandwagon with China, hedge against the United States)." Instead, it is close to being that of a partner of China.

The Philippines' political dependent triangle from 2001 to 2018 is depicted in Figure 3.

The Economic Dependent Triangle of the Philippines, the United States, and China

Since independence in 1946, the Philippines has not only depended on the United States politically but has also been very dependent on it

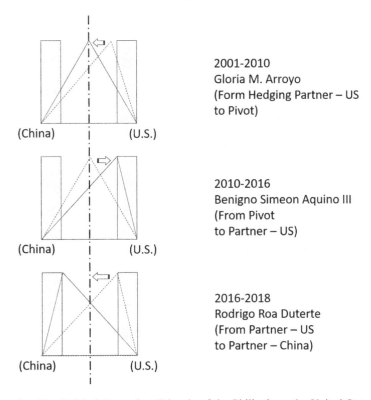

2001-2010
Gloria M. Arroyo
(Form Hedging Partner – US
to Pivot)

(China)   (U.S.)

2010-2016
Benigno Simeon Aquino III
(From Pivot
to Partner – US)

(China)   (U.S.)

2016-2018
Rodrigo Roa Duterte
(From Partner – US
to Partner – China)

(China)   (U.S.)

Figure 3: The Political Dependent Triangle of the Philippines, the United States, and China by Philippines' Presidency, 2001–2018

economically. In 2001, when Arroyo was in power, she emphasized that the government would give top priority to economic development and introduce a diversified foreign economic policy to reduce the Philippines' economic dependence on the United States and Japan. During Arroyo's administration, trade between the Philippines and China increased substantially, gradually bringing total trade closer to that between the Philippines and the United States (see Figure 6). In addition, during this period, the Philippines' imports and exports with both countries were relatively balanced (see Figures 4 and 5). Although Arroyo was using the "equi-balancing" strategy to balance the Philippines' trade relations with the United States and China, regional integration within ASEAN was also

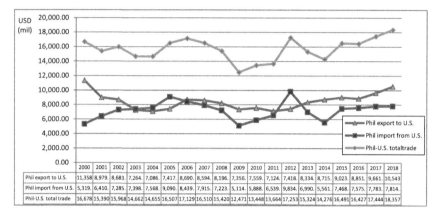

	2000	2001	2002	2003	2004	2005	2006	2007	2008	2009	2010	2011	2012	2013	2014	2015	2016	2017	2018
Phil export to U.S.	11,358	8,979.	8,683.	7,264.	7,086.	7,417.	8,690.	8,594.	8,196.	7,356.	7,559.	7,124.	7,418.	8,334.	8,715.	9,023.	8,851.	9,661.	10,543
Phil import from U.S.	5,319.	6,410.	7,285.	7,398.	7,568.	9,090.	8,439.	7,915.	7,223.	5,114.	5,888.	6,539.	9,834.	6,990.	5,561.	7,468.	7,575.	7,783.	7,814.
Phil-U.S. total trade	16,678	15,390	15,968	14,662	14,655	16,507	17,129	16,510	15,420	12,471	13,448	13,664	17,253	15,324	14,276	16,491	16,427	17,444	18,357

Figure 4:   Trade between the Philippines and the United States, 2000–2018

Source: Philippines Statistics Authority 2019.

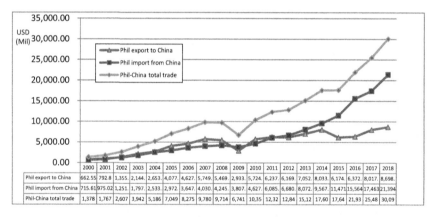

	2000	2001	2002	2003	2004	2005	2006	2007	2008	2009	2010	2011	2012	2013	2014	2015	2016	2017	2018
Phil export to China	662.55	792.8	1,355.	2,144.	2,653.	4,077.	4,627.	5,749.	5,469.	2,933.	5,724.	6,237.	6,169.	7,052.	8,033.	6,174.	6,372.	8,017.	8,698.
Phil import from China	715.61	975.02	1,251.	1,797.	2,533.	2,972.	3,647.	4,030.	4,245.	3,807.	4,627.	6,085.	6,680.	8,072.	9,567.	11,471	15,564	17,463	21,394
Phil-China total trade	1,378	1,767	2,607	3,942	5,186	7,049	8,275	9,780	9,714	6,741	10,35	12,32	12,84	15,12	17,60	17,64	21,93	25,48	30,09

Figure 5:   Trade between the Philippines and China, 2000–2018

Source: Philippines Statistics Authority 2019.

on the rise. In November 2000, China first proposed the idea of a free trade area in Southeast Asia, and 10 years later, the ASEAN–China Free Trade Area (ACFTA) became the world's largest free trade area in terms of population and the third-largest in terms of nominal GDP. The Philippines' imports from China also grew rapidly, but less so than exports. Imports increased 5 times between 1996 and 2006, while exports increased 14 times. As with the Philippines' exports, the commodity

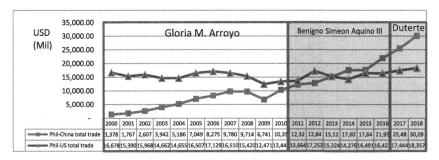

Figure 6: Philippines–U.S. Trade vs. Philippines–China Trade, 2000–2018
Source: Philippines Statistics Authority 2019.

groups with the largest share of total imports were electronic components (37%), parts for office equipment (12%), and telecommunications equipment (9%) (Medeiros *et al.* 2008, p. 104). In this period, the Philippines was enjoying a trade surplus with China.

In November 2011, after Aquino took office, the governments of the Philippines and the United States agreed to a Partnership for Growth to address constraints on economic growth and development in the Philippines. The Philippines was one of just four countries selected to join this Partnership for Growth and the only one in Asia. The partnership supports the Philippines' priorities, which are to achieve inclusive and resilient economic growth. It stimulates institutional reform at the national and local levels to mobilize domestic and foreign investment (USAID 2020). This economic partnership resulted in an increase in trade between the Philippines and the United States, but trade between the Philippines and China under ACFTA increased even more. In 2013, the volume of trade between the Philippines and China exceeded that between the Philippines and the United States (see Figure 6). Although economic opportunities derived from China's rapid growth can offset overdependence on the U.S. economy, the Philippines, along with other ASEAN states, also fears overdependence on the Chinese economy and that Beijing might in the future use that dependence to exert pressure on Manila (Cho and Park 2013, p. 85).

In the context of regional economic integration and China's rapid economic growth, almost all the ASEAN countries have increased their trade with China significantly, so this is not entirely due to the pro-China attitude of President Duterte. In the 2 or 3 years up to 2018, the Philippines might have built some major infrastructure with Chinese assistance, but from the perspective of trade data, the Philippines showed significant trade surpluses with China during the period 2016–2018 which may not have been beneficial to them. Meanwhile, the Philippines still enjoyed a trade surplus with the United States (see Figure 5).

The Political Dependent Triangle of Taiwan, the United States, and China

After the government of the Republic of China retreated to Taiwan in 1949, the Kuomintang (KMT) ruled the island until 2000, when Chen Shui-bian from the opposition Democratic Progressive Party (DPP) was elected president. In 2008, the KMT returned to power with the election of President Ma Ying-jeou, and then in 2016, the DPP came to power again when President Tsai Ing-wen was elected, completing a third change of ruling party.

In its early years on Taiwan, the KMT regarded the Chinese Communist Party (CCP) as its enemy. Eventually, although the party realized that the growth in China's national power would make it difficult for the KMT to recover the mainland, most KMT leaders came to believe that the two sides of the Taiwan Strait should be reunited peacefully sometime in the future. The DPP also regards the CCP, which has never given up the option of reunifying China by force of arms, as an enemy, and most DPP supporters would prefer Taiwan to be independent. In view of the threat of force from China, no matter which political party is in power, Taiwan automatically depends on the United States to guarantee its national security.

Given that the DPP had long advocated independence for Taiwan, the election of Chen Shui-bian in 2000 soon led to a deterioration in Cross-Strait relations. President Chen's expressions of goodwill in his first term did not win a satisfactory response from China. In order to differentiate himself from the KMT candidates during his reelection campaign in 2004, Chen took a harder line, and that won him the election. Determined to forestall any attempt by Chen to declare Taiwan's independence, in 2005 the People's Republic of China passed an Anti-Secession Law which set out its legal red line. At this time, when President Chen needed more support from the United States, Washington proved reluctant to get involved in Cross-Strait political disputes, even criticizing Chen for troublemaking. Although Chen hoped to become a political partner of the United States in the latter part of his administration, he still did not receive a positive response from the Americans. In this situation, he was not confident enough to show his hostility to China, and he could only become a hedging partner of the United States.

The pro-peaceful unification KMT returned to power with the election of Ma Ying-jeou in 2008. President Ma made active efforts to repair relations with China. He managed relations between Washington, Beijing, and Taipei by "being close to Washington, being friendly to Tokyo, and being at peace with Beijing." He did not achieve much in terms of enhancing relations with the United States and Japan, but his administration signed 23 agreements with China, including a deal on the "three links"(direct flights, shipping, and postal services) and a Cross-Strait Economic Cooperation Framework Agreement (ECFA). In 2015, the last year of Ma's presidency, a historic summit meeting took place in Singapore between Ma and the leader of the CCP, Xi Jinping. This was the first time the leaders of the KMT and CCP had met since Mao Zedong founded the People's Republic of China in 1949. To summarize the achievements of Ma's administration, although the president may have believed that he had placed Taiwan in a pivot position between China and the United States, most people criticized him for being a little too close to China.

In 2016, the DPP candidate, Tsai Ing-wen, won the presidential election, becoming Taiwan's first female head of state. President Tsai pledged to "maintain the *status quo*" in Cross-Strait relations but refused to recognize the 1992 Consensus, a vague agreement reached between the CCP and the KMT. President Tsai emphasizes Taiwan's autonomy in its relations with China, holding that only by reinforcing a Taiwanese identity can Taiwan exercise national independence and freedom. On December 2, 2016, President Tsai had a telephone conversation with Donald Trump and congratulated him on his victory in the U.S. presidential election. This inconspicuous phone call was the first time that the leaders of the two countries had spoken directly since Washington broke off diplomatic relations with the Republic of China in 1979. As the international situation changed, the Trump administration identified China as a strategic competitor in the National Security Strategy of the United States of America 2017, calling for the use of all possible means to deter China in all dimensions, including declaring a "trade war." Taiwan therefore became a

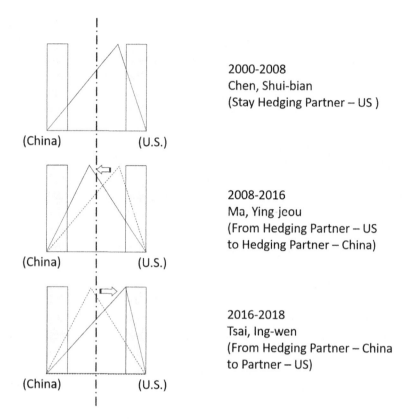

2000-2008
Chen, Shui-bian
(Stay Hedging Partner – US)

(China)   (U.S.)

2008-2016
Ma, Ying jeou
(From Hedging Partner – US
to Hedging Partner – China)

(China)   (U.S.)

2016-2018
Tsai, Ing-wen
(From Hedging Partner – China
to Partner – US)

(China)   (U.S.)

Figure 7:   The Political Dependent Triangle of Taiwan, the United States, and China by ROC (Taiwan) Presidency, 2000–2018

political card used by the United States against China, which resulted in closer relations between Taipei and Washington. In contrast to the period of the Chen Shui-bian presidency, the United States wanted Taiwan to become its political partner. For the political dependent triangle from 2001 to 2018, see Figure 7.

The Economic Dependent Triangle of Taiwan, the United States, and China

After the KMT retreated to Taiwan in 1949, the ROC government was heavily dependent on the United States both politically and economically.

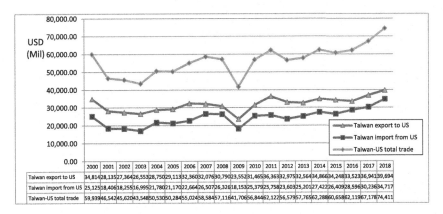

Figure 8: Trade between Taiwan and the United States, 2000–2018

Source: Bureau of Foreign Trade 2019.

According to statistics provided by the ROC Bureau of Foreign Trade, trade between Taiwan and the United States accounted for 25.6% of Taiwan's total trade volume in 1992, and it remained above 20% until 2000 (Figure 8).

When he came to office in 2000, President Chen introduced a policy of "proactive liberalization with effective management" with regard to trade and economic exchanges with China. From 2001 to 2004, Cross-Strait economic and trade relations developed rapidly under the impetus of this policy, and Taiwan's economic dependence on Mainland China also increased (Figure 9). In 2004, China overtook the United States to become Taiwan's largest trading partner (see Figure 10). By 2006, the Chen administration was worried that Taiwan's economy might have become too dependent on China, a situation which might lead the business community to start promoting unification. At that point, Chen changed his economic and trade policy to one of "proactive management with effective liberalization," slowing the growth rate of investment in China slightly.

Ma Ying-jeou, once he came to office in 2008, was committed to institutionalizing Cross-Strait economic and trade relations, and he signed a succession of agreements with China. The ECFA was signed in June 2010, signaling further integration between the economies on the two sides of the Taiwan Strait. Two major follow-up treaties to the ECFA were planned: the Cross-Strait Service Trade Agreement (CSSTA) and the

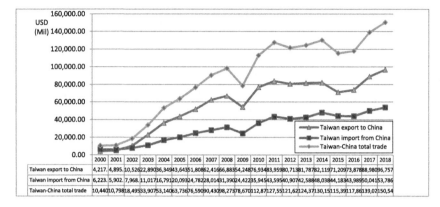

Figure 9:   Trade between Taiwan and China, 2000–2018

Source: Bureau of Foreign Trade 2019.

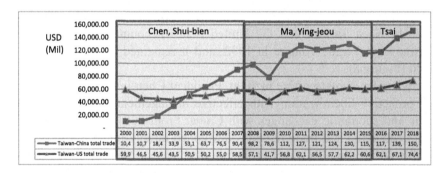

Figure 10:   Taiwan–U.S. Trade vs. Taiwan–China Trade, 2000–2018

Source: Bureau of Foreign Trade 2019.

Cross-Strait Goods Trade Agreement (CSGTA). The first of these was signed in 2013, but when it went before Taiwan's legislature for ratification, it sparked a massive social movement, the Sunflower Student Movement or 319 Movement. As a result, it was never ratified. At the time of writing, the second treaty has yet to be negotiated.

President Tsai rejected both the "one China" principle and the 1992 Consensus, causing a significant decline in Cross-Strait economic and trade activities. In order to compensate for this, the Tsai administration launched the New Southbound Policy which was designed to increase trade with Southeast Asia. At the same time, the Trump administration's efforts to attract foreign investment, combined with improved Taiwan–U.S. relations, prompted many Taiwanese business people to invest in the United States. This led to an increase in the volume of trade between Taiwan and the United States.

Taiwan has a trade surplus with both China and the United States. Like other Asian countries, as China's economy has grown significantly, Taiwan's total trade with China has continued to increase. Even the New Southbound Policy did not cause an immediate reversal of this trend. In both 2017 and 2018, total trade between Taiwan and China continued to increase.

Comparisons and Analysis

As mentioned earlier, the Philippines has not had to deal with a relationship as complicated as that between Taiwan and China, but as a small power caught between two big powers, it is faced with similar strategic choices. According to the logic of rational choice, in a strategic triangle, the best position for a small country should be that of a pivot between the two big countries. In a changing international environment, it is quite difficult, or near impossible, to maintain this ideal position either economically or politically for a long time. Therefore, when a small country is more dependent on one big country economically, it usually finds ways to balance that and reduce risk by relying on another big country politically.

During the Arroyo administration, the Philippines was committed to the "equi-balancing" strategy to achieve a balance between China and the United States both economically and politically in order to occupy the pivot position. Before Arroyo stepped down, this strategy seemed to be quite successful. Of course, it was also necessary to respond to changes in the international situation and retain domestic support. President Aquino felt that the Philippines was becoming increasingly dependent on China economically, so he adopted a pro-American policy politically, which according to our argument above, seems to have been a rational choice. Under President Duterte, the Philippine economy became even more dependent on China, but Duterte adopted a pro-China political strategy, which does not fit our argument. Some observers believe Duterte's anti-American outlook was the result of his own personal background and experience (Parameswaran 2016).

Returning to the case of Taiwan, when President Chen feared that the economy was becoming too dependent on Mainland China, he also adopted a pro-U.S. policy. Like Duterte, Chen's successor, Ma Ying-jeou, leaned toward China both economically and politically, which does not fit our pattern. However, we should remember that on account of Taiwan's complicated relationship with China, Ma's overall strategy was to pre-serve peace across the Taiwan Strait. His administration may have believed that a more pro-China political strategy combined with deeper economic integration had the potential to reduce the chance of war between the two sides. President Tsai's adoption of a pro-U.S. strategy to offset economic dependence on China is in line with our pattern.

Another important issue is the extent to which excessive dependence occurs. It would be unrealistic to expect to find an answer to this question in terms of economic dependence that applies in every case, but in the cases of the Philippines and Taiwan, we note that economic dependence seems to peak when trade volume with one country reaches nearly 25% of the country in question's total trade (see Figures 11 and 12). At what point a country becomes excessively dependent on another politically is a subjective judgment. Basically, there are no permanent enemies or friends in politics. It is unrealistic for a small country to believe that big countries will sacrifice their national interests on its behalf. When the big country uses the dependent relationship as a bargaining chip, the small country's policy alternatives are limited.

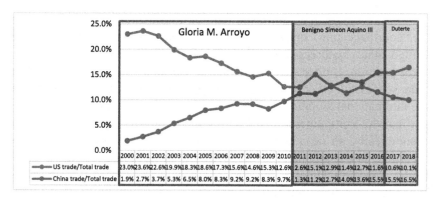

Figure 11: Philippines–U.S. Trade vs. Philippines–China Trade as Percentage of Philippines Total Trade, 2000–2018

Source: Philippines Statistics Authority 2019.

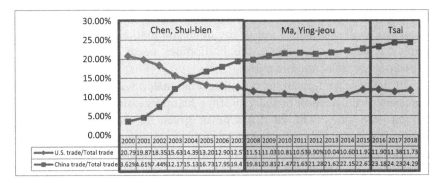

Figure 12: Taiwan–U.S. Trade vs. Taiwan–China Trade as Percentage of Taiwan Total Trade, 2000–2018

Source: Bureau of Foreign Trade 2019.

Furthermore, there is another situation worthy of consideration: that is, when a small country is heavily dependent on one big country economically, and for the purpose of balancing, it is also heavily dependent on another big country politically. Whether the security of the small country is improved when both kinds of dependence become over-dependence is a question that will only be answered when we have more historical evidence.

Conclusion and Recommendations

In order to understand the strategic choices of small powers caught between two big powers, this chapter has examined political and economic dependence in two triangles: that of the Philippines, China, and the United States, and that involving Taiwan, China, and the United States during the period 2000–2018. I find that of the three administrations in this period only that of President Duterte did not conform to our assumptions concerning rational decision making in a strategic triangle. However, at the time of writing, Duterte seems to have adjusted his pro-China policy and begun to repair the Philippines' political and economic relations with the United States. The more urgent challenge for him is how to reduce the Philippines' trade deficit with China. It turns out that the country's exports to China, such as electronic components, parts for office equipment, and telecommunications equipment, are no longer competitive, whereas the cheap goods imported from China have squeezed local companies out of the domestic market. According to the statistical data shown above, the Philippines needs to make a timely adjustment to its economic policy.

In the case of Taiwan, its complex relationship with China involving the issue of unification or independence hampers rational decision making on both sides. The CCP has never given up the option of taking Taiwan by force. The idea that closer economic integration between the two sides will reduce the chance of war is uncertain and lacks sufficient support among the Taiwan people. According to statistics provided by Taiwan's Bureau of Foreign Trade, Taiwan's trade with the United States continued to grow after 2018 while trade with China decreased. Although at the time of writing, it appears that President Tsai's economic policy of reducing dependence on China has achieved little, it is undisputed that Taiwan's political dependence on the United States has reached its highest level. In August 2019, Taiwan's foreign minister, Joseph Wu, said that Taiwan's relations with the United States were very good and probably better than at any time in the past. Has Taiwan reached the point where it is overdependent on China economically and overdependent on the United States politically? If this is the case, has a perfect balance been achieved or is Taiwan at increased risk? Only time will tell. In order to reduce this uncertainty, while reducing Taiwan's economic dependence on Mainland China, Taiwan's leaders should perhaps think about how they can reduce its political dependence on the United States while that is still possible.

References

Blanchard, Ben. 2016. Duterte Aligns Philippines with China, Says U.S. Has Lost. *Reuters*, October 20. https://www.reuters.com/article/us-china-philippines/duterte-aligns-philippines-with-china-says-u-s-has-lost-idUSK CN12K0AS.

Bureau of Foreign Trade, MOEA, ROC (Taiwan). 2019. https://cus93.trade.gov.tw/.

Cho, Il Hyun and Seo-Hyun Park. 2013. The Rise of China and Varying Sentiments in Southeast Asia toward Great Powers. *Strategic Studies Quarterly* 7(2): 69–92.

De Castro, Renato Cruz. 2007. China, the Philippines, and U.S. Influence in Asia. *Asian Outlook*. Washington, DC: American Enterprise Institute.

De Castro, Renato Cruz. 2014. The Aquino Administration's Balancing Policy against an Emergent China: Its Domestic and External Dimensions. *Pacific Affairs* 87(1): 5–27.

Dittmer, Lowell. 1987. The Strategic Triangle: A Critical Review. In *The Strategic Triangle: China, the United States and the Soviet Union*, edited by Ilpyong J. Kim, 29–47. New York: Paragon House Publishers.

Keohane, Robert O. and Joseph S. Nye. 2012. *Power and Interdependence*. 4th edn. Boston, MA: Longman.

Medeiros, Evan, Keith Crane, Eric Heginbotham, Norman Levin, Julia Lowell, Angel Rabasa, and Somi Seong. 2008. "The Philippines." In *Pacific Currents: The Responses of U.S. Allies and Security Partners in East Asia to China's Rise*, 97–124. Santa Monica, CA; Arlington, VA; Pittsburgh, PA: RAND Corporation.

Parameswaran, Prashanth. 2016. Why the Philippines' Rodrigo Duterte Hates America. *The Diplomat*, November 1. https://thediplomat.com/2016/11/why-the-philippines-rodrigo-duterte-hates-america/.

Philippines Statistics Authority, Republic of the Philippines. https://psa.gov.ph/statistics/foreign-trade.

USAID. 2020. Partnership for Growth with Equity. https://www.usaid.gov/philippines/partnership-growth-pfg.

Waltz, Kenneth N. 1979. *Theory of International Politics*. Reading, MA: Addison-Wesley Pub. Co.

Wu, Yu-Shan. 2017. Pivot, Hedger, or Partner: Strategies of Lesser Powers Caught between Hegemons. In *Taiwan and China: Fitful Embrace*, edited by Lowell Dittmer, 197–220. Berkeley, CA: University of California Press.

Chapter 5

From Pivot to the Indo-Pacific: U.S., India, and Their Strategic Convergence, Opportunities and Challenges With Vietnam Under QUAD

Roger Chi-feng Liu

Introduction

This chapter is to evaluate Vietnam's strategic existence in the context of the increased attention on the Indo-Pacific area by great powers mainly the United States and India. My main arguments are that Vietnam has been more important in the strategic planning of Washington and Delhi as the rise of China in the region. Since the 1990s, U.S. and India have both begun to approach Vietnam at the same time but on different paths. While the end of the Cold War with the thawing of political relations makes Washington and Hanoi to walk closer, for the Look East Policy economy is behind India's decision to work closely with Vietnam against the back-drop of a good Indo-Vietnamese relations since the Soviet Era. That being said, there had been no coordinated policy for India and the U.S. toward Vietnam. However, with the continuing and increasing presence of China in regions like the South China Sea and the Indian Ocean region, a strategic convergence between India and other great powers such as the U.S. is becoming a reality. This chapter also attempts to explore the opportunities and challenges of India's policy toward and strategy collaborations with Vietnam in the fabric of QUAD.

Background: U.S. and India Approaching Vietnam

The end of Cold War saw new opportunities for U.S., India, and Vietnam to improve their relations. Washington and Hanoi established their diplomatic relations in 1995. However, for the first 15 years of the bilateral relations, the U.S.–Vietnamese mutual security collaboration had developed slowly due to the lack of trust (caused by the difference in the political systems and historical experience of antagonism) and common threat. China's increased presence in the South China Sea in late 2000s accelerated the pace of U.S.–Vietnam strategic cooperation. In 2013, the two countries archived a joint statement to establish a comprehensive partnership following the visit by State Secretary Hillary Clinton in 2010 to upgrade the relations with Vietnam (Nguyen and Nguyen 2021). The Chinese oil rig *"Haiyang Shiyou 981/ Hải Dương 981"* incident in 2014 saw the worsening of SCS situation between China and Vietnam and the boost of U.S.–Vietnam collaboration. In 2015, Nguyễn Phú Trọng made the first-ever visit as the General Secretary of the Communist Party of Vietnam to the United States. In 2016, the U.S. President Barack Obama, during his visit to Vietnam, lifted the arms embargo that U.S. posed on Vietnam for decades. In 2017, the Joint Statement on Establishment of a Comprehensive Partnership was announced (Tomotaka 2018).

China's adventurism, especially after Xi Jinping assumed his position as the General Secretary of the Communist Party of China, contributed much for Vietnam and the U.S. to get strategically closer after 2014. However, the U.S. had attempted to adjust its policy toward East Asian since 2010. In 2011 Hillary R. Clinton announced the *Pivot to Asia* or Rebalance strategy. To fulfill its goal, the U.S. needed to strengthen the bilateral relations with Asia-Pacific countries such as Vietnam to Mongolia; to enhance its participation in the multilateral web of regional organizations, and to adjust to increase its military deployment in the region (Campbell 2016). In the Shangri-La Dialogue held in Singapore from May 30 to June 2014, the representatives from the U.S., Australia, Japan, and Vietnam spoke against China's oil rig adventurism. Chuck Hagel, the U.S. Defense Secretary directly warned his Chinese counterpart that "the United States will not look the other way when fundamental principles of the international order are being challenged" (Vorsatz and de Leon 2014). As a major component of the *Pivot*, the Trans-Pacific Partnership (TPP) also included Vietnam into the negotiation process in 2008, which aimed to reduce economic reliance of Vietnam on China and consequently give Vietnam more autonomy when it comes to the Bien Dong/SCS issues (Le 2016).

Around the same time, U.S. upgraded its security collaboration with India as well. In 2015, Barack Obama was invited to attend the Republic Day event as the chief guest, making him the first U.S. President to attend. In 2016, the Obama Administration declared India to be America's first "Major Defense Partner." India would have access to "a wide range of dual-use technologies" as U.S.'s closest allies and partners (Panda 2017). The strategic adjustment of U.S. has continued into the Trump era, although it looked more unilateral in appearance. In 2017, Trump made it clear that "a free and open Indo-Pacific" is the vision of U.S. in the APEC CEO Summit held in Da Nang, Vietnam, a symbolic location chosen to reflect the importance of Vietnam in QUAD 2.0 — the revival of idea raised by the Japanese Prime Minister Shinzo Abe in 2007 with a lost momentum (U.S. Mission to ASEAN 2017). In the *Indo-Pacific Strategy Report* (U.S. Department of Defense 2019), the Trump Administration put Vietnam in the first place when it comes to prioritizing new relationship of strategic collaboration in ASEAN, indicating that the strengthened U.S.–Vietnam partnership is based upon common interests and principles including freedom of navigation and rule-based order, referring to the South China Sea (p. 36). After Biden assumed office in January 2021, in the beginning there were doubts and suspicions that he and his administration might "reset" the relations with China and relinquish the Indo-Pacific Strategy relying heavily on QUAD. However, so far the Democrat Administration under Biden seems to have still followed the way of Trump, especially on the competition mode with China, continuation of the FONOPs in South China Sea and the reliance on QUAD. On March 12, 2021, Biden had an online QUAD Summit with the Japanese Prime Minister Yoshihide Suga, the Australian Prime Minister Scott Morrison, and the Indian Prime Minister Narendra Modi. In the post-Summit Joint Statement, the four leaders reiterated the commitment to "promoting a free, open-rules-based order, rooted in international law to advance security and prosperity and counter threats to both in the Indo-Pacific and beyond" (Biden 2021). In the Interim National Security

Strategic Guidance released 9 days before the QUAD Summit, Biden mentioned that the U.S. will keep deepening "our partnership with India and work alongside New Zealand, as well as Singapore, Vietnam" and other ASEAN members states, "to advance shared objectives" (The White House 2021).

The United States and India tried to approach Vietnam in the 1990s after the Cold War ended. For both, the momentum was mainly for the economy. In the case of the U.S., with the trade embargo lifted in 1994 and the normalization of bilateral relations in the 1995, the Vietnam under the guidance of *Doi Moi* appeared a growing market for Washington, as the diplomatic normalization comes with a good symbolic meaning of reconciliation between the U.S. and its archenemy in the 1960s and 1970s, marking a new start of the American diplomacy in the Southeast Asian region.

For India, the collapse of Soviet Union destroyed a role model, based on whose politico-economic system New Delhi had made its economic policy and development models since its independence in 1947. This constitutes the basic logic of the "Look East Policy" announced in 1991 by the Narasimha Rao, then Prime Minister of India. India going eastbound was not only for the models to emulate but also for emerging and potential markets and investments. Based on such consideration, Singapore became the first country approached by India due to the colonial social network laid down by the Brits, as well as the economic model of Singapore — the national capitalist model — was more imitable for the traditional planned economic system of India. Other than Singapore, however, Vietnam is the most approachable for India: both emulating the Soviet planned economy model, Hanoi and New Delhi were close to Moscow diplomatically and politically. That India supported the anti-American struggles of Vietnam in the 1970s, however, was not necessarily because of the fact that they both had the U.S.S.R. as the most important ally, but because India was in an inimical relationship with the U.S. in the 1960s and 1970s.

The U.S. support of Pakistan and Central Treaty Organization (CENTO) and Southeast Asia Treaty Organization (SEATO) had positioned itself on the enemy side of India, as the standoff between the U.S. and Indian Navies in the Bay of Bengal during the Third India–Pakistan War (aka the Bangladesh Independence War) in 1971 not only prompted New Delhi to sign the *Treaty of Amity* with the Soviet Union in 1972 but also made it more sympathetic to the Communist Vietnam fighting a war with the U.S. at that time. The slogan *"Tera Naam Mera Naam, Vietnam*

Vietnam" (Your name is my name, Vietnam Vietnam)" shouted out on university campuses from students supporting Vietnam's cause during the Vietnam War apparently reflected the sentiments among Indian intellectuals in the 1970s. The official positive stance by the Government of India on the invasion of Cambodia in 1978 by the Vietnamese military was also reflected on the Indian support of the Communist government.

Although Vietnam and India had a good baseline in diplomacy, the first phase of *LEP* had not seen closer interactions between Delhi and Hanoi, especially not in the security and defense aspect. The improvement was made when Atal Bihari Vajpayee of the Bharatiya Janata Party (BJP) became the Prime Minister of India in 1998. Vajpayee is deemed the political mentor of Narendra Modi who became the PM in 2014. Guided by Vajpayee's "extended neighborhood" policy, India kept reaching out to the Southeast Asian region, not only multilaterally via ASEAN but also bilaterally to individual countries. In 2000, Delhi signed the first Defense Protocol with Hanoi, focusing on the collaboration on anti-piracy, intelligence swap, and the support of Russian-made weapon systems of the Vietnamese armed forces (Pant 2018). In 2003, there was a more comprehensive relationship built in defense affairs. In the *Joint Declaration on the Framework of Comprehensive Cooperation between the Republic of India and the Socialist Republic of Vietnam as they enter the 21st Century*, the two countries agree to remain comprehensive and regularized high-level meetings along with exchanges among various levels in government and politics. Also, India and Vietnam agreed to cooperate in multilateral organizations and forums, especially in the UN, ASEAN, ARF, and the Mekong–Ganga Cooperation (MGC). Finally, gradual steps would be taken to enhance the cooperation in security and military affairs (MEA India, 2003).

China has begun to extend its influence toward the Indian Ocean Region in the 2000s. The September 11 Incident gave Beijing the opportunities and reasons to dispatch its naval vessels to the Middle East via the Indian Ocean for multinational anti-terrorism efforts (Kondapalli 2018, pp. 195–196). In 2006, ONGC Videsh Limited (OVL), the international branch of the Oil and Natural Gas Corporation (ONGC) of India acquired the 7,000-km^2 Block 128 in the Vietnamese EEZ and a smaller one Block 06/1. When India signed an agreement with Vietnam on the drilling in Block 128, it was warned by China (Panda 2020). In 2014, China moved its oil rig *Haiyang Shiyou 981* to the Vietnam-claimed area of SCS, which triggered a series of diplomatic events between Beijing and Hanoi.

In 2019, China sent a taskforce fleet with its maritime survey ship *Haiyang Dizhi 8* to again approach controversial areas close to the India-acquired oil block (Saha 2021).

China's growing assertiveness is most likely the product of its ambitious Belt and Road Initiative. It was announced in 2013, the next year when Xi Jinping became the fifth generation of leadership in the Communist Party of China (CPC). In 2014, the right-wing BJP leader, former Chief Minister of Gujrat Narendra Modi became the Prime Minister of India. In the initial years China and India had attempted to reset the bilateral relations as the new leadership started in both countries. In September 2014 Xi made a state visit to India and Modi visited Xi'an, Beijing, and Shanghai in May 2015 in return. However, the two highest-level visits with agreements on investment and exchanges in a wide spectrum of social and economic levels could not prevent the territorial crisis of Doklam stand-off from happening in July 2017.

It is against this backdrop of India–China strategic competition that India under Modi keeps strengthening collaboration in security areas with Vietnam. India announced its Look East Policy in 1991, and around the time Modi assumed his prime minister seat, Vietnam had become the second closest ASEAN country with India (only second to Singapore, Blank *et al.* 2015). In 2018, the late Vietnamese President Trần Đại Quang visited Delhi and signed three memoranda of understanding (MoUs) on further collaboration in areas of nuclear, agriculture, and trade. Trần also voiced the support for India's bid for the permanent membership in the UN Security Council (*The Indian Express* 2018). In the joint statement Modi stressed that the two countries will work together for "an open, independent and prosperous Indo-Pacific region where sovereignty and international laws are respected" (*News18* 2018), echoing Trump's "free and open Indo-Pacific region" announced in APEC Da Nang CEO Summit in 2017.

India was more cautious and had taken a more gradual step toward QUAD between 2017 and late 2019. After the Doklam standoff, Delhi had taken a series of policies to ameliorate the negative diplomatic results. Vijay Gokhale, the Ambassador to China during the Doklam event, was promoted in January 2018 to be the Foreign Secretary to manage relationship with China from MEA. Two informal summits between Xi and Modi were held respectively April 2018 in Wuhan, and October 2019 in Mamallapuram, Tamil Nadu. However, the two informal summits — along with all the other communication channels at various levels between the two governments — intended to improve the communications between India and China started to fail as COVID-19 spread from Wuhan in March 2020 to different cities of India. The Galwan Valley conflict between the Indian Army and the People's Liberation Army officers and soldiers in the Western Sector of Aksai Chin that erupted in the mid-June of 2020 — the deadliest one after the 1975 border standoff in Arunachal Pradesh — provided the momentum for India to further incorporate itself into the QUAD scheme. As Modi said in the address of the first-ever QUAD leadership Summit, that the members — including India — will become "closer than ever before" (*The Hindu* 2021).

How the Indian-Vietnamese Relations Can Grow Under, and Better Converge with QUAD

As India has decided to embed itself more into the fabric of QUAD, in the future it has to inevitably coordinate its own Act East Policy with the quadrilateral scheme. How would this change India's approach to ASEAN countries, as well as Vietnam, one of its most secure partners in Southeast Asia? Positively speaking, QUAD serves as an umbrella to incorporate different bilateral mechanisms, boosting them with reinforced collective goals, protecting them from being canceled out by the changes in domestic politics of certain great powers, creating more spaces for micro-multilateral connections, as well as instilling more power and capacity for the execution of plans in this framework. QUAD can reinforce bilateral security cooperation (including the India–Vietnam one) in the following ways:

Better coordination, accommodation, and moderation of strategic goals for countries of different backgrounds of strategic cultures. Originated from the "democratic diamond," QUAD is the idea of Shinzo Abe, the former Prime Minister of Japan in 2007. The geostrategic idea to bring four Asian democracies together to counter the expansion of the Chinese influence was dormant in 2008 when the governments of Japan, U.S.A., and Australia turned "left." It was revived when the American President Donald J. Trump was in office in 2017, while the governments of Japan, Australia, and India were in the hands of right-wing parties. Among these four democracies, each has different sets of strategic planning toward the regional threat, i.e., China. Compared with Washington, Tokyo, and Canberra, Delhi talks more about the importance of remaining a "free and open Indo-Pacific," while the Indian version of "Indo-Pacific Ocean Initiative/IPOI" is different than the unilateral American "Indo-Pacific Strategy" (especially under the Trump Administration). Other than India, the rest of the QUAD members do not have land territorial issues with China, which the Government of India has to deal with constantly. It becomes specifically significant after a series of border conflicts that took place mainly in the Western Sector of the Line of Actual Control (LAC) and culminated into the deadly Galwan Valley conflict in mid-June of 2020.

The multilateral nature of the QUAD creates a framework to accommodate a variety of strategic conditions and plans, not only for the original four members but also for the late-joiners in the form of QUAD-plus, such as France, U.K., Germany, and the ones that joined even later, such as Canada, South Korea, and Vietnam. Among the QUAD countries, none of them are more similar than the India–Vietnam pair. First, both share land borders with China, and have fought with China over territorial issues (India: 1960–1962; 1962–present, and Vietnam 1974, 1979, 1980–1990). Second, both have maritime issues and claims with China. For Hanoi, it's Biển Đông/South China Sea; for Delhi, it is the growing Chinese presence in the Indian Ocean Region. Third, for both India and Vietnam, the regional geopolitical environments are facing threats with the expansion of China: while China is developing closer politico-economic relations with Cambodia and Laos through the Belt and Road Initiative (BRI), it also poses a great threat to India's Sphere of Influence by entering into IOR countries such as Sri Lanka, Nepal, Bangladesh, and Pakistan.

Other than geopolitics, Vietnam and India are most likely to benefit from the U.S.–China economic and trade standoff, or as it was called in the Trump era, the "Trade War." While the European countries and the U.S. are looking to reduce their reliance on China in supply chains, the needs to build new supply chains in which Vietnam and India play important roles are also growing. This new situation not only creates opportunities for the two countries but also the similar issues and concerns rising from it. Governments of India and Vietnam can take advantage of the QUAD-plus framework for more dialogues and necessary coordination for their own industrial policies.

Affinity in strategic cultures: Non-alignment movement and limited alignment. Most of the QUAD/plus members are developed industrialized economies, other than India and Vietnam. As for strategic cultures, India and Vietnam are also more similar than others. India has a long tradition of "non-alignment" which can be traced back to the Independence and the 1950s. During the Third Indo-Pakistan War (the Bangladesh War of Independence), the strategic conception of "Strategic Autonomy" was further developed. India would make sure that its decision in defense, diplomacy, and security affairs are free from too much interference of great powers, especially the United States. Although in recent years Delhi has apparently moved closer to the U.S. in strategic and security aspects, it still tries to maintain some distance for maneuvering. One example is that the Indian Navy refused to co-patrol with its U.S. counterpart because it did not benefit India's strategic goals.

India's strategic practices and thoughts have much in common with Vietnam's. According to the 2019 Viet Nam National Defense, officially issued by the Ministry of National Defense of Vietnam, some of the most essential principles in the security affairs include: "…developing defence relations with all nations, especially its neighbouring ones, strategic partners, comprehensive partners, building confidence, and garnering international support and assistance to preclude and respond to the risk of wars of aggression" (VNMND 2019, pp. 26–27), and "[a]ctively and proactively preventing and repulsing the danger of wars are among essential tasks of Viet Nam's national defence in peacetime in order to implement the national defence strategy to its optimal effectiveness which necessitates the protection of national sovereignty, territorial unity and integrity, and interests without resorting to warfighting" (VNMND 2019, p. 30).

The principles of multilateral security and preventive diplomacy are well stipulated in the official document of the Government of Vietnam. Hanoi also has embedded itself in the network woven by multiple international/regional security fora and mechanisms such as ADMM+, as well as bilateral agreements of defense and security collaboration. Hanoi avoids taking sides with a specific great power against another, engaging in practices that Ciorciari (2010) terms as "the limited alignment," which shares similar forms and spirits of India's Non-aligned Movement (NAM). The similarities that Hanoi and Delhi share would make them the pair within the QUAD with the highest level of affinity. This special bilateral relationship would not only strengthen the bond within the QUAD/plus but in reverse would also be reinforced by the multilateral nature of QUAD.

QUAD can empower the bilateral security bond (mechanisms and dialogues) between Delhi and Hanoi: Since the Indian Defense Minister George Fernandez's monumental visit to Vietnam in 2000 raising the curtain of bilateral collaboration in security affairs, many have been achieved, including the establishment of strategic partnership (2007) and its upgrade to a "comprehensive strategic partnership" in 2016; 13 rounds of the India–Vietnam (Defense) Security Dialogues (2003–2021). In the defense technology, since 2014 India began the offering of *BrahMos* anti-ship missile co-produced with Russia to the Vietnamese Navy. That is, before the revival of QUAD by the Trump Administration in 2017 marked by the State Secretary Rex Tillerson at CSIS, India and Vietnam have long been engaging in security collaboration. However, the re-launch of QUAD inevitably created more momentum to boost explicit gestures in bilateral security collaborations, such as the first Indo-Vietnamese army exercise VINBAX and the first maritime bilateral exercise in Da Nang, both in 2018 (Solanki 2021).

Although Vietnam has sent a representative to participate in the multilateral MILAN exercise hosted by the Indian Navy long back in 2008, the meaning of holding bilateral military exercises is apparently stronger, especially to the potential threats. The reconstruction, growth, and expansion of the QUAD/plus framework has provided more incentives for Hanoi and Delhi to send stronger signals to China both in the Indian Ocean and the Biển Đông/South China Sea Regions.

Another function that QUAD can provide for the India-Vietnamese bilateral security collaboration is a platform for expanding their collaborative relations to a third even fourth party. One example is the triangular team formed by India, Japan, and France within the framework of QUAD beginning in the form of a workshop in January 2021 with a focus on the maritime surface and underwater domains as well as the defense technology area (Nayak 2021).[1] The "social space" created in QUAD allows members to form coalitions based on similar geopolitical and/or geo-economics interests. For example, Japan, India, and Vietnam have great potentials to form its coalitions in the framework of QUAD to deal with regional maritime issues. In issues regarding Biển Đông/SCS, Hanoi, Tokyo, and Delhi have overlapped interests in keeping the area "free and open."

---

[1] https://www.orfonline.org/research/maritime-opportunities-await-the-india-japan-france-trilateral/.

On the other hand, the collectiveness of QUAD can also reduce the pressure of each member or a set of specific members when they are facing China alone. The growing strategic proximity between Hanoi and Delhi often draws the criticism from Beijing. QUAD would give more political support to its members to act collectively toward China. This is especially important to Vietnam and India who have embraced multilateralism and limited alignment/non-alignment for a long time. Although the collective responses and actions within the framework of QUAD have yet to establish the protocols, it is more likely now than pre-2017 to see co-patrols, passex/passage exercises in bilateral or multilateral forms to take place in the Indo-Pacific region. Either the Vietnamese Navy or the Indian Navy would have opportunities to coordinate not only with each other but also with navies of the U.S., France, UK, or the Japanese Maritime Self-defense Force (JMSDF).

QUAD would also help diluting the U.S. unilateral influence and interference in the domestic politics of specific countries: Vietnam is now the only non-democratic, one-party socialist republic in the QUAD/plus framework. During the Trump Administration, this can be a lesser issue since the Republican administration had not (at least in the Trump Administration) attempted to put much emphasis on the spread of democracy via "peaceful evolution" (Diễn biến hòa bình; Le and Tsvetov 2018, p. 24; Tomotaka, 2020a). However, Biden's victory in 2020 presidential election could bring some uncertainty for closer strategic cooperation between Washington and Hanoi, although the U.S. government has shown some flexibility to take a more realist (and practical) stance toward the domestic political issues with Vietnam. Kurt Campbell, the "Asia Tsar," who heads the newly created position of Coordinator for the Indo-Pacific in the National Security Council, has proposed that "…a sustainable and stable relationship with Vietnam will require a pragmatic approach to human rights. The United States should forgo public shaming in favor of dialogue, private counsel, and support for Vietnamese reforms" (Campbell 2016).

In fact, some minor political conflicts emerged between the liberal U.S. government and the right-wing, nationalistic BJP government of India in the first months after Biden's inauguration. The Government of India accused international activists — such as the Greta Thunberg and Meena Harris, an American human right lawyer and niece of the Vice President Kamala Harris — of launching "motivated campaigns" over farmers' protests around the national capital region of Delhi with India as the target (*Mint* 2021).

For democratic members in the QUAD/plus, the multilateral mechanism has well protected the strategic goals shared among the members, although the political stances might vary due to the results of the elections of chief executives. The first official high-level communication between India and the U.S. was not the conversation between Biden and Narendra Modi, but between Jake Sullivan, the U.S. National Security Advisor, and his Indian counterpart Ajit Doval. What will be the takeaway lesson for Vietnam is that, within a multilateral framework like QUAD/plus, the unilateral great power's influence is diluted, as other bigger members within the organization — when they are sided with smaller members — would somewhat balance out the dominating forces of the leading great power. Vietnam being a one-party communist country within QUAD led by the Democrat U.S. for which peaceful evolution is usually a favorable strategy in foreign affairs does not worry too much. With Asian regional powers such as India and Japan being the members, the social networks would cancel out the influence of the U.S. should there be intention to further interfere with Vietnam's domestic politics.

Potential Challenges for India and Vietnam to Cooperate under QUAD

There are some potential concerns of India and Vietnam's security collaboration under QUAD. *First, as it is expanding, how QUAD/plus is going to impose itself upon the geopolitical realities without challenging the so-called "ASEAN Centrality" is worthy of much observation.* As many like to use this concept (many times, though, in a casual and under-defined way), *ASEAN Centrality* has been challenged in at least the trade as well as the security areas. India has been using *ASEAN Centrality* with emphases on official announcements as a context when conceptualizing its own IPOI.

Nevertheless, New Delhi's withdrawal from the RCEP negotiation process without a prospective of rejoining the largest free-trade area agreement soon has distanced itself from ASEAN, both economically and politically. In contrast, India has shown much more interest and made progress in the participation of QUAD activities, which makes much sense considering the security challenges that it has faced for the past few years from China: along the LAC in both Eastern and Western Sectors; from the Indian Ocean, and from China's diplomatic offensives carried out in the name of BRI toward its neighboring countries. These geopolitical challenges can only be answered by QUAD rather than by ASEAN.

Vietnam, similarly, needs more from the QUAD to buttress its "Biển Đông/SCS-centered" security strategy. According to Zhang (2017), after the 11th National Congress of the Communist Party of Vietnam (Đại hội đại biểu toàn quốc lần thứ XI), the agenda of Vietnam's foreign policy has begun to be occupied by the Biển Đông/SCS-related issues. The South China Sea issue has appeared everywhere, both in the foreign policy processes and is the major if not the most important goal of Vietnam's foreign policy (pp. 19–20). The SCS issue between Sino-Vietnamese relationship is more conflictual than cooperative, which is totally different than other pairs regarding SCS issues such as the Vietnamese-Filipino, the Vietnamese-Malaysian, and the Vietnamese-Brunei bilateral relations (p. 21). In 2020, Vietnam used its chairmanship of ASEAN to reaffirm the United Nations Convention on the Law of the Sea (UNCLOS) as the basis to determine the rights, entitlements, claims, and jurisdictions in the South China Sea. However, China began to play through different members of ASEAN such as Laos, Cambodia, Myanmar, the Philippines, and Malaysia, so as to dissuade them from being proactive or committed on the SCS issues (Tomotaka 2020b).

Due to the consensus nature and the lack of "big players," ASEAN is a forum where powers stand off against each other. Compared with it, QUAD is more powerful, committed, and useful. As the situation becomes more confrontational, how Delhi and Hanoi can maintain well the balance between the rule-and-consensus-based ASEAN and the power-equipped QUAD, could determine the route for further collaboration between each other and within the QUAD for the future (Iwamoto 2021).

Second, whether and how India can deliver on the strategic synthesis with Vietnam in the framework of QUAD could also influence the potential of further collaboration: Delhi has begun to reach out to Southeast Asian countries including Vietnam via multilateral organizations or projects in the 1990s; for example, the BIMSTEC (1997) and the Mekong Ganga Commission (MGC, November 2000) were launched early to boost the connection with countries including those on the continental SE Asia such as CLMV (Cambodia, Laos, Myanmar, and Vietnam). However, other than the "soft infrastructure," big connectivity projects such as the India–Myanmar–Thailand Highway and the Kaladan Multi-modal Transit Transport Project (KMTTP) designed to further improve the connection between India and countries on the Indochina Peninsula are still behind schedule (Liu 2018).

Delivery has been a major concern in the strategic cooperation between Vietnam and Southeast Asia countries. According to a report made by the leading U.S. think tank RAND in 2015, delay in delivery of strategic plans or projects has affected SE Asian countries' reliance and impression on India *vis-à-vis* China. Some SE Asian countries feel disappointed by India for being passive or sluggish, as Indian government officials are satisfied by participating in the meetings and conferences only without further commitment on deliveries (Blank *et al.* 2015). The RAND report might reflect some of the U.S. mainstream policymakers' evaluation about India in SE Asia. How much has changed in the QUAD framework? The successful delivery in strategic collaboration still very much depends on the domestic management and politics of India. However, QUAD would help adjust strategic plans when accidents take place. In the online QUAD Summit in March 2021, leaders of the U.S., Japan, Australia, and India reached consensus that Delhi would be producing vaccines needed for the others as well as for the regions to use. But the unexpected surge of cases in the worst-so-far second wave of COVID-19 altered the route of the original plan. With the resilience of QUAD, the U.S. fills up the shortage and promises to deliver 500 million vaccines to the world and the WHO. This could be a microcosm for the collaboration in strategic affairs later within the QUAD.

The third factor that might influence India and Vietnam's collaboration in the QUAD is Russia: Both India and Vietnam have maintained close strategic relationships with Russia, and their respective relations with Moscow even have played a connecting role to facilitate the Indian-Vietnamese collaboration in security affairs. The training programs for the Vietnamese Navy's Kilo-class submarines, the tech transfer of *BrahMos* Anti-ship missiles as well as coordination through Russian-made weapon systems are examples. On the SCS/Biển Đông-related issues and disputes, Moscow has officially had a "neutral position" and objected the interference of outside powers. Albeit supporting UNCLOS and the Conduct of the Parties in the South China Sea (DOC) as well as the Code of Conduct (COC), Russia sided with China in objecting the Permanent Court of

Arbitration (PCA) ruling in 2016 (Kapoor 2021). From QUAD's perspective, the inclusion of India and Vietnam would help further checking on Moscow's stance and behavior on SCS, but it can also be a potential issue, hinging on the development of the U.S.–Russia relations. If the Biden Administration chooses a more realist path toward Russia instead of focusing too much on its domestic politics, then a conciliated U.S.–Russia relations should be a plus for the QUAD. But if the bilateral relations between Moscow and Washington worsen in the years to come and Russia chooses to side with China more — the SCS issues included — then Delhi and Hanoi might appear to be more detached from major agenda items that the QUAD is pursuing. And, if the U.S. has any change on the waiver for purchasing Russian-made weapons for India and Vietnam, it might create negative atmosphere as well.

What India and Vietnam Would Do, and Could Do?

Under current circumstances, there is still much Delhi and Hanoi can try to accomplish within the framework of QUAD. Hanoi might want to remain low-profile to observe its multilateral, non-aligned foreign policy stance. But QUAD does increase the opportunities for further interactions among members. India and Vietnam could form a working group-like mechanism in the QUAD to expand their relations with other key stakeholders in this quadrilateral collective security mechanism. First, Vietnam and India should strengthen the coordination in the QUAD framework. Second, based on the existent bilateral relationship, the two countries that share similar geopolitical challenges should well identify the issues and choose to work with likely QUAD/plus members based on various issues.

Japan can be the first country that the India–Vietnam duo can reach out. All three have maritime territorial issues with China respectively in the East China Sea, the Indian Ocean, and Biển Đông/South China Sea. Trade- and investment-wise, Tokyo also has common interest with Delhi and Hanoi. As major investors are moving their bucks out of China, both Vietnam and India now have become the new destinations to relocate and rebuild the supply chains (Onose 2020). Japan has also engaged in key infrastructures in both countries such as the metro/subway systems and the high-speed rails. Militarily, the three have held exercise or capacity building activities frequently in pairs. The Japanese Maritime Self-Defence Force (JMSDF) has had exercises of different topics and levels with the Indian Navy, while it has more capacity-building operations with

Vietnam People's Navy (VPN); the Indian Navy has done passex, port calls, and anti-submarine-focused drills with VPN. There is more space, however, to expand the scale of military and strategic dialogues and practices in a three-way format. One of the merits of this kind trilateral working group is that with the help and prompt of India, Vietnam could integrate in the QUAD framework with more willingness and incentives.

Other areas that India and Vietnam can further explore to elaborate include:

(1) *Maritime law and practice*: Although still in development, Delhi's IPOI that Modi announced in 2019 in Bangkok focuses more on the "inclusiveness"; the seven pillars that include "maritime security, maritime ecology, maritime resources, capacity building and resource sharing; disaster risk reduction and management; science, technology and academic cooperation; and trade connectivity and maritime transport" (MEA 2020) are still an umbrella framework that needs more substantial plans and efforts to support this idea. Other than development and capacity-building-related goals, a key aspect that Vietnam and India can work together regarding maritime cooperation and security is the collaborative study in international maritime law and the preparation for stronger arguments regarding the South China Sea issues. India's abundance in legal talents, networking with Western legal practitioners and academicians, and enthusiasm in SCS issues shall be the strength that Hanoi can take advantage of. On the other hand, Hanoi and Delhi should also look for opportunities to work closely in the UN system as well as other multilateral organizations and forums.

(2) *Collaboration on studying territorial and geostrategic issues*: Vietnam and India are in similar situations when facing the geostrategic challenges from China. The two states not only are trapped in the territorial problems with China but also face the same intrusion of the Chinese presence and influence in the region. For Vietnam, the increasing political and economic clout of China into Laos and Cambodia has created strategic pressure encircling Vietnam along with China's presence from the Sea. For India, the Chinese presence in the name of BRI has created some influence in the neighboring Nepal, Sir Lanka, and Bangladesh, let alone the long-term friendship with Pakistan. The resemblance in geostrategic problems actually create vast space for collaboration. For example, India could explore the possibility to involve Vietnam more into its regional multilateral

organizations or forums such as Indian Ocean Rim Association (IORA) or the India Ocean Naval Symposium (IONS), while Vietnam can involve India more into the scientific and commercial exploration of the South China Sea. Other collaborative areas can be the influence of BRI, the People's Liberation Army (PLA) studies and/or other strategically related topics.

(3) *Enhance the think-tank, strategic-community- and college-level collaboration*: The talks between strategic communities or researchers of related disciplines (political science, international relations, legal studies and international laws, petroleum, geology, marine biology, etc.) are important and more significant than short-term meetings or conferences regarding some specific issues. A prestigious scholar and commentator of international relations and strategy in India has commented in one of the SCS conferences — where the Vietnamese Embassy diplomats were present — on the eve of PCA results in 2019 that "in the last year there are at least 200 meeting regarding South China Sea taking place in Delhi, but little has been changed." Thus, to establish more solid and lasting dialogue mechanisms is important, and this is what India and Vietnam can do in the context of multilateral security dialogues, including the QUAD.

As indicated by Kurt M. Campbell, the senior coordinator of Indo-Pacific Affairs in the National Security Council, the U.S. engagement with China has "come to an end" and competition has now become the "dominant paradigm" (Zheng 2021). Predicably as a result QUAD will stay on the U.S. foreign policy agenda as an essential item and a powerful tool for use in the coming decade. Both Delhi and Hanoi should plan their future geostrategies in the context of QUAD. A rising regional power, India has greater resilience and capacity to resist China's pressure on any important geostrategy it makes. A flexible regional power that enjoys social relations that other QUAD members might not have (such as with Iran, Russia, Afghanistan), Delhi has great potential to play the key linkage between QUAD members and smaller but important countries such as Vietnam.

References

Biden, J. R. 2021. Renewing America's Advantages: Interim National Security Strategic Guidance. Whitehouse.gov. https://www.whitehouse.gov/wp-content/uploads/2021/03/NSC-1v2.pdf (accessed July 14, 2021).

Blank, Jonah, J. Moroney, A. Rabasa, and B. Lin. 2015. *Look East, Cross Black Waters: India's Interest in Southeast Asia.* Santa Monica, CA: Rand Corporation.

Campbell, Kurt. 2016. *The Pivot: The Future of American Statecraft in Asia.* New York: Grand Central Publishing. Kindle Edition.

Ciorciari, J. D. 2010. *The Limits of Alignment: Southeast Asia and the Great Powers since 1975.* Washington, DC: Georgetown University Press.

Iwamoto, Kentaro. 2021. ASEAN Defends Its Indo-Pacific 'Centrality' between Quad and China. *Nikkei Asia.* https://asia.nikkei.com/Spotlight/Asia-Insight/ASEAN-defends-its-Indo-Pacific-centrality-between-Quad-and-China (accessed July 15, 2021).

Kapoor, Nivedita. 2021. Russia's Conduct in the South China Sea. *Commentaries (ORF).* June 18, 2021. https://www.orfonline.org/research/russias-conduct-in-the-south-china-sea/ (accessed July 20, 2021).

Kondapalli, S. 2018. China's Evolving Naval Presence in the Indian Ocean Region: An Indian Perspective. In David Brewster ed., *India and China at Sea: Competition for Naval Dominance in the Indian Ocean.* Chennai: Apple Books.

Le, Hong Hiep and Anton Tsvetov. 2018. *Vietnam's Foreign Policy under Doi Moi.* Singapore: ISEAS-Yusof Ishak Institute.

Le, Thu Huong. 2016. High Hopes and a Big Let-Down: Vietnam and the TPP. *The Interpreter.* https://www.lowyinstitute.org/the-interpreter/high-hopes-and-big-let-down-vietnam-and-tpp (accessed July 21, 2021).

Liu, Roger C. 2018. The Evolution of Trump Administration's 'Indo-Pacific Strategy' and the Role of India. [川普「印太戰略」構想的演變與印度的角色] *Studies on Chinese Communist* [中共研究] 52 (2): 29–45.

Ministry of External Affairs (MEA India). 2003. *Joint Declaration on the Framework of Comprehensive Cooperation between the Republic of India and the Socialist Republic of Vietnam as they Enter the 21st Century.* MEA.gov. https://www.mea.gov.in/bilateral-documents.htm?dtl/7658/Joint (accessed July 01, 2021).

Ministry of External Affair (MEA India). 2020. Indo-Pacific Division Briefs. MEA.gov. https://mea.gov.in/Portal/ForeignRelation/Indo_Feb_07_2020.pdf (accessed July 10, 2021).

Mint. 2021. Jaishankar Slams Rihanna, Greta for "Motivated Campaign" over Farmers' Protest. Livemint.com.https://www.livemint.com/news/world/jaishankar-slams-foreign-celebs-for-motivated-campaign-over-farmers-protest-11612411592197.html (accessed July 24, 2021).

Nayak, Sohini. 2021. Maritime Opportunities Await the India-Japan-France Trilateral. *Special Report No. 13* (ORF). https://www.orfonline.org/research/maritime-opportunities-await-the-india-japan-france-trilateral/ (accessed July 20, 2021).

News18. 2018. Vietnam, India Cement Modi's Act East Policy, Sign 3 Agreements. News 18.com. March 4, 2018.https://www.news18.com/news/india/vietnam-india-cement-modis-act-east-policy-sign-3-agreements-1677861.html (accessed July 24, 2021).

Nguyen, K. V. and X. T. Nguyen. 2021. Vietnam and the United States: A Strategic Partnership in the Future? *India Quarterly* 77 (2): 238–251.

Onose, Takahisa. 2020. Japanese and Vietnamese Economies are Substantially Intertwined. EY.com. https://www.ey.com/en_vn/ey-news/japanese-and-vietnamese-economies-are-substantially-intertwined (accessed July 15, 2020).

Panda, Ankit. 2017. US Implementation of 'Major Defense Partner' Perks for India Underway. *The Diplomat.* https://thediplomat.com/2017/04/us-implementation-of-major-defense-partner-perks-for-india-underway/ (accessed July 19, 2021).

Panda, Rajaram. 2020. Chinese Incursions Into Vietnamese Waters, Security Implications for the Region, and the Potential Role of India. *China Brief* 20: 10. https://jamestown.org/program/chinese-incursions-into-vietnamese-waters-security-implications-for-the-region-and-the-potential-role-of-india/ (accessed July 24, 2021).

Pant, Harsh. 2018. Defence Cooperation. In *India and Vietnam: A "Strategic Partnership" in the Making.* Singapore: S. Rajaratnam School of International Studies, Nanyang Technology University. http://www.jstor.com/stable/resrep 17644.5 (accessed July 10, 2021).

Saha, Premesha. 2021. India Calibrates its South China Sea Approach. *Issue Brief (ORF) 477.* https://www.orfonline.org/wp-content/uploads/2021/07/ORF_IssueBrief_477_India-SouthChinaSea_FinalForUpload.pdf (accessed July 24, 2021).

Solanki, Viraj. 2021. India-Vietnam Defence and Security Cooperation. *India Quarterly* 77 (2): 219–237.

The Hindu. 2021. First Quad Summit: Quad Leaders For 'Open, Free' Indo-Pacific. Thehindu.com. March 12, 2021.https://www.thehindu.com/news/national/first-quad-summit-meeting/article34054156.ece (accessed July 24, 2021).

The Indian Express. 2018. Vietnamese President Praises PM Modi on Act East Policy, Bats for India's UNSC Membership. *The Indian Express.* March 4, 2018.http://indianexpress.com/article/india/vietnamese-president-praises-pm-modi-on-indias-act-east-policy-5085490/ (accessed July 24, 2021).

The White House. 2021. Quad Leaders' Joint Statement: 'The Spirit of the Quad'. Whitehouse.gov. https://www.whitehouse.gov/briefing-room/statements-releases/2021/03/12/quad-leaders-joint-statement-the-spirit-of-the-quad/ (accessed July 16, 2021).

Tomotaka. Shoji. 2018. Vietnam's Security Cooperation with the United States: Historical Background, Present and Future Outlook. *Boei Kenkyusho Kiyo* [NIDS Security Studies] 20(2): 3–16.

Tomotaka, Shoji. 2020a. Vietnam's Security: Challenges and Responses. http://ssdpaki.la.coocan.jp/en/proposals/73.html (accessed July 24, 2021).

Tomotaka, Shoji. 2020b. ASEAN's Growing Concern About China's Assertive Stance in the South China Sea. *International Information Network Analysis.* https://www.spf.org/iina/en/articles/shoji_12.html (accessed July 24, 2021).

U.S. Department of Defense. 2019. *Indo-Pacific Strategy Report: Preparedness, Partnerships, and Promoting a Networked Region.* Defense.gov. https://media.defense.gov/2019/Jul/01/2002152311/-1/-1/1/DEPARTMENT-OF-DEFENSE-INDO-PACIFIC-STRATEGY-REPORT-2019.PDF (accessed July 15, 2021).

U.S. Mission to ASEAN. 2017. Remarks by President Trump at APEC CEO Summit | Da Nang, Vietnam. Usmission.gov. https://asean.usmission.gov/remarks-president-trump-apec-ceo-summit-da-nang-vietnam/ (accessed July 22, 2021).

VNMND (Ministry of National Defence, Socialist Republic of Viet Nam). 2019. *2019 Viet Nam National Defence.* Hanoi: National Political Publishing House.

Vorsatz, B. and R. de Leon. 2014. Revisiting the Shangri-La Dialogue: Candid and Heated Conversations are Encouraged. *Center for American Progress.* https://www.americanprogress.org/issues/security/reports/2014/08/14/95661/revisiting-the-shangri-la-dialogue-candid-and-heated-conversations-are-encouraged/ (accessed July 20, 2021).

Zhang, Mingliang. 2017. The South China Sea Issue of Vietnam's Foreign Policy. ["南海问题化"的越南外交] *Southeast Asian Studies* 1 (2017): 19–34.

Zheng, Sarah. 2021. US–China Ties: Competition, Not Engagement From Now On, Kurt Campbell Says. *South China Morning Post.* May 27, 2021.https://www.scmp.com/news/china/diplomacy/article/3135066/us-china-ties-competition-not-engagement-now-kurt-campbell (accessed July 20, 2021).

Part II
Alternative Fields for Regional Cooperation

Chapter 6

The Efforts of ASEAN Countries on Establishing Technology-Led and Knowledge-Based Economies and Non-ASEAN Countries' Cooperation

Akio Egawa

Introduction

Malaysia and Thailand, the upper middle-income countries of the Association of Southeast Asian Nations (ASEAN), achieved rapid economic growth and middle-income status before the early 2000s by introducing labor-intensive manufacturing from abroad and exporting cheap but low value-added products. Now, these countries will lose their main engine of economic growth unless they shift from input-based industries to technology-led and knowledge-based ones. As they can no longer import technology suitable for their stage of economic development, they need domestic experts to generate their own technology, so a national strategy for human capital formation and human resource development becomes of great importance.

How, then, have the two countries dealt with the necessity of upgrading their industries and developing human resources, and what are their policy responses on human capital formation and human resource development? This chapter will examine recent policy responses by ASEAN and its middle-income member-states leading to the establishment of technology-led and knowledge-based economic structures, focusing on human capital formation and human resource development. In the next section, I will consider how these countries' economic development policies should be changed and discuss the importance and urgency of human resource development. I will present an overview of human capital formation through higher education in the third section, using the case of Thailand as an example, noting how delivery of this policy has failed to increase higher education enrollment. As Thailand cannot address all its problems alone, in the fourth section I examine the contribution of international cooperation, specifically with Japan. From my overview, it is clear that the international community can do very little in developing human resources for ASEAN countries. In section five, I draw my conclusions.

ASEAN Middle-Income Countries: Past Development Paths and Current Limitations on Further Economic Development

Past advantages become current limitations

ASEAN's upper middle-income countries, Malaysia and Thailand (soon to be joined by Vietnam), have recorded rapid economic growth, but unless they upgrade their industrial structures, they will fall into what is known as the "middle-income trap." This means that factors that supported their rapid economic growth in the past may now become limitations. These past advantages/current limitations are as follows:

(1) Relatively high productivity in the agricultural sector: Asian countries had systems and conditions that were ideal for agricultural production, such as climate and soil quality, a cultivation-oriented community, and improvement of breeds (Birdsall *et al.* 1993). While the acreage of agricultural land remained roughly stable, increases in efficiency led to a labor surplus in agriculture. The marginal productivity of surplus labor is zero in the agricultural sector, but once that labor is absorbed into labor-intensive manufacturing, it can produce something at a very low level of wages. As the number of factories increased, this intersectoral shift of labor raised these countries' overall productivity, resulting in rapid economic growth.

Now, whereas ASEAN's low-income and lower middle-income countries can still benefit from this advantage because their wage levels are still low enough to attract foreign direct investment (FDI), Malaysia and Thailand have already exhausted their supplies of surplus labor. In those countries, companies introduce labor-saving equipment into their factories instead of employing more workers at higher wages. Their governments face the difficult task of shifting their agricultural labor force to a growing industrial sector (typically not a labor-intensive one).

(2) A highly competent bureaucracy able to formulate an economic development strategy: In the early 1980s, Singapore, Malaysia, and Thailand began amending legislation to create a framework more favorable to FDI from Japan. Vietnam amended its industrial policies and foreign exchange regime in line with international standards in the late 2000s, which resulted in a huge inflow of FDI. Cambodia, Laos, and Myanmar began to formulate legislation promoting foreign investment once they had achieved political stability. Legislation governing the promotion of foreign investment was originally designed to attract labor-intensive industries, and the ASEAN countries were able to learn from the experiences of Asia's developed economies (such as Japan and South Korea) when they were designing the economic and social systems necessary for economic development. In fact, Singapore, Malaysia, and Thailand were in close dialogue with the Japanese government and business sector when they were formulating their own development strategies which included the efficient facilitation of investment from Japanese businesses.

Now, ASEAN middle-income countries risk falling into the middle-income trap (ADB 2011),[1] if they are not already caught in it (OECD 2014).[2] An economic growth strategy that relies heavily on utilizing cheap

---

[1] The middle-income trap was first identified in a World Bank report (Gill and Kharas 2007) as pertaining to the situation of resource-rich Latin American countries in the 1980s. A resource-rich country can easily reach middle-income status by just exporting its natural resources, but it would find it difficult to become a high-income country because of its heavy reliance on one industry (mining) and lack of industries that are based on productivity growth.

[2] Although there is no criterion for judging whether a country is caught in a middle-income trap, Eichengreen *et al.* (2011) estimated the conditions that lead to a sharp drop in a country's GDP growth rate and used the result in their analysis of the Chinese economy.

labor will hit a limit, because these countries can no longer compete with others with lower income levels. The key to a successful economic development strategy is no longer short-term cost incentives but the development of technology-led, knowledge-based industries. People in ASEAN countries are generally educated to a higher standard than they were in the past, and industry is seeking a more talented or highly skilled labor force. Therefore, the best policy options for overcoming the middle-income trap may be: (1) avoiding a mismatch between university students' choice of major and the requirements of businesses, and (2) the universal provision of vocational and higher education. However, policymakers tend to be hesitant when it comes to adopting long-term and costly policy measures such as those affecting education and publicly funded research and development (R&D), because they do not bear enough fruit in the short-term to attract voters.

(3) An open trade policy and logistics infrastructure development, including ASEAN connectivity: The ASEAN countries formulated the economic development strategy known as export-oriented industrialization (EOI) during their early stage of development to attract foreign businesses that needed an abundance of low-wage labor. EOI involved granting special privileges to foreign investors and the development of export-related infrastructure (such as seaports, special industrial zones, and roads), on condition that the foreign-owned businesses would not be permitted to sell their products on the domestic market. Under the business strategy known as the "flying geese model" (this will be discussed later in this chapter), EOI suited foreign investors' need to produce parts or materials rather than finished products, and to export them elsewhere for the next stage of the production process. This strategy was facilitated by ASEAN's vision, since 1992, to establish an ASEAN free-trade area. Foreign (typically Japanese) manufacturing companies tried to establish Asia-wide supply chain networks and locate the labor-intensive production of parts and materials and assembly in accordance with the stage of economic development in each individual country. This influenced the creation of the tariff-free ASEAN Economic Community (AEC) at the end of 2015.

This estimate is used as a criterion by some scholars. For example, Jitsuchon (2012), based on the Eichengreen, Park, and Shin analysis, argued that Thailand was already caught in such a trap.

Now, free intra-regional movement of persons (person-to-person connectivity) under the AEC has yet to be realized. The need for highly skilled personnel has to be satisfied within each individual ASEAN country, as it is still difficult to import overseas talent either from within or outside ASEAN. Without amending regulations on the movement of labor, adjustment of the industrial structure is unlikely to be successful. And these countries will have to develop their information and communication infrastructure as well as their logistics infrastructure if they are to utilize technology and become a regional hub for the digital economy.

Thus, ASEAN upper middle-income countries may face problems in the following areas when formulating policies aimed at establishing a technology-led and knowledge-based economy: shifting from an input-based economic structure to a productivity-based one; improving higher education (both in terms of quality and quantity); and devising schemes to promote the international movement of persons, including facilitation of person-to-person connectivity.

Theoretical considerations concerning technology needs of middle-income countries

While these countries had lower-middle income status, their governments collaborated with the private sector in carrying out basic and applied research for domestic technological development, and private-sector companies were able to utilize the fruits of this research. To improve this collaboration, the governments developed the necessary infrastructure and supported the development of human resources. Nowadays, however, technological development and the development of workforce skills and knowledge is conducted by individual private companies through R&D investment. This is because the characteristics of technology changes as a country's economy develops.

Technological development consists of three main elements: invention, innovation, and diffusion, although the distinction between these three elements has become increasingly blurred (Bell and Pavitt 1993). Developing countries have neither sufficient technicians nor facilities to develop new technologies, so they tend to focus first of all on the "diffusion" of existing imported technologies to the manufacture of various goods and services without making any drastic changes. However, Nelson (1980) argues that developing countries face difficulties in innovation and diffusion in four respects: (1) knowing which technologies are best suited to their stage of economic development; (2) knowing from which company they can obtain such technologies; (3) knowing whether they can adapt (innovate) these technologies to make them suitable for their economic development or consumer markets; and (4) being able to protect adapted or imported technologies from leakage.

However, if technology imports could be conducted as a form of FDI (i.e., by means of within-company international transfer), those difficulties would be eliminated altogether. At the same time, as a developing country accumulates experience in utilizing imported technologies, it will gradually develop the ability to innovate domestically (Romer 1990). The second model, that of the flying geese pattern of development (hereinafter, the flying geese model), applies to technology transfers within Asia through FDI. As the economy of a country develops and its wage level rises, foreign businesses shift their labor-intensive production processes out of that country and concentrate on capital-intensive production processes and innovation and invention. This shift also triggers economic and industrial development within the recipient country. In Asia, Japanese companies initially shifted their labor-intensive production to the newly industrialized economies (NIEs) of Asia, that is, South Korea, Taiwan, Hong Kong, and Singapore, when wage levels in Japan became too high. Then, after the Plaza accord of 1985 triggered a lasting surge in the Japanese yen and the Asian NIEs attained upper middle-income status, Japanese firms moved their labor-intensive production from the Asian NIEs to the ASEAN countries and their capital-intensive production from Japan to the Asian NIEs. Knowing this, the ASEAN countries formulated industrial development strategies based on the flying geese model since they had adopted EOI with the expectation of receiving Japanese FDI accompanied by transfers of appropriate technology.

Even so, the ASEAN countries still faced the difficulties identified by Nelson (1980) when trying to develop invention potential. As new technologies are the only source of profit for companies in advanced countries nowadays, they tend to conduct their own R&D and seldom share its (firm-specific) fruits as that would involve huge uncertainties concerning its success and also carry the risk of leakage. If the results of a particular R&D program are likely to be useful for industries nationwide, the R&D should be conducted publicly or receive public support in terms of the construction of research facilities and the development of information and communication infrastructure. This would mean that public expenditure

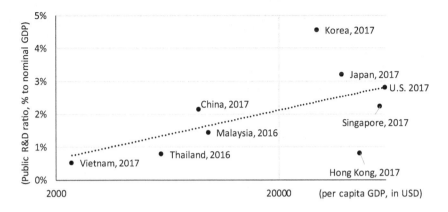

Figure 1: Public R&D Ratio
Source: World Bank Data (accessed October 30, 2019).

on R&D would be greater for countries with a higher national income. Figure 1 shows the relationship between the ratio of public expenditure on R&D to GDP and per-capita GDP as a measure of national income. The dots indicating middle-income countries (Malaysia, Thailand, and Vietnam) are located below the asymptotic line, which suggests that the governments of these countries were not spending enough on R&D at that time.

Technological development vs. cross-sector shift of labor

Public R&D would improve individual workers' efficiency, or "pure productivity" at a national level, through the development of skills and knowledge. However, instead of facilitating public R&D, ASEAN countries could opt for a cross-sectoral shift of the labor force. When the workforce in a low-productivity sector shifts to a high-productivity sector, productivity increases at the national level without there being any technological development. The flying geese model worked as a good strategy for realizing a cross-sectoral shift of labor as the economies of the ASEAN countries began to take off. In fact, the success or otherwise of this shift of labor to some extent determined the differences in countries' economic growth in this century. According to an Oxford Economics (2016) estimate, the average growth rates of pure productivity for Malaysia, Thailand, and Vietnam for the years 2000–2015 differed by only

2.3–2.5 percentage points, but the contribution of sectoral shift to productivity growth was 0.0% in Malaysia and 0.1% in Thailand, against 1.7% in Vietnam.

According to Watanabe (2009), per-worker productivity in the manufacturing sector was almost triple that in the services sector among upper middle-income countries, although it is still higher in services than in the agricultural sector. Therefore, the best way to improve economic productivity is to shift the labor force from the agricultural sector to manufacturing. However, as the discussion concerning the middle-income trap indicates, high value-added or high-productivity manufacturing that requires workers to have a high level of talent or skill should be promoted in upper middle-income countries. As farmers lack the education required to engage in manufacturing, they would either stay in farming or shift to low-productivity tertiary industries. In the case of Thailand, for example, there is an abundance of labor in the agricultural sector (32% of the total workforce in 2015, although there is no longer a surplus of labor), but as we can see from Figure 2, that workforce remained in agriculture, which lowered the productivity growth rate. In 2015, only 17% of the total workforce was engaged in the manufacturing sector, lower than the value, 23%, that Eichengreen *et al.* (2011) estimated would minimize the risk of a sharp drop in the economic growth rate. This means that governments should not *either* improve pure productivity in advanced industries *or* facilitate labor mobility from agriculture to manufacturing, but should facilitate labor mobility by improving pure productivity of labor at all

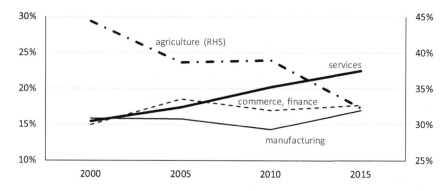

Figure 2:   Sectoral Share of Labor Force in Thailand, 2000–2015

Source: National Statistical Office of Thailand "Labour Force Survey (annual)."

levels of the industrial sector. Concerning investment promotion policies, the governments of upper middle-income countries are nowadays expected to do more than simply attract FDI with tax and other cost incentives; they also have to provide poorly educated workers with the skills necessary to work in "new" industries to facilitate a shift of the labor force toward the high value-added manufacturing sector.

Nowadays, the term "Industry 4.0" frequently appears in discussions of new industrial structures for advanced countries.[3] Individual ASEAN member-states, especially those with upper middle-income status, recognize the importance of developing Industry 4.0, and ASEAN itself is beginning to form a vision of future economic and industrial systems, known as ASEAN's fourth industrial revolution (4IR hereinafter). ASEAN is stepping up joint efforts in key areas such as infrastructure, regulatory reform, e-commerce (harmonization of rules, data protection, digital payment, etc.), intellectual property rights protection, consumer protection, and so on.[4] In addition, the ASEAN member states are discussing how to upgrade the skills level of the labor force so that it can be utilized in high-tech and high value-added manufacturing and service sectors. Economists call the process of developing and accumulating skills and talent by learning and experience "human capital formation." As the ASEAN middle-income countries have come to recognize that higher education will facilitate their workers' employment in high value-added manufacturing sectors, they have carried out reforms of higher education, such as establishing more universities and vocational schools. In the next section, I will provide an overview and assessment of the state of human capital formation and policies for its improvement, taking the case of Thailand as an example.

---

[3] Industry 4.0 derives its name from the inventions that triggered successive industrial revolutions. Industry 1.0 was triggered by the invention of the steam engine, 2.0 came with the harnessing of electricity and its transmission, and 3.0 was driven by the development of information and communication technology, especially the Internet. Now, advanced and upper middle-income countries are trying to work out what Industry 4.0 will involve.

[4] The information in this paragraph regarding 4IR is cited from a lecture delivered by Dr. Aladdin D. Rillo, Deputy Secretary-General of ASEAN for the AEC, at the ASEAN–Japan Center, August 26, 2019, entitled "Update on AEC — What Has (and Hasn't) Changed?"

The State of Human Capital Formation and Efforts Taken to Improve It: The Case of Thailand

Now that Thailand has achieved upper middle-income status, its economic strength no longer comes from the mass production of low value-added goods or cost efficiencies. Recognizing this, the Thai government launched the "Thailand 4.0" initiative to identify the next generation of industries and to promote them. Thailand 4.0 is, unlike Industry 4.0 or ASEAN 4IR, an attempt to foster new, growing industries by upgrading existing key industries using information and communication technology.[5] However, even if the government can attract FDI in the new industrial sectors, foreign investors will need sufficient numbers of highly skilled domestic (Thai) workers who can operate the new machines, acquire new skills, and conduct innovation and invention. Therefore, human resource development and human capital formation become increasingly important. This section is dedicated to an overview of the actual policy efforts undertaken in Thailand.

Human capital formation in Thailand

The World Bank has developed a Human Capital Index (HCI) which measures the average state of human capital formation in a country and can be used in drawing international comparisons. A country's HCI is, in general, positively correlated with its income level. From Table 1, we can see that, in contrast to the ranking based on per-capita GDP, Vietnam is ranked higher than Thailand or Malaysia, whose per-capita national income is greater than that of Vietnam. In Malaysia and Thailand, health-related scores are higher than those in Vietnam, whereas Vietnam's score for educational attainment is higher than those of the other two countries. This means that improving the quality of education may be important in Thailand. Although young Thais can attend school for longer than they did in the past, educational attainment in Thailand may not be high enough to enable the workforce to utilize its knowledge. This view is supported by the OECD (2014, p. 3), which points out that the quality of

---

[5]The Thai Ministry of Industry explains that Thailand 1.0 was agriculture, Thailand 2.0 was light manufacturing industries, and Thailand 3.0 was heavy and petrochemical manufacturing industries, which is where Thailand's industrial structure is today.

Table 1: Human Capital Index (Comparison)

Rank	Country	Human Capital Index (HCI)	Probability of Survival to Age 5	Expected Years of School	Harmonized Test Scores	Learning-Adjusted Years of School	Fraction of Kids Under 5 Not Stunted	Adult Survival Rate
1	Singapore	0.884	0.9972	13.885	580.865	12.905	—	0.950
2	Korea	0.845	0.9967	13.580	563.126	12.236	0.975	0.940
3	Japan	0.844	0.9974	13.640	563.358	12.295	0.929	0.945
4	Hong Kong	0.822	0.9907	13.428	561.893	12.072	—	0.951
46	China	0.673	0.9907	13.250	456.000	9.667	0.919	0.921
48	Vietnam	0.666	*0.9791*	12.298	519.100	10.214	*0.754*	0.878
55	Malaysia	0.622	0.9921	*12.164*	468.068	9.110	0.793	0.879
65	Thailand	0.604	0.9905	12.365	*436.497*	*8.636*	0.895	*0.855*
84	Philippines	0.548	0.9719	12.799	408.921	8.374	0.666	0.801
87	Indonesia	0.535	0.9746	12.308	402.906	7.935	0.664	0.828
100	Cambodia	0.493	0.9708	9.547	451.890	6.903	0.676	0.833
107	Myanmar	0.473	0.9514	9.854	424.631	6.695	0.706	0.808
111	Lao PDR	0.452	0.9366	10.842	368.142	6.386	0.670	0.813
115	India	0.440	0.9606	10.170	354.991	5.776	0.621	0.825

Source: World Bank "Human Capital Index 2018."

secondary education there is too low to meet the standards required for university entrance. The ADB (2018, p. 281) raises the problem of the quality of university education and the existence of a mismatch between the skills of new graduates and the demands of the labor market.

Thailand carried out a reform of higher education in the early 2000s which was aimed at raising vocational technological colleges to the status of universities (called Rajamangara universities), in response to requests from the business sector. However, the survey by the Japanese Chamber of Commerce in Bangkok (2020) indicates that one of the biggest concerns for Japanese affiliates in Thailand is "shortage of workforce." This was a bigger concern for manufacturing companies than it was for non-manufacturing companies. Looking at the share of students across faculties in Thailand (Figure 3), the ADB (2018) concluded that "universities are not turning out enough graduates in science, technology, engineering, and mathematics" (ADB 2018, p. 281). It also pointed out that "greater

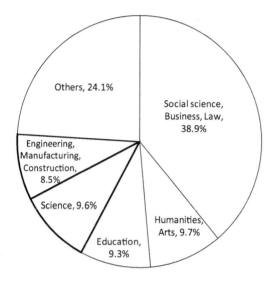

Figure 3:   Enrollment in Tertiary Education in Thailand by Subject, 2014
Source: ADB (2018).

cooperation between local educational institutions and universities abroad can help boost the number of students with the technical skills." One reason why students (or their families) choose to study the arts or social sciences rather than the natural sciences is lower tuition fees, shorter period of schooling, and higher post-graduation salaries. This indicates that the government should get rid of the obstacles that prevent students from choosing to study the natural sciences.

In ASEAN upper middle-income countries (Thailand and Malaysia), the substitution of labor with automation and artificial intelligence (AI) seems to have already begun. According to an analysis by the Thai National Economic and Social Development Board (NESDB 2018), employment levels among university graduates fell between 2016 and 2018, the period of economic expansion, whereas total employment increased. NESDB argues that this was partly due to the private sector's reluctance to expand its workforce, substituting it instead with labor-saving processes including automation and AI, which have already begun to be introduced into areas such as personnel management and accounting. As AI advances further, the employment of arts and social science graduates is likely to be further reduced. The employment situation will

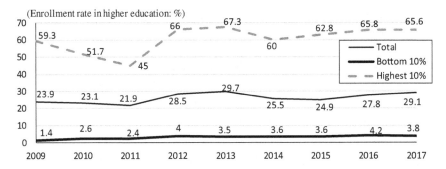

Figure 4: Enrollment Rate in Higher Education in Thailand by Income Level, 2009–2017

Source: National Statistical Office of Thailand (2018).

worsen and growth potential will be diminished in the medium to long term unless the share is more balanced.

Income inequality has resulted in lower enrollment in higher education. Even though the Gini coefficient, an index of income inequality, has declined in Thailand since 2002, it was as high as around 0.46 in 2017, according to an NESDB estimate. Figure 4 shows differences in enrollment rates in higher education by household income level in Thailand. The enrollment rate for households in the lowest 10% income group remains low at around 4%, while that for households in the highest 10% income group is much higher. Someone with a relatively low level of educational attainment would need longer than a university graduate to acquire skills and knowledge through vocational training. Besides, employment opportunities for those with only modest skills will be reduced as automated manufacturing processes and AI become more widespread in both the manufacturing and service sectors. Therefore, the strategy for human capital formation should be compatible with schemes to promote FDI (internalization of technology procurement) and should support schemes for human capital formation within businesses and in society.

Addressing the issues concerning human capital formation discussed above will become increasingly important if Thailand is to develop a technology-led and knowledge-based economy. In summary, the issues are:

(1) Removal of obstacles to studying the natural sciences, such as income inequality and/or difficulty accessing higher education and schooling for those on low incomes.

(2) Improvement of the quality of higher education through collaboration between business and government so that human resources can be developed in a way that is suitable for the economy.
(3) Development of talent and public efforts in R&D.
(4) Changes in the primary and secondary curriculum to make it more suitable for internationalization and the information society.

Household behavior in relation to higher education enrollment

It would be useful to establish a model of household decision making on enrollment in higher education. Thailand provides 12 years of free elementary and secondary education, but higher education is subject to tuition fees, and students (or their parents) have to bear the cost of schooling. Besides, given the increasing risk of unemployment after graduation and the prospect of no increase in salaries for graduates to offset the cost, households may become more hesitant about letting their children go to university. This hesitancy will only be mitigated if the following applies:

$$\sum_{t=g}^{R}\left[\left(1-E\left(u_t^h\right)\right)\cdot E\left(Y_t^h\right)\right]-C>\sum_{t=0}^{R}\left[\left(1-E\left(u_t^s\right)\right)\cdot E\left(Y_t^s\right)\right]$$

where u_t is unemployment rate at the year t (the same hereinafter), Y_t is income level, g is the minimum number of years of schooling for tertiary education, and C is the total cost of tertiary education (including tuition fees, schooling, stationery, etc.) for g years. If the actual cost C exceeds a household's ability to afford it (denoted by $\bar{C}$), then the household will not choose to let their child go to university. R is the number of years between graduation from secondary education and retirement age. $E(\cdot)$ is the expected value for a future event, and superscripts denote the final stage of education (h for higher education and s for secondary). In this situation, if the government is to raise the university enrollment rate, policy measures should have the following objectives: (1) to raise $\bar{C}$ or to reduce C; (2) to raise $E(Y_t^h)$; (3) to lower $E(u_t^h)$; and (4) to shorten g.

(1) **To raise $\bar{C}$ or to reduce C:** The high cost of higher education makes low-income households hesitant about allowing their children to go to university. According to NESDC (2019), almost 670,000 children lost educational opportunities due to income inequality, which results in an

opportunity loss equivalent to 200 billion baht. Therefore, it is necessary to improve income distribution, but that takes time. Instead, the government has other options, such as increasing the affordability of higher education and easing the burdens associated with schooling for low-income households. Students already have access to scholarships, but not every student can receive a monetary scholarship. Some students take out bank loans instead, but they then face the additional burden of interest payments after graduation, and it would require a higher $E(Y_t^h)$, including interest payments as well as the cost of university education (greater C).

If an increasing number of young people go into higher education, society as a whole will benefit in terms of efficiency and profit-making (external economies). If this is the case, society should bear some of the burden of the cost of higher education through policy delivery. The government has taken an additional step since 2018 by legislating for the establishment of the "equitable education fund," whose objectives include financial support for low-income households that cannot afford their children's education and for children who lack educational opportunities. Although the main targets are those households with pupils at elementary and secondary schools, (prospective) students of higher education can also receive benefits through the fund.

(2) **To raise $E(Y_t^h)$:** Possible policy options that would increase $E(Y_t^h)$ include the promotion of the Thailand 4.0 initiative (policies for fostering new industries), public R&D, collaboration with business, reform of the primary-, secondary-, and tertiary-level curricula, and abandonment of grass-roots policies which result in reluctance to take advantage of a university education.

First, the government should foster new industries to the extent that they can absorb graduates of university courses in natural sciences and engineering, as this would result in increased $E(Y_t^h)$ and more stable employment. The government has already launched the Thailand 4.0 initiative and selected ten industries (called S-curve industries) for promotion in the Eastern Economic Corridor (EEC) area. It also plans to construct a science park in Chon Buri prefecture and invite domestic and foreign research institutes and universities to conduct government-led R&D there. Thailand's large publicly owned petrochemical company will locate two science and technology colleges of its own in the EEC, and these will collaborate with ten Thai universities in the development of renewable energy and R&D on petrochemicals.

Second, collaboration involving the government administration, universities, and businesses should be facilitated to ensure that university graduates are not replaced by machines or AI technology. A new ministry in charge of this was established in 2019 and allotted 130 billion baht from the national budget. It already has a target of increasing public expenditure on R&D from 155 billion baht (1% of GDP) in 2017 to more than 340 billion baht (2% of nominal GDP) by 2026. Besides this, the Ministry of Digital Society Development launched a program of collaboration with 20 Thai universities to foster talented individuals to work in the digital economy. But since there is a shortage of this kind of talent in Thailand, as seen from the Japanese Chamber of Commerce's survey, the government will have to invite personnel from abroad until a sufficient number of talented Thais has been trained up for work in the EEC. The government has amended immigration legislation and introduced a "smart visa" scheme for talented overseas personnel. Smart visa holders are guaranteed to be able to stay in Thailand for longer than holders of normal business visas, and their individual income taxes are reduced.

Third, the curriculum at primary, secondary, and tertiary levels should be updated to facilitate internationalization and development of the information and communication society. Rural communities in Thailand prefer to protect their traditions and would rather not change (Harada 1988), so farmers are unwilling to change their jobs as long as they can earn enough to survive in the countryside. Traditions are valuable, and the UNDP (2007 and 2014) argues that Thailand's moral education has benefitted human development. Even so, this way of thinking is no longer suitable for an internationalized economy and an information and communication society. The OECD (2014) warned that Thailand's outdated curriculum that emphasizes morality rather than education about the world economic and social system may become an obstacle when it comes to avoiding the middle-income trap. However, no improvements to the curriculum have been introduced since then.

Fourth, the government should abandon unnecessary policy measures that benefit farmers and others living in rural areas, known as grass-roots policies. These benefits are directed mainly at those without higher education and they increase their $E(Y_t^s)$, which makes university education less attractive to low-income rural residents.

(3) **To lower $E(u_t^h)$:** $E(u_t^h)$ has increased recently due to the introduction of automation into manufacturing and advances in AI technology, which

may reduce the need for normal university graduates (NESDB 2018). Nonetheless, the number of students who choose to study natural sciences is still small, and the problem of the mismatch between graduates' qualifications and the jobs market has not been solved. If the risk of graduate unemployment becomes greater in the future, and lifetime income is insufficient to offset the cost of a university education, students may opt not to go on to higher education. To reduce the risk of unemployment, two approaches can be considered. One is the accumulation of skills and talent that AI technology and automation cannot cover, and the other is the elimination of the mismatch between subjects studied at university and the requirements of business. If the government provides more favorable scholarships for prospective natural science students, fewer students will be forced to opt for the arts or social sciences, and more students will tailor their education to the expectations of business.

(4) **To shorten *g*:** Shortening higher education courses in the natural sciences and engineering would not only reduce the burden of tuition fees and other expenditures but also increase lifetime total income by extending working life. In this regard, the Thai government has begun to introduce the "Kosen" system, an overview of which is presented in the next section.

The discussion in this section can be summarized as follows. First, enrollment in university education has improved, but it is still costly. This problem has been partly addressed by policy measures that provide low-income households with financial support. The problem of the quality of higher education and mismatch between the subjects students study and the requirements of business may be solved through collaboration between academics, the business community, and the government administration, but relevant policies have yet to be formulated. There has been no progress with reform of the elementary and secondary curriculum. There has been too little progress in the cultivation of a highly skilled work force so there is still a need for international cooperation to help address this problem.

Cooperation with Non-ASEAN Countries on Education: The Case of Japan

Even though Thailand has not been able to address two of the problems listed above — the cultivation of a skilled workforce and reform of the

school curriculum — it may be able to do so through international cooperation. However, it would be difficult for foreign countries to intervene
in curriculum reform as that is closely linked with Thailand's fundamental
strategy for social development. But there has already been some transfer
of knowledge regarding teaching methods in elementary and secondary
schools under a project initiated by the Japanese Ministry of Education,
Culture, Sports, Science and Technology (MEXT) in 2016. The private
sector has also been making efforts in this area, in collaboration with the
public sector. In this section, I discuss how international society can
cooperate with higher education institutions and present an overview of
projects conducted in Thailand (and in Vietnam) in collaboration with the
Japanese private and public sectors.

Private sector collaboration in the establishment of higher education institutes

As discussed above, R&D is usually conducted at company level for reasons of firm-specificity, confidentiality, and fear of leakage. Besides,
public sector efforts in human capital formation through higher education
(i.e., the production of graduates with sufficient knowledge) take too long
to bear fruit. Consequently, each company will build its capacity based on
existing employees. Even so, public provision of more institutes of higher
education and the cultivation of a larger pool of talent (not just university
graduates) are still essential for Thailand's economic and industrial
development.

In this regard, the private sector (both Thai and Japanese) began to
establish higher education institutes, with Japanese government support.
In 2007, a non-profit organization in Thailand, the Technology Promotion
Association Thailand-Japan (TPA), established the Thai-Nichi Institute
(TNI) in Bangkok. The objective of the TNI is to educate its students to
take active roles in Japanese companies in Thailand, such as those in the
automotive sector. It has faculties for educating technicians as well as
office workers familiar with Japanese accounting systems and business
practices, and some subjects are taught in Japanese. The TNI was established by the TPA, but many Japanese manufacturing companies have
helped to fund it, and the Japanese government has provided technical
assistance under its official development assistance (ODA) scheme. The
TNI is a Thai university, but the Thai government amended its legislation

in 2018 to enable foreign higher educational institutes to establish branches in the EEC. Foreign universities are allowed to teach their own curriculum, so they may contribute not only to educating a greater number of young Thais but also to compelling Thai universities to modernize their curriculum in order to compete, as the ADB (2018, p. 281) has suggested.

In Vietnam, the Vietnam–Japan Institute, a school with a very similar structure to the TNI, opened in 2017. Prior to that, in 2002, the Japan International Cooperation Agency (JICA), the body in charge of implementing Japanese ODA, established the Vietnam-Japan Human Resources Cooperation Center (VJCC) within the campus of the Foreign Trade University (FTU) in Hanoi. The VJCC offers courses in business for the FTU, but these are targeted not at FTU students but at Vietnamese business people and Vietnamese companies. It also offers Japanese language teaching for business people and students, and provides information about studying in Japan.

Exporting the Japanese education system: The EDU-Port Nippon Project

In 2016, the MEXT launched a pilot project to export Japanese methods of education at elementary, secondary, and tertiary levels, named the EDU-Port Nippon Project. This project shares information among Japanese government agencies, educational institutions, and private companies concerning models for exporting Japanese teaching methods, fulfilling a need among local administrations in developing countries. Once a foreign country shows an interest in the Japanese education system, Japanese entities will come forward to collaborate with each other to devise the project and export it, sometimes backed by the Japanese government. Although this project is focused mainly on primary and secondary education rather than higher education, Malaysia, Vietnam, and Thailand had expressed an interest in it as of the end of 2019 and, based on their requirements, cooperation in the provision of higher vocational education is, or will be, conducted in those countries. In one example cited in the information brochure provided by the MEXT, Chiba University in Japan has conducted a pilot project to provide knowhow on teaching robot technology to Hanoi National University in Vietnam. As this project did not involve many students it is uncertain whether it will be expanded to include other Vietnamese universities or whether Hanoi National University will disseminate its experience to other institutes.

One project in Thailand is worthy of note. The Thai government believes that the Japanese technological college (Kosen) system could help the country rapidly develop a pool of talent, and since 2018, two Thai universities have begun to offer Kosen courses. Japanese Kosen has the advantage that students can acquire basic techniques and technologies that are normally taught in high schools and then in university courses and become expert in them over a period of only 5 years. In 2020, King Mongkut University of Technology in Bangkok was due to open its own independent Kosen college. Together with the establishment of Kosen, the Japanese government sends technicians to Thailand to teach at college level, developing teaching materials, designing curricula, and so on.

Conclusion

For the ASEAN upper middle-income countries, creating a technology-led and knowledge-based industrial structure is the key to escaping the middle-income trap. However, for reasons discussed above, FDI no longer comes with automatic transfers of technology. What is more, university graduates may face a greater risk of unemployment in the near future because of advances in automation and AI.

In this chapter, I have identified factors behind the low appetite for acquiring university education from the perspective of household behavior, using a cost-benefit approach to analyze the relationship between the increase in lifetime income that comes with a university degree and the cost of obtaining it. The mismatch between students' choice of courses and the requirements of the business sector is also important, and this increases the risk of unemployment. The shortage of talented technicians will continue if this problem is not addressed. Therefore, the issue of human capital formation should be tackled at both the national and ASEAN levels. ASEAN is now focused on responding to the fourth industrial revolution and is discussing possible collaboration with countries outside the bloc. In Thailand, the Thailand 4.0 initiative is aimed at fostering new industries and attracting more talented individuals into the EEC area.

It is essential that strategies for human resource development are formulated and firmly implemented. The level of enrollment in higher education has not improved in Thailand, partly due to the problem of affordability for low-income households, although the government has recently introduced policy measures aimed at reducing the cost burden for those on low incomes. However, neither the above-mentioned mismatch nor the longer enrollment period for science courses has been addressed. The former could be addressed by the government offering households inducements to choose natural science subjects, together with the facilitation of collaboration with academics and businesses to respond to both detailed demand and the supply of labor. The latter may be partly solved by the introduction of Japan's unique education system and allowing foreign education institutes to operate, even if only in the EEC. Anyway, since education in Thailand is an integral part of the basic national development strategy, foreign intervention in Thai education policy is likely to be quite limited. Even so, collaboration with the advanced countries and among academics, the business community, and the government administration is essential if human capital formation is to be strengthened.

References

ADB (Asian Development Bank). 2011. *Asia 2050: Realizing the Asian Century*. Manila.
ADB (Asian Development Bank). 2018. *Asian Development Outlook: How Technology Affects Jobs*. Manila.
Bell, Martin, and Keith Pavitt. 1993. Accumulating Technological Capability in Developing Countries. *Proceedings of the World Bank Annual Conference on Developing Economics*. World Bank: Washington, DC, 122–154.
Birdsall, Nancy M., Jose Edgardo L. Campos, Chang-Shik Kim, W. Max Corden, Lawrence MacDonald (ed.), Howard Pack, John Page, Richard Sabor, and Joseph E. Stiglitz. 1993. *The East Asian Miracle: Economic Growth and Public Policy: Main Report (English)*. New York: Oxford University Press. http://documents.worldbank.org/curated/en/975081468244550798/Main-report.
Eichengreen, Barry, Donghyun Park, and Kwanho Shin. 2011. When Fast Growing Economies Slow Down: International Evidence and Implications for China. NBER Working Paper Series, 16919.
Gill, Indermit and Homi Kharas. 2007. *East Asian Renaissance: Ideas for Economic Growth*. Washington, DC: World Bank.
Harada, Y. 1988. *Thai Keizai Nyuumon* [Economic Development in Thailand]. Tokyo: Nippon Hyoronsha.

Japanese Chamber of Commerce, Bangkok. 2020. *Survey on Business Sentiment of Japanese Corporations in Thailand for the 2nd Half of 2019*. https://www. jcc.or.th/download/index.

Jitsuchon, Somchai. 2012. Thailand in a Middle-Income Trap. *TDRI Quarterly Review* (Thailand Development Research Institute) 27 (2): 13–20.

NESDB (National Economic and Social Development Board). 2018. *Phawasangkhomthaitraimartsi laekarnruampee 2560* [The Social Situation in Thailand and Its Outlook — The Fourth Quarter of 2017 and the Whole Year of 2017]. http://social.nesdb.go.th/social/Portals/0/Documents/ Social%20Press_Q4-2560_final_1254.pdf.

NESDC (National Economic and Social Development Council). 2019. *Thailand's Social Situation and Outlook in Q1/2019*. http://www.nesdb.go.th/nesdb_en/ download/document/Social%20Press_Q1-2562.pdf.

National Statistical Office of Thailand. 2018. *Household Socio-Economic Survey — Whole Kingdom*. http://www.nso.go.th/sites/2014en/Survey/ social/household/household/2017/whole%20kingdom/Full%20Report.pdf.

Nelson, Richard. 1980. Production Sets, Technological Knowledge and R&D: Fragile and Overworked Constructs for the Analysis of Productivity Growth? *American Economic Review Papers and Proceedings* 70(2): 62–67.

OECD (Organisation for Economic Co-operation and Development). 2014. *Economic Outlook for Southeast Asia, China and India 2014: Beyond the Middle-Income Trap*, 215–230. http://dx.doi.org/10.1787/saeo-2014-en.

Oxford Economics. 2016. *Economic Insight: South East Asia Quarterly Briefing Q2 2016*. www.indonesia-investments.com/upload/documents/Economic-Insight-SEA-Q2-2016.pdf.

Romer, Paul. 1990. Endogenous Technical Change. *Journal of Political Economy* 98(5): 71–102.

UNDP (United Nations Development Program). 2007. *Thailand Human Development Report 2007 — Sufficiency Economy and Human Development*. Bangkok.

UNDP (United Nations Development Program). 2014. *Thailand Human Development Report 2014 — Advancing Human Development Through ASEAN Community*. Bangkok.

Watanabe, T. 2009. *Kaihatsu Keizaigaku Nyuumon* [*Introduction to Development Economics*]. 3rd edn. Tokyo: Toyo-Keizai Shimposha.

Chapter 7

Japanese Capitalism After Globalization: The Distinct Japanese Accounting System in East Asia and Its Implications

Masahiro Matsumura and Yoshiaki Ozawa

Introduction

Today, globalization under U.S. economic hegemony is slowing down at an increasing rate and may even have regressed, while its corresponding international economic system is weakening and disintegrating. Although hyper-globalization facilitated the efficient global allocation of resources through the market mechanism, it was also the cause of serious local deindustrialization, involving a stark decline of the middle class and resultant socio-political polarization. This resulted in the rise of populism in the major liberal democracies, most notably with the election of President Donald Trump in the United States and in the United Kingdom, the vote in favor of exit from a European Union in thrall to rampant Union-wide populism and growing centrifugal dynamics. Given that those two countries have been generally considered to constitute the Anglo-Saxon capitalist engine of globalization, the current trend will most likely continue and remain irreversible.

The U.S. economic hegemonic system is facing a growing need for adjustment, downsizing, and restructuring. This need is a natural consequence of the significant strengthening, widening, and deepening of the system that underwent during the period of U.S. predominance and the fact that the unipolar moment has long been over. Consequent on the financial crisis of fall 2008 and its after-effects, the United States faced potential insolvency and other structural vulnerabilities after it had successfully weathered the unprecedented liquidity crisis with the aid of an unparalleled level of quantitative easing. This meant that the United States was less and less able to finance ambitious arms buildups and other large defense expenditures to maintain its overstretched military hegemonic system.

Thus, it is most important to examine the durability of U.S. economic hegemony after globalization. Some international trade and investment will probably continue thanks to the cumulative effects of existing supply chains and overseas financial assets, but these will be at the mercy of the major power's domestic politics which is ridden with growing populism. Each country will surely strive to expand domestic demand, improve its employment situation, and keep wages rising. Also, each will enhance its international competitiveness by diverting the interests of its companies from overseas to domestic markets. These evolving circumstances are already producing significant divisions in global markets, as demonstrated by the decoupling of U.S.–China interdependence in the making.

Put more analytically, according to the theory of hegemonic stability, a power that is economically, technologically, and militarily predominant can exert a preponderant influence or authority over other countries, so its growing debility will inevitably destabilize the international order and eventually lead to its breakdown (Gilpin 1981, 1987). On the other hand, the theory of international regimes argues that regimes can maintain an international order because they are "principles, norms, and decision-making procedures around which actor expectations converge in a given issue-area" (Krasner 1983). If international regimes are intervening variables between international distribution of power as the basic causal variable and the stability of an international order as the outcome (Krasner 1983), U.S.-led international regimes may enable continuation of the existing order even after globalization consequent on U.S. predominance.

In this light, this chapter will examine accounting standards as a key issue area from which to examine the durability of the U.S. economic hegemonic system. Given that there is no world government, there are no *de jure* global accounting standards, only local ones legislated in individual countries. However, there can be *de facto* standards, particularly when a hegemon sets them and they are explicitly or implicitly adopted by other major powers — followed by an overwhelming majority of other states.

The United States took advantage of the unipolar moment and attempted to set *de facto* global accounting standards based on market price, having exercised great influence, although not control, over the shaping of them. This involves exclusion of other possible standards, especially Franco-German accounting standards on impairment basis[1] (Gunji 2018) and Japanese eclectic accounting standards that amalgamate the two different bases with unique path-dependent circumstantial needs. Generally, the Anglo-Saxon standards value fairness and are based on pragmatism that emphasizes the importance of practical business operation and the need to protect the interests of stockholders and investors. On the other hand, the Franco-German standards respect impartiality and are grounded on rationalism that attaches importance to state taxation and related legal measures and emphasize the necessity of protecting creditors' interests (Kuroda 2011). Naturally, the Anglo-Saxon and the Franco-German standards often stand in opposition to each other in matters of principle while exhibiting significant discrepancies in practice with the Japanese standards.

Different standards reward certain types of business transaction and corporate operation, while penalizing others, though the choice of a particular basis appears purely technical and politically neutral. However, this choice involves a heavy political bias toward a specific creed, philosophy, or priority on certain types of business transaction and corporate operation and, therefore, the interests of particular economic, social, and political forces. The bias either contributes to or harms the development of specific individual companies, industries, and/or national economies, which will inevitably affect the rise and fall of a specific variant of capitalism.

Thus, this chapter will focus its analysis on Japan's limited adoption of *de facto* international accounting standards in contrast to the full adoption of those standards by other major East Asian countries. Then, based on the findings, the chapter will briefly discuss a future path for Japanese

---

[1] In German, this is known as *dynamische Bilanz*, or "accounting for the impairment or disposal of long- lived assets."

capitalism *vis-à-vis* U.S. capitalism after globalization, and make a rudimentary prediction concerning the implications of this for the East Asian countries.

A Comparative Analysis of Accounting Standards of Major East Asian Countries

An overwhelming majority of countries, particularly those in East Asia, have already adopted the International Financial Reporting Standards (IFRS) for listed companies, while continuing to use local Generally Accepted Accounting Principles (GAAP) for non-listed companies. The IFRS aims to help international investors compare rigorous financial statements on a market price basis to facilitate investment decision-making. The IFRS is not only directly instrumental for international investors and global companies but is also indirectly instrumental for domestic companies wishing to establish important business relationships with them.

In this chapter, we will first present a comparative analysis of the evolving accounting standards used in China, Taiwan, Mongolia, South Korea, and Japan, with a focus on the Japanese case as the crucial outlier, and consider the changing relative importance of the IFRS and the GAAP. Only the Japanese system allows its listed companies to voluntarily adopt the IFRS, while the other countries' systems require full adoption by all listed companies. We will then analyze the peculiar set of conditions in the Japanese political economy that has made the country the outlier, on the basis of which we will discuss a plausible future path for the adaptation of Japan's accounting standards that would internalize the norms embedded in the current system.

Japan

The IFRS is the *de facto* international standard for corporate financial reporting that is set by the International Accounting Standard Board (IASB), a non-governmental international association of professional certified public accountants. In 2005, the European Union and Australia introduced domestic legislation concerning mandatory adoption of the IFRS. Other countries have followed their example since then. As of

December 2016, 175 countries and separate customs territories have followed suit.[2]

Under the evolving dynamics of reform, Japan also accelerated a review of its accounting standards system in the late 1990s, which led in 2001 to the establishment of the Accounting Standards Board of Japan (ASBJ), a private-sector independent standard-setting body. Having kept pace with the IASB's move, the ASBJ initiated a convergence project in May 2005, and decided in August 2007 to work on the convergence of the Japanese GAAP and the IFRS.

Against this background, in June 2009, the Japanese Financial Services Agency (FSA) released an interim report entitled, "Opinion on the Application of the IFRS," that included a roadmap for IFRS adoption. It set a principle that voluntary adoption of the IFRS would be accepted for financial statements after early 2010.[3] We will discuss below the specific conditions under which the IFRS was to be adopted.

Japan has now established the principle of voluntary adoption, with 251 Japanese listed companies having already adopted or being scheduled to adopt the IFRS as of the end of February 2022. Yet, this is less than 6.7% of the total number of companies listed on the Tokyo Stock Exchange (TSE) (Japan Exchange Group 2022a). However, because many of the early adopters are big companies, with a total market capitalization of 326 trillion yen, they account for 42% of the total market capitalization (742 trillion yen) of the TSE-listed companies as of the end of June 2021. Also, in 2022, the TSE authorities indicated that 167 companies were considering adoption of the IFRS in the near future (Japan Exchange Group 2022b).

China (*PricewaterhouseCoopers (PwC) China 2013*)

The Chinese government has two accounting rules: the Accounting System for Business Enterprises (ASBE) and the Accounting Standards

---

[2]For comprehensive information on international financial reporting in general and the activities of the International Accounting Standards Board (IASB) in particular, see "Use of IFRS by Jurisdictions," July 2019, https://www.iasplus.com/.en/resources/ifrs-topics/use-of-ifrs (accessed October 20, 2019).

[3]https://www.fsa.go.jp/en/news/2009/20090701-1.html (accessed October 20, 2019).

for Business Enterprises 2006 (CAS 2006). The Chinese Financial Service Agency (CFSA) has applied them to all types of companies since January 1, 2001. The ASBE consists of 16 specific sets of accounting standards and other related accounting regulations. It sets out the necessary accounting treatment rules for major line items in financial statements, such as assets, liabilities, equities, income, and expenses.

The CFSA established the CAS on February 15, 2006, as a comprehensive basis for accounting in China and it has been applied to all listed companies in the country since January 1, 2007. The IASB acknowledged that there was substantive convergence between the CAS and the IFRS, which indicates China's commitment to the adoption of IFRS standards and their application to some domestic companies, albeit without a fixed deadline for completion (IFRS 2019). Yet CAS 2006 requires different accounting treatment for several categories of transaction and operation under distinctive local Chinese conditions. For example, one PricewaterhouseCoopers (PwC, 2013) assurance partner pointed out that there was insufficient description in the accounting standards of some important differences in rule implementation (PricewaterhouseCoopers (PwC) China). In fact, Beijing has achieved "perfect" emulation of the IFRS in form alone, as the international standards are not always enforced in practice. This superficial, deceptive emulation will never lead to what the IFRS is designed to achieve; instead, it will result in Chinese free-riding in financing through U.S. and international markets. Thus, it is no wonder that the U.S. Congress has introduced a bill to strengthen the auditing of foreign-affiliated companies listed on U.S. stock markets (Kawazoe 2019). Having taken this situation into consideration, the Holding Foreign Companies Accountable Act (HFCAA) became law December 2020. Under HFCAA, SEC can delist Chinese companies from U.S. exchanges if American regulators cannot review company audits for three consecutive years.

South Korea (*Samil PwC 2015*)

As a consequence of the foreign exchange crisis of 1997, the South Korean government followed the recommendations of the International Monetary Fund (IMF) and the World Bank to fully revise Korean business accounting standards to correspond with the IFRS. This stipulated the replacement of the traditional standards with the IFRS. In July 2007, the Financial Supervisory Commission (FSC) of Korea commissioned the Korean Accounting Institute (KAI) to set new business accounting standards as well as to revise and interpret the existing ones. South Korea has introduced the IFRS without any modifications and applied it to all listed companies and financial institutions.

Taiwan (PwC Taiwan 2015)

The Taiwanese government has applied the IFRS to most companies. The non-governmental Accounting Research and Development Foundation (ARDF) translated the text of the IFRS and the official IASB interpretations of it. These ARDF-endorsed translations and the implementation guidance are referred to as Taiwan-IFRS or T-IFRS. Since 2013, listed companies and financial institutions, with the exception of credit cooperatives, credit card companies, and insurance intermediaries, have been required to produce their financial reports in line with T-IFRS. Also, the unlisted public companies, credits cooperatives, credit card companies, and insurance intermediaries are required to prepare financial reports using T-IFRS starting in 2015 and are permitted to apply them starting in 2013.

Mongolia (PwC Mongolia 2015)

The Mongolian government has formally adopted the IFRS and required all listed companies to apply it. Yet private unlisted companies remain restricted by local Mongolian accounting and tax regulations in several areas, so there are discrepancies in practice between the two systems.

The following analysis has identified Japan's partial adoption of the IFRS, the *de facto* international accounting standards, which makes it an outlier among the East Asian countries, all of which have adopted the IFRS. Under Japan's existing accounting system, Japanese listed companies voluntarily follow the IFRS when they are or plan to be active in international business transactions and operations. When they are only active in the domestic economy, they choose to follow local standards.

Some Major Features of the Japanese Case

Four sets of accounting standards

Japanese companies are required in principle to produce non-consolidated financial statements in accordance with the ASBJ-endorsed, generally

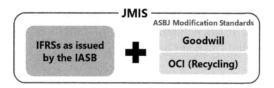

Figure 1:   Contents of JMIS

Source: ASBJ. https://www.asb.or.jp/en/ifrs/about.html (accessed October 20, 2019).

accepted accounting principles (J GAAP). Listed companies are also obliged to produce consolidated financial statements[4] pursuant to J GAAP, IFRS standards (Designated IFRS), Japan's Modified International Standards (JMIS), or U.S. GAAP. The JMIS is a new set of accounting standards that the ASBJ instituted in 2015, while having endorsed IASB principles. However, this constitutes a *de facto* IASB accreditation given the worldwide endorsement of the IFRS. No listed company in Japan has chosen to use the JIMS to produce its financial statements. So listed companies in Japan have a choice of four sets of standards, but as discussed earlier, more and more of them follow the IFRS.

The JMIS (ASBJ, 2018) combines the IASB IFRS and the ASBJ Modification Standards. Currently, there are two Modification Standards: ASBJ Modification Standard No. 1 "Accounting for Goodwill"[5] and ASBJ Modification Standard No. 2 "Accounting for Other Comprehensive Income." As shown in Figure 1, in June 2015, the ASBJ endorsed the IFRS of December 31, 2012, and used it to institute the JMIS, and, in July 2016, the ASBJ endorsed the IFRS of 2013, according to which the ASBJ amended the JMIS.

Differences between the IFRS and the J GAAP

In August 2007, the ASBJ and the International Accounting Standards Board (IASB) concluded the Tokyo Agreement to accelerate convergence

---

[4]According to International Accounting Standards 27, consolidated financial statements are the "financial statements of a group in which the assets, liabilities, equity, income, expenses and cash flows of the parent company and its subsidiaries are presented as those of a single economic entity."

[5]Goodwill is the established reputation of a business regarded as a quantifiable asset.

between the J GAAP and the IFRS. It set an outline according to which the major differences between the two systems would be eliminated by the end of 2008 and all differences eliminated by June 30, 2011. However, there are still several differences remaining. Given that the IFRS itself is still in the making, its revisions and newly added standards will call for further convergence measures.

The first major difference between the IFRS and the J GAAP lies in the non-amortization of goodwill. In mergers and acquisitions (M&A), the purchase price of an acquired company is normally higher than its net asset value due to the value of its brand and the assessed growth potential of profit. This difference is called goodwill and is recorded as an intangible asset. According to the J GAAP, the value of goodwill depreciates and thus requires regular amortization over 20 years. The IFRS does not allow systematic amortization if an M&A activity is successful. This difference involves a veiled heavy bias against or in favor of predatory M&A, particularly when there is a significant difference in financial standing and business prospects between the parties concerned. This kind of M&A is unfavorable to industrialists who prioritize corporate survival and development and basically do not see a corporation as a target of trading.[6] It does favor investors who prioritize profit-making. Furthermore, the different priorities are embedded in dissimilar structural constraints under variants of the existing capitalist systems, particularly the Anglo-Saxon, the Franco-German, and the Japanese.

The second major difference is the booking of impairment loss. The IFRS is better suited to immediate identification of loss on revaluation of fixed assets. The J GAAP recognizes loss from impairment when the future cash flow before discount of assets is less than the book value and it records the difference between the future recoverable amount and the present value as impairment loss. The IFRS, in contrast, recognizes an impairment loss when the future cash flow, including discount rate, is less than the book value. This means that the IFRS likely accelerates the

---

[6]Japan is an unparalleled case given that it has 7 companies which have been in business for more than 1,000 years and some 28,000 that have been around for more than 100 years. *Riku Nabi Jyanaru Next.* November 12, 2014. "Sekai-Saiko No Kaisha: Kongo-Gumi No Tosan-Kiki Wo Sukutsuta Kokuhokyuu To Takumiwaza To Naniwa-Bushi [The World's Oldest Company: National-Treasure-Class Craftmanship and Old-Fashioned Sense of Loyalty and Human Feeling That Saved Kongo-Gumi from Impending Bankruptcy]. https://next.rikunabi.com/journal/20141112/ (accessed October 13, 2019).

timing of recording impairment loss when interest rates increase discount rates, and that the IFRS, but not J GAAP, allows the reversal of losses when circumstances improve. But the IFRS requires costly regular impairment tests, disincentivizing cost-averse, often small and medium-sized companies from adopting it. The above difference appears technical in nature, but the cost factor significantly influences a company's choice of accounting standard — the IFRS or the J GAAP.

The third major difference exists in the capitalization of research and development (R&D) expenses. The IFRS records a part of development costs as an intangible asset, while research expenses are fully charged as expenses. Because the success or failure of R&D is uncertain, the J GAAP records the entire amount as expenses. The IFRS does not capitalize all development costs, only those that are expected to be profitable through commercialization. The recorded intangible assets have to be amortized over the expected period of earnings. Naturally, R&D-intensive companies or industries, such as those in the pharmaceutical sector, prefer to adopt the IFRS. Thus, countries prefer the IFRS when they have key industries of this kind that exert significant national politico-economic influence. For example, the major Japanese pharmaceutical companies have opted for the IFRS, and Germany has done so as a country.

The fourth major difference is the "recycling," or reclassification, of other comprehensive income, which in reality means cross-shareholding. The IFRS recognizes certain items as other comprehensive income and does not reclassify them as profit or loss in subsequent periods. On the other hand, the J GAAP reclassifies all the items of comprehensive income as profit or loss.

The J GAAP makes Japan an outlier among the East Asian countries in this analysis, and this reflects the unique structure of the Japanese capitalist system. Although it is beyond the scope of this study to go into detail, it is generally accepted that Japan's prewar capitalist system was in many ways similar to its Anglo-Saxon counterpart until the late 1920s, in terms of corporate governance, financing, and employment. As World War II approached, however, Japan, in common with the United States and the other major capitalist powers, transformed itself into a total war regime, despite superficial ideological differences, that is, democracy versus totalitarianism. The United States dismantled this regime soon after the war was over and returned to prewar normalcy, but post-war Japan essentially continued the regime of the 1940s, especially the state-guided wartime priority production system, while it carried out post war economic reconstruction and development. The collaborative relationship between the state and the private sector was known as "Japan Inc." It facilitated the country's rapid economic growth from the mid-1950s to the late 1970s, giving Japan the world's second largest GDP after the United States. Under the U.S.-led occupation, the pre-war *zaibatsu* concerns were forcibly dismantled into six across-all-industries corporate groups through substantial cross-shareholdings. Their head-to-head domestic and international competition greatly contributed to the rapid growth of the Japanese economy. When this period was over, and following the bursting of the economic bubble in the early 1990s and the ensuing two-decade-long depression, "Japan Inc." gradually dissolved while the six powerful corporate groups have reorganized themselves into three loose and weakened groups (Kobayashi *et al.* 1995; Noguchi, Yukio 1995; Okumura 1991, 1994). And yet the Japanese system retains some of the basic structure of the postwar period, although TSE-listed Japanese companies have recently reduced their cross-shareholding from 34.1% in 1990 to 9.5% in 2017 and 10.1% in 2019 (*Nikkei Shimbun* 2019).

The Political Economics of Japanese Opposition to the IFRS

On June 30, 2009, the ASBJ published an interim report entitled "Opinion on Handling the IFRS in Japan" (Wagakuni niokeru kokusai-kaikei-kijyun no toriatsukai nikansuru ikensho), after four continuous rounds of deliberation on the convergence of the J GAAP and the IFRS from October 23, 2008 to June 11, 2009. Based on this report, the FSA allowed voluntary adoption of the IFRS for consolidated financial statements until March 31, 2010. However, the adoption was limited to listed companies that operate internationally and have an appropriate accounting system in place. The adoption also required international comparability of consolidated financial statements, involving prior adjustment of the existing financial statements consonant with traditional Japanese business and accounting practices.

Thus, the FSA chose to take a "consolidation first," rather than a big bang, approach to implementing convergence. This approach was generally considered a necessary evil due to the anticipated mandatory application of the IFRS at the end of 2012.

However, Dr. Shozaburo Jimi,[7] the then minister of finance, delivered a speech on June 21, 2011, arguing against accelerated convergence and in favor of a postponement of mandatory IFRS adoption. He emphasized the need to heed requests from Japanese business people opposed to accelerated convergence to avoid taking risks at a time when Japan was suffering from the negative economic impacts of the Great East Japan Earthquake of March 2011, to make sure that convergence was in line with Japan's unique accounting and related systems, and, last but not least, to make sure of the policy dynamics of the U.S. Securities and Exchange Commission (US-SEC). Embedded in the minister's thinking was the idea that accounting standards are not only technical but also closely related to a country's history, economic culture, corporate structure based on that culture, corporate laws, related systems such as the tax system, and companies' international competitiveness (Jimi 2011). He expressed a great sense of conservatism and caution regarding the differences between the IFRS and the J GAAP as discussed earlier; he was opposed to predatory M&A and thus the non-amortization of goodwill, and favored corporate survival over profit-making and industrialists over investors. Jimi's position was consonant with voluntary adoption of the booking of impairment loss and the capitalization of research and development expenses according to the differing interests of individual Japanese companies. Finally, his position could potentially be invoked by those who supported cross-shareholding and thus the continuation of the existing structure of the Japanese capitalist system.

Thereafter, the FSA deliberated five times between June 30 and December 22, 2011, before it issued another interim report on July 2, 2012, entitled "Discussion on How to Respond to the IFRS."[8] The report emphasized, as appropriate policy criteria, selective application of the IFRS to consolidated, but not non-consolidated, financial statements; the exemption of small and medium-sized enterprises from IFRS requirements; and the expansion of voluntary adoption of the IFRS. This remained consistent with its 2009 interim report that attached importance

---

[7]At that time, Jimi was a member of the Diet. Born on November 5, 1945, he had an early career as a medical doctor/scientist and was awarded a doctoral degree in medicine from Kyushu University in 1977. He was generally considered to have little expertise in accounting and the related legal measures.

[8]https://www.fsa.go.jp/inter/etc/20120702-1/01.pdf.

to the promotion of voluntary adoption and Japan's unique local conditions.

Then, the FSA reversed its proactive policy on voluntary adoption of the IFRS. After five deliberations from March 26 to June 19, 2013, the Business Accounting Council (BAC), an advisory body of the FSA, released on June 21 an interim policy statement on convergence measures with the IFRS, entitled "Report on the Use of the International Financial Reporting Standards [IFRS] in Japan"[9] that analyzed the evolving IFRS policies of the United States and other major countries. The statement only superficially reconfirmed Japan's need to adopt the IFRS and to make "significant use of it," as well as Japan's continued commitment to provide the IFRS Foundation with human and financial resources. Yet, in response to the requests of the IFRS Foundation, the FSA reconsidered the policy recommendations of the two interim reports of 2009 and 2013 regarding IFRS adoption, with a focus on the three requirements (listed companies, maintenance of appropriate accounting systems, and international business activities). As a result, the FSA proposed to waive these requirements from listed companies, particularly those engaged in international business activities. In addition to policy goals set by the IFRS Foundation for Japan's convergence project, Japan's ruling Liberal Democratic Party proposed that 300 companies should adopt the IFRS by the end of 2016.[10]

Based on these internal and external requests, the interim policy statement of 2013 called for a J-IFRS to be developed according to Japan's needs and conditions and with a curve-out option with IASB consent to delete or modify some standards. Consequently, the J GAAP, pure IFRS, JMIS, and U.S. GAAP exist side-by-side in Japan, and all Japanese listed companies have voluntarily adopted one of them. Japan therefore suffers from a lack of comparability between its multiple accounting standards (Itoh 2013). The reasons for the above development may be found in the pros and cons of Japan's mandatory adoption of the IFRS contained in the BAC deliberation. Two-thirds of its membership — accounting researchers, other researchers, tax accountants, manufacturers, representatives of

---

[9] https://www.fsa.go.jp/en/news/2013/20130621-1.html (accessed October 20, 2019).
[10] "Proposals for Compliance with International Accounting Standards," joint paper adopted by the subcommittee of the Financial Research Committee of the Liberal Democratic Party's Policy Research Council, June 13, 2013. https://www.jimin.jp/policy/policy_topics/pdf/pdf111_1.pdf (accessed October 19, 2019).

chambers of commerce, and representatives from the ASBJ — opposed voluntary adoption because they prioritized the preservation of the domestic *status quo* involving unique local conditions and their institutional complementarity over adaptation to globalization through full IFRS adoption. On the other hand, with the exact opposite rationale, the remaining one-third of the membership — representatives from the Japan Institute of Certified Public Accountants (JICPA), the financial services industry, the pro-big business Japan Business Federation (Nippon Keidanren), the TSE, and analysts — supported full adoption (Tsunogaya 2014).

It remains to be seen whether the IASB will recognize the J-IFRS as IFRS, particularly on account of the coexistence of multiple accounting standards that hinders sufficient comparability, and whether Japan's rejection of full mandatory adoption of the IFRS and its resultant isolation in terms of accounting standards from other East Asian countries will benefit or harm the country.

Conclusion

This study has analyzed how and why Japan weathered the once-intense globalization dynamics under U.S. economic hegemony that pressed the country to accept full mandatory adoption of the market-price-based IFRS characteristic of Anglo-Saxon capitalism. With its low-profile, maneuvered opposition, Japan introduced voluntary adoption of the IFRS. As a result, the country has ended up with four accounting standards and limited international comparability of financial statements, while maintaining the *status quo* in its domestic capitalist system. In the foreseeable future, Japan will be unlikely to face similar external pressure because, with the relative decline of U.S. economic hegemony, globalization has stalled and even receded, and this has considerably weakened the dynamics of international regime building in accounting standards.

Yet if regime dynamics of this kind are built into the Japanese system of accounting standards, the IFRS will become more influential even after globalization. In fact, as mentioned earlier, the number of Japanese listed companies that have voluntarily adopted the IFRS has steadily increased because their activities have become more internationalized with the growing liberalization of capital markets and consequent demand for a high degree of international comparability of financial statements. This may be a natural consequence of the growing importance of foreign shareholders of these companies, whose percentile distribution grew from some 20% to 30% in the decade up to 2018.[11] These companies cannot but adopt the IFRS if they are to meet the needs of foreign shareholders and investors who demand high international comparability. Also, these companies are increasingly financed through international corporate bond markets where high comparability is also required. As long as Japanese listed companies have to rely on foreign investors and international financial markets, the built-in regime dynamics will surely be reinforced.

However, built-in regime dynamics of this kind may weaken if Japanese listed companies depend significantly less on foreign investors and international financial markets. Japan is now the only major creditor nation, while the United States and the major European countries face serious insolvency and other structural vulnerabilities. This situation would make Japan the major capital-flight haven in the event of a global financial crisis. With such financial power, Japanese listed companies could rely solely on Japanese investors and Japanese financial markets and invest in other East Asian countries, taking advantage of high international comparability of financial statements with those of other East Asian companies.

Any discussion of these two possibilities will remain inconclusive in the foreseeable future, but it will be reduced to the question of the international competitiveness in investment of the Japanese financial sector, particularly venture capitalists and other risk-taking investors. It is well known that Japan lacks competitive investment banks and other risk-taking institutional investors, while "Japanese money" is circulated in international financial markets through the yen carry trade by foreign investors and comes back to Japanese markets. If Japan does not have a competitive financial sector, it will have to rely on foreign investors for risk-taking investment and innovation. Otherwise, the dynamism of Japanese capitalism will be significantly reduced.

Thus, the Japanese capitalist system will continue to be a major pole in the international economy because it has successfully retained system integrity amidst the politics of international accounting standards. However, its long-term viability remains uncertain. East Asian countries should be

---

[11] This data are based on the "Research Paper Regarding Results of the 2018 Stock Distribution Survey," issued by the Japan Exchange Group, June 19, 2019. https://www.jpx.co.jp/markets/statistics-equities/examination/nlsgeu0000043n00-att/j-bunpu2018.pdf.

aware that U.S. dominance in accounting standards is over, while Japanese as well as West European influence in this area remains significant. This is particularly the case because China's atypical "socialist market" has only superficially adopted the IFRS, and because China cannot be a "normal" economic partner on an equal footing with the United States, Japan, and other major West European countries. Thus, the countries of East Asia must understand Japan's unique accounting standard system in the context of the three major variants of capitalism and the Chinese "socialist market," particularly when they retain and develop supply chains through Japanese, American, West European, and Chinese investment.

More specifically, given that most large East Asian companies, with the notable exception of China's state-owned enterprises, have already adopted the IFRS, they will enjoy a high degree of comparability in financial statements with the large Japanese companies that have voluntarily adopted it. This will help East Asian investors merge with or acquire Japanese companies in search of superior individual technologies and, to a lesser extent, brands, as demonstrated by the increasing number of M&A cases and the growing investment in them by Chinese, Taiwanese, and Korean investors. On the other hand, those investors must be careful in cases involving companies that use the J GAAP because they will entail considerably higher accounting consulting costs.

References

ASBJ. https://www.asb.or.jp/en/ifrs/about.html (accessed October 20, 2019).

Gilpin, Robert. 1981. *War and Change in World Politics.* Cambridge: Cambridge University Press.

Gilpin, Robert. 1987. *The Political Economy of International Relations.* Princeton, NJ: Princeton University Press, 92–97.

Gunji, Takeshi. 2018. Theoretical Changes of the Viewpoint of Balance Sheet. *Osaka Gakuin University Review of Commerce and Business Administration* 43(2): 1–31.

Ibid., 5–10.

IFRS. 2019. Use Around the World: Who Uses IFRS Standards? https://www.ifrs. org/use-around-the-world/use-of-ifrs-standards-by-jurisdiction/china/ (accessed October 20, 2019).

Itoh, Kunio. 2013. IFRS Heno Torikumi No Genjyo, Ronten, Kadai [Current Status, Issues, and Challenges of IFRS Initiatives]. In *Kigyo-Kaikei-Seido*

No Sai-Kochiku [Rebuilding the Corporate Accounting System], edited by Kunio Itoh. Tokyo: Chuo Keizaisha, 2–19.

Japan Exchange Group. 2022a. Voluntary Application of IFRS (Current and Scheduled). https://www.jpx.co.jp/english/listing/others/ifrs/ (accessed February 2022).

Japan Exchange Group. 2022b. Voluntary Application of IFRS (Current and Scheduled), Japan Exchange Group, 2022. https://www.jpx.co.jp/english/equities/improvements/ifrs/02.html (accessed February 2022).

Jimi, Shozaburo. 2011. Considerations on the Application of IFRS. June 21. https://www.fsa.go.jp/en/announce/state/20110621-1.html (accessed October 20, 2019).

Kawazoe, Keiko. 2019. Hong Kong Wa Bei-Chu No Shu-Senjyo [Hong Kong as a Major Battlefield], *WILL* (November 2019): 306.

Kobayashi, Hideo, Seichiro Yonekura, and Tetsuji Okazaki. 1995. *'Nihon-Kabishi-Gaisha' No Showa-Shi: Kanryo-Shihai No Kozo* [The History of 'Japan Inc.' During the Showa Period: The Structure of the Bureaucratic Rule]. Tokyo: Sogen-Sha.

Krasner, Stephen D. 1983. Structural Causes and Regime Consequences: Regimes as Intervening Variables. In *International Regimes*, edited by Stephen D. Krasner, 1. Cornell University Press.

Kuroda, Masatoshi. 2011. Nihon Niokeru Kaikeigaku No Deno — Ichi-Shiron [An Inquiry into the Tradition of Accounting Studies in Japan], *Kokusai Kaikei Kenkyu Gattsukai Nenpo* [Annual of the Japan Association for International Accounting Studies] 2. http://jaias.org/2011bulletin_2/07_JPN. pdf#search='日本＋伝統的会計基準 (accessed October 6, 2019).

Nikkei Shimbun. September 5, 2019. https://www.nikkei.com/article/DGXMZO 49410140U9A900C1MM8000/ (accessed October 6, 2019).

Noguchi, Yukio. 1995. *1940nen Taisei [The 1940 Regime]*. Toyo Keizai Shimpo Sha. Okumura, Hiroshi. 1991. *Hojin-Shihon-Shugi: Kaisha-Honi No Taikei [Corporate Capitalism: A Company-Centered System]*. Osaka: Asahi Shimbun Sha.

Okumura, Hiroshi. 1994. *Nihon No Rokudai-Kigyo-Shudan* [Japan's Six Major Corporate Groups]. Osaka: Asahi Shimbun Sha.

PricewaterhouseCoopers (PwC) China. Doing Business in China. https://www.pwccn.com/en/migration/pdf/iic-full.pdf (accessed October 20, 2019).

PricewaterhouseCoopers (PwC) China. 2013. Doing Business and Investing in China. https://www.pwccn.com/en/migration/pdf/iic-full.pdf (accessed October 20, 2019).

PwC Mongolia. 2015. Doing Business in Mongolia 2015. https://www.pwc.com/mn/en/publication/assets/dbg_2015.pdf (accessed October 20, 2019).

PwC Taiwan. 2015. Doing Business in Taiwan. https://www.pwc.tw/en/publications/doing-business-in-taiwan.html (accessed October 20, 2019).

Samil PwC. 2015. Doing Business and Investing in Korea. https://www.pwc.de/de/internationale-maerkte/assets/doing-business-and-investing-in-korea.pdf (accessed October 20, 2019).

Tsunogaya, Nobuyuki. 2014. Diversity of Views on the Mandatory Adoption of IFRS in Japan: Based on Analysis of the Minutes of the Business Accounting Council. *Annual Report of the Japanese Association for International Accounting Studies*, 1, 9–24.

Chapter 8

Japan's Data Free Flow with Trust: Progress and Prospects in Data Governance

Mark Bryan Manantan

Introduction

During his speech at the 2019 World Economic Forum (WEF), Prime Minister Shinzo Abe made the bold claim that he would make the Osaka G20 the "summit that started world-wide data governance" (Abe 2019a). Recognizing that the "the engine for growth ... is fueled no longer by gasoline, but more and more by digital data," Abe proposed Data Free Flow with Trust (DFFT) as the blueprint that would guide the laying down of rules and principles in the fast-emerging data-driven economy under the auspices of multilateral platforms such the World Trade Organization (WTO) (Abe 2019a).

However, one critical question is whether Japan's bid to make the rules in data governance is likely to be hindered by the increasing competition in harnessing data to lead digital transformation, rising geopolitical and technological competition, and fragmentation of the Internet governance regime. Thus, it came as no surprise when, during the Osaka Summit some countries, such as India and Indonesia, did not signal their support for DFFT. This was evidence of a growing trend toward data localization led by China and Russia. In these circumstances, the Japanese will surely struggle in their efforts to rebuild trust in global digital trade.

However, despite such challenges, Japan's ambition to write the rules, principles, and standards of digital trade and e-commerce is gaining momentum, with a growing coalition of like-minded partners who embrace cross-border data flows while strengthening data privacy and protection and intellectual property.

This chapter examines Japan's ambition to write the rules for global data governance under its flagship framework of DFFT. It provides a conceptual roadmap of Japan's approaches to rulemaking in the emerging digital economy through the example of DFFT. Two pathways are explored to illustrate Japan's attempt to demonstrate its commitment to translating DFFT into a practical set of principles: (1) Japan's coalition building in various multilateral forums such as the WTO, and (2) its leading role in the implementation of the e-commerce and digital trade provisions embedded in the Comprehensive and Progressive Agreement for Trans-Pacific Partnership (CPTPP). Finally, the chapter examines the prospects for further advancing DFFT as a fundamental reference in driving data governance initiatives. The findings in this chapter are drawn from the author's fieldwork as part of the U.S.–Japan–Southeast Asia Partnership in a Dynamic Asia Fellowship. Interviews were conducted with various sources from government institutions, academia, industry associations, and civil society organizations, all of whom have first-hand knowledge of ongoing efforts and collaboration between the United States, Japan, and Southeast Asia. My conclusion is that despite the fragmentation of global consensus, Japan remains steadfast in capitalizing on the role of multilateral institutions while compensating for their limitations through engagement in multistakeholder platforms. Through its convening power, Japan can facilitate dialogue between tech companies and governments to overcome barriers that lead to siloed policymaking. In this context, Japan's two-pronged strategy of complementing multilateralism with a multistakeholder approach to data governance presents a practical way of realizing mutually beneficial outcomes.

Defining DFFT

The fundamental hallmarks of DFFT are two-fold: Removing barriers to the free flow of data through the development of interoperable international standards and mitigating the growth of data hegemony and protectionism to promote deeper collaboration. As 5G networks and the Internet of things (IoT) become even more embedded in everyday lives, data is being produced at an unprecedented rate of around 2.5 quintillion bytes per day. With the world rapidly shifting from an information society to Society 5.0 where the physical and digital realms are very much integrated data is regarded as the new oil that will fuel the next frontier in global value creation (*METI-Journal* 2019).

Realizing the game-changing impact of data on value creation, Japan has positioned itself as a pioneer in rulemaking for the emerging data-centered era. DFFT, as it was unveiled by the late Prime Minister Shinzo Abe at the WEF in 2019, represents an attempt by Japan to seize the emerging digital economy and trade. Japan was setting the stage for a deeper interrogation of how the power of data can be harnessed in the Fourth Industrial Revolution. DFFT proposes a more nuanced approach by zeroing in on the fundamental issue of categorizing data (Abe 2019a). The flow of data that are classified as personal — intellectual property or national security intelligence — must be restricted, while non-personal data, such as "medical, industrial, traffic and other most useful non-personal anonymous data" would be allowed to cross borders under specific and agreed-upon conditions (Figure 1) (Abe 2019a).

Following the annual WFT summit, Abe reiterated his proposal on DFFT, also known as the Osaka Track, as the centerpiece of Japan's chairmanship of the G20 summit. The Osaka Track aims to jumpstart the

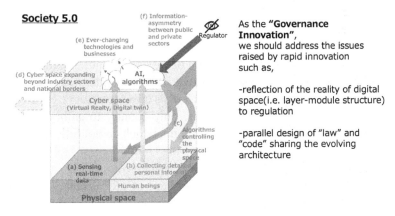

Figure 1: Society 5.0

Source: Study Group on a New Governance Models in Society 5.0, *Governance Innovation: Redesigning Law and Architecture in the Age of Society 5.0.* https://www.meti.go.jp/english/press/2019/pdf/191226001.pdf.

process of building consensus on the establishment of a framework that will guide the anticipated e-commerce and digital economy negotiations in the WTO. Trust will be the enabler in such deliberations, with the aim of realizing interoperability to maximize productivity and achieve innovation (Kodama 2019). Countries which rely on an open, rules-based global trading system must agree on common principles on electronic commerce and data flow (Table 1).

The Osaka Track was launched against the backdrop of growing geopolitical competition between the United States and China. In the months leading up to the G20 summit, the Sino-American tit-for-tat on tariffs was on full display. What started as an effort to curb China's unfair trade practices and address its trade deficit with the United States rapidly bled into the area of technological competition, with Chinese ICT giant Huawei caught in the crossfire. The trade-turned-technological war signaled the potential decoupling of the world's two largest economies marked by the Trump administration's decision to block access by suspected state-owned Chinese enterprises to key U.S. technologies (Manantan 2020a). At the same time, the China made the bold announcement that they would fast-track their efforts to produce their own indigenous technology (Manantan 2020b).

The unraveling of U.S.–China relations thus bring to the fore the philosophical divide on how the two great powers view the world. And this played out especially in the technological terrain which lies at the heart of their bitter rivalry. In 2018, Xi Jinping voiced an aspiration for China to write the rules of global cyber governance in a way that would deviate from the open Internet model of the United States (Sacs 2018). The idea is for China to be independent of foreign technologies and for its indigenous companies to take an active role in standard setting in the world of tech. Data is fundamental to China's effort to achieve cyberspace sovereignty. However, China is not the only country to embrace such a model — developing countries such as India which do not fully align with the free and open Internet advocated by the United States, Japan, and the European Union (EU) find the Chinese alternative appealing.

Given that they generate the lion's share of global data, China and India are leading proponents of data localization where data must be collected and stored in their geographic jurisdictions. China has launched its data flow regulatory regime grounded on "local storage and outbound assessment" (Liu 2018). Foreign businesses operating in China are subject to security assessments before they can transfer data overseas (Livingston 2017).

Table 1: Excerpts from the G20 Osaka Leader's Declaration on DFFT

Trade and Investment	8. We welcome the G20 Ministerial Statement on Trade and Digital Economy in Tsukuba. We strive to realize a free, fair, non-discriminatory, transparent, predictable and stable trade and investment environment, and to keep our markets open. International trade and investment are important engines of growth, productivity, innovation, job creation and development. We reaffirm our support for the necessary reform of the World Trade Organization (WTO) to improve its functions. We will work constructively with other WTO members, including in the lead up to the 12th WTO Ministerial Conference. We agree that action is necessary regarding the functioning of the dispute settlement system consistent with the rules as negotiated by WTO members. Furthermore, we recognize the complementary roles of bilateral and regional free trade agreements that are WTO-consistent. We will work to ensure a level playing field to foster an enabling business environment.
Innovation: Digitalization, DFFT	10. Innovation is an important driver for economic growth, which can also contribute to advancing towards the SDGs and enhancing inclusiveness. We will work toward achieving an inclusive, sustainable, safe, trustworthy and innovative society through digitalization and promoting the application of emerging technologies. We share the notion of a human-centered future society, which is being promoted by Japan as Society 5.0. As digitalization is transforming every aspect of our economies and societies, we recognize the critical role played by effective use of data, as an enabler of economic growth, development and social well-being. We aim to promote international policy discussions to harness the full potential of data.
Innovation: Digitalization, DFFT	11. Cross-border flow of data, information, ideas and knowledge generates higher productivity, greater innovation, and improved sustainable development, while raising challenges related to privacy, data protection, intellectual property rights, and security. By continuing to address these challenges, we can further facilitate data free flow and strengthen consumer and business trust. In this respect, it is necessary that legal frameworks, both domestic and international, should be respected. Such DFFT will harness the opportunities of the digital economy. We will cooperate to encourage the interoperability of different frameworks, and we affirm the role of data for development. We also reaffirm the importance of interface between trade and digital economy, and note the ongoing discussion under the Joint Statement Initiative on electronic commerce, and reaffirm the importance of the Work Programme on electronic commerce at the WTO.

(Continued)

Table 1:   *(Continued)*

12. To further promote innovation in the digital economy, we support the sharing of good practices on effective policy and regulatory approaches and frameworks that are innovative as well as agile, flexible, and adapted to the digital era, including through the use of regulatory sandboxes. The responsible development and use of Artificial Intelligence (AI) can be a driving force to help advance the SDGs and to realize a sustainable and inclusive society. To foster public trust and confidence in AI technologies and fully realize their potential, we commit to a human-centered approach to AI, and welcome the non-binding G20 AI Principles, drawn from the Organization for Economic Cooperation and Development (OECD) Recommendation on AI. Further, we recognize the growing importance of promoting security in the digital economy and of addressing security gaps and vulnerabilities. We affirm the importance of protection of intellectual property. Along with the rapid expansion of emerging technologies including the Internet of Things (IoT), the value of an ongoing discussion on security in the digital economy is growing. We, as G20 members, affirm the need to further work on these urgent challenges. We reaffirm the importance of bridging the digital divide and fostering the adoption of digitalization among micro, small and medium enterprises (MSMEs) and all individuals, particularly vulnerable groups and also encourage networking and experience-sharing among cities for the development of smart cities.

Source: Japan Ministry of Foreign Affairs, *G20 Osaka Leaders Declaration*. https://www.mofa.go.jp/policy/economy/g20_summit/osaka19/en/documents/final_g20_osaka_leaders_declaration.html#:~:text=We%20strive%20to%20realize%20a,innovation%2C%20job%20creation%20and%20development.

Such a move by China is part of its larger strategic ambition to become a cyber power, a fundamental component of which is the rewriting of the rules on data governance (Kania *et al.* 2017). India also adheres to the same conditional principle on the transfer of data across borders. Sensitive transfers of personal information must satisfy a level of protection under specific conditions. It gives the Indian government the right to classify data that are deemed fit to be stored and processed within its territory (Basu 2020). This underscores India's opposition to the concept of data colonization that predominantly Western IT tech companies impose when they engage in large-scale data collection among Indian citizens (Basu and Sherman 2020).

Abe's ambition to build a system of data governance was therefore seen as ludicrous, given the conflicting perspectives of nation-states that transcend geopolitical competition and are cast in the larger narrative of technical divides rooted in philosophical differences. However, according to Tetsuya Watanabe, Director-General for trade policy at the Japanese Ministry of Economy, Trade and Industry (METI), Japan's bold move is premised on using the G20 summit as an intermediary and "not aiming to simply react to the actions of U.S. and China" (*Genron-NPO* 2019). Watanabe added that Japan, along with the other 15 members of the G20, aspires to strengthen the rules of the international order to alleviate the tension that is afflicting the global trading system. But Kenji Okamura, Director of the International Bureau at the Ministry of Finance, asserted that there is obvious concern among emerging economies about China's actions in building alternative value systems that challenge existing frameworks like the G20 and which may lead to even more confusion and complications (*Genron-NPO* 2019).

Despite the looming fragmentation on the global stage, Japan was able to achieve modest results with the signing of the Osaka Declaration on Digital Economy by 24 countries, including the United States, China, Russia, and the EU. The signatories were seeking to provide a political stimulus to the elimination of barriers to the free flow of data. They described the Osaka Track as the "process which demonstrates our commitment to promote international policy discussions, *inter alia*, international rule-making on trade-related aspects of electronic commerce at the WTO" (*G20* 2019). The agreement also noted the support of 78 WTO members who signed the Joint Statement on Electronic Commerce issued in Davos on January 25, 2019. While the general agreement with the Osaka Track exemplified consensus, specific items have yet to be settled before pathways for implementation can be set out (*Mizuho* 2019). Furthermore, some significant states that are known to generate data on a massive scale, such as Indonesia, India, and South Africa, opted out of the digital governance declaration. But Tamaki Tsukada, Deputy Assistant Minister of Japan's Economic Affairs Bureau, claimed that overall, Japan maximized the G20's inherent value as a platform for agenda-setting and rulemaking by putting forward the concept of DFFT to reflect the evolving landscape of the global trading system (*Genron-NPO* 2019). Thus, it demonstrated Japan's convening power in a multilateral institution to arrive at mutual and common understanding.

Sustaining the Osaka Momentum

Crystallizing a global agenda for DFFT was the longer-term ambition of the Abe government. Japan aims to position DFFT as an enduring and sustainable engagement, confirming Abe's pronouncements that the G20 was not the culmination but only the springboard for a worldwide conversation about global data governance. Saudi Arabia was the incoming chair of the G20 Summit in 2020, and commentators were quick to stress that issues relating to data governance might not receive the emphasis they had at the Osaka summit in 2019. But whatever global issues Saudi Arabia may decide to focus on during its chairmanship, DFFT has already gained a positive momentum. Within a span of one year, DFFT strengthened its own narrative through various international policy forums in a way that transcended the summitry of the G20.

Leading reform at the WTO

In the aftermath of the diplomatic showmanship at the G20 summit, Japan has increased the velocity of DFFT despite the increasing trend toward the exploration or introduction of data localization laws and policies by other countries, most notably in the Asia-Pacific region. Through its persistent engagement with regional and multilateral platforms, Japan capitalized on its coalition-building approach and promoted DFFT as the fundamental reference in shaping policy discussions. It was clear from the start that Prime Minister Abe was determined to make DFFT the guiding principle of the long overdue reforms at the WTO.

In recent years, Japan's convening power as the "flag-bearer of free trade," premised on its commitment to WTO reform, has been evident. According to Minister Hiroshige Seko of METI, Japan's intermediary role builds on its track record in forming coalitions with like-minded states at the global level (*METI-Journal* 2019a). In 2017, Japan, Australia, and Singapore issued a joint statement on revisiting WTO trade rules and addressing digitalization. Seko added that Japan's convening power was also instrumental in facilitating the trilateral meeting of the United States, Japan, and the EU (*METI-Journal* 2019a). These three discussed how rulemaking could play a crucial role in the areas of industrial subsidies, forced technology transfers, and the digital economy. Cementing their commitment to lead the reforms at the WTO, the trilateral grouping presented a proposal on compliance with notification obligations on industrial subsidies (*METI-Journal* 2019a).

After Japan called for a global consensus on data governance at the G20 summit, the road forward led to the WTO. Japanese policymakers argued that success in institutionalizing broader reforms of the global digital economy would depend on Japan's ability in the WTO to encourage member-states to create a framework based on DFFT. As a testament to Japan's commitment, METI, along with the Ministry of Foreign Affairs (MOFA), embarked on a series of engagements in various international policy forums (Table 2).[1]

Japan participated in a series of WTO rulemaking negotiations in the lead-up to the much-anticipated WTO Ministerial Conference in Nur-Sultan, Kazakhstan, in June 2020. Since the signing of the Osaka Declaration, the number of state signatories had increased from 78 to 83.[2] New additions, including Indonesia and the Philippines, evinced the positive traction that Japan had gained in the WTO e-commerce negotiations. Participating countries have now progressed to formulating the negotiation texts and will hopefully codify them for operationalization. However, Japanese officials were also cognizant of the prevailing challenges to consensus building that exist in any multilateral set-up: more participants means less agreement, and the higher the quality of the

---

[1] Interview with officials from the Ministry of Economy, Trade, and Industry (METI), Tokyo, Japan.
[2] Interview with METI.

Table 2:   Key Elements Proposed in the WTO e-Commerce Negotiations

Facilitation	Electronic signatures and authentications
	Electronic documentation of trade documents (paperless trading)
	Access to online payment solutions/electronic payment
Liberalization	Non-imposition of customs duties on electronic transmissions
	Free access to the Internet (prohibition of arbitrary blocking by the government)
	Non-discriminatory treatment of digital products
	Free cross-border transfer of information by electronic means
	Prohibition of data localization barriers including using or locating computing facilities
	Improving commitments on goods and services market access
Reliability (Trust)	Online consumer protection
	Unsolicited commercial e-mail (spam)
	Protection of personal information (privacy)
	Protection of important information such as trade secrets, including source codes and proprietary algorithms
Transparency/ Cooperation	Publication and exchange of information on regulatory measures and procedures
Development	Technical assistance and capacity building

Source: https://www.mizuho-ri.co.jp/publication/research/pdf/eo/MEA190726.pdf.

agreement, the less the commitment.[3] In this regard, interoperability and the need to balance both freedom and trust while considering national interests continue to surface as areas of contention.

Expanding multilateralism into a multistakeholder approach: The OECD and WEF

Recognizing the potential limitations of the WTO decision-making process and the urgent need to resolve the debate between values and national security, Japanese officials used other avenues that embrace inclusivity and an evidenced-based policymaking approach to fortify their case for adopting DFFT. The Japanese government's engagement has expanded

---

[3] *Ibid.*

from multilateral frameworks to intergovernmental institutions like the Organization for Economic Cooperation and Development (OECD) and multistakeholder platforms such as the WEF.[4]

To address the "specific" interventions that were not clearly laid out during the 2019 G20 summit, the Japanese government collaborated with the OECD to operationalize the DFFT principles through an approach called governance innovation.[5] As METI has stated, "The issues of how and by whom the increasingly integrated architectures of cyberspace and physical space are to be designed, and how the regulating elements, including laws, market mechanisms and social norms, should function are becoming crucial for the governance of the economy and society" (*METI* 2019b, p. 6). The proposed governance innovation process entails three primary actors — the state/government; businesses; and communities and individuals — in three major stages: (1) rulemaking, which consists of identifying mechanisms to regulate behavior based on agreed standards, market principles, and social norms; (2) monitoring, which is the collection of information for evaluation from businesses, individuals, machines, and programs; and (3) enforcement or resolving certain issues or problems through litigation or improvement measures (*METI* 2019, p. 9). Through its partnership with the OECD, Japan was able to achieve three objectives: (1) an expanded collective engagement with critical actors beyond government that include industries and consumers; (2) resolution of the practical and itemized issues that were deemed unresolved by critics after the launch of the Osaka Track; and (3) the setting of a path toward operationalizing DFFT as a fundamental reference among participating countries in the WTO or as a reference in devising national data governance frameworks (Table 3).[6]

Since unveiling DFFT at the WEF in January 2019, Davos has been an important venue for Japan. Although no concrete agreements are reached, the WEF embraces a multistakeholder approach that allows governments to explore partnerships with companies in undertaking pressing global issues.[7] The WEF enabled Japan to shape the policy agenda among key decisionmakers from the private sector. At the January 2020 forum, Japanese state minister for foreign affairs Kenji Wakamiya had the

---

[4] *Ibid.*
[5] *Ibid.*
[6] *Ibid.*
[7] Interview with the Ministry of Foreign Affairs, Tokyo, Japan.

Table 3:   Governance Model Framework for Governance Innovation

Process	Actor		
	Government	Businesses	Communities/individuals
Rule-making	<Establish, design, provide or review a mechanism that regulates human activities>		
	• Law	• System architecture	• Market mechanisms
		• Source code	• Social norms
Monitoring	<Collection of information necessary to evaluate businesses, machines or programs>		
Enforcement	<Actions taken in response to an incident>		

Source: Study Group on a New Governance Models in Society 5.0, *Governance Innovation: Redesigning Law and Architecture in the Age of Society 5.0*. https://www.meti.go.jp/english/press/2019/pdf/191226001.pdf.

opportunity to engage with various private sector CEOs from all over the world (*Japan Times* 2020). This gave Wakamiya the opportunity to reinforce the principles of DFFT and introduce the concept of governance innovation into the operationalization of the framework so that digital issues could be tackled on a global platform.

Achieving interoperability through the CPTPP

Aside from the WTO, Japan is also determined to demonstrate the specific principles of DFFT using the e-commerce and digital trade provisions embedded in the CPTPP.[8] In essence, the DFFT principles are iterations of the CPTPP aimed at enhancing the regulatory governance of data management to protect intellectual property and strengthen cybersecurity. The CPTPP provides Japan with the leverage to shape the preferences of participating economies in the Asia-Pacific by adopting high standards on e-commerce and digital trade, while promoting cross-border data flow and mitigating the growth of data sovereignty. According to experts consulted for this study, trade agreements provide the most feasible route to achieving interoperability between domestic and international standards. CPTPP members, like Vietnam, and other interested parties such as Malaysia, Brunei, Thailand, and Indonesia, could realign their existing policies to

---

[8] Interview with METI.

accommodate a less restrictive approach to data flow in exchange for broader economic incentives. The CPTPP serves as a neutral venue for devising compatibility mechanisms to implement a more nuanced approach to personal and non-personal data that may persuade CPTPP members to enact data policies to meet their economic objectives.

Exploring Prospects in Southeast Asia

The evolution of DFFT from being a flagship framework at the G20 to becoming an item on the global agenda will not happen in a linear fashion. The dynamic route undertaken by the framework demonstrates how policymaking in the increasingly multipolar world requires nimbleness, inclusivity, and collaboration. But as competition in setting the rules of the road on data governance intensifies, exacerbated by the current COVID-19 crisis, Japan's coalition building is beset with a high degree of uncertainty. Notwithstanding the limitations that the "new normal" imposes on Japan's rulemaking initiatives, Japan can capitalize on the foundational gains of DFFT pre-pandemic. This section offers potential touch points for DFFT to continue toward its ultimate goal of fortifying trade rules in the data-driven international economy in the current climate.

Cultivating inclusivity and a multistakeholder approach in local and international settings

Given the complexity of local and international rulemaking on the flow of data and its potential impact on data-reliant industries, the idea of multilateralism is attractive. But arriving at a definitive consensus is fraught with challenges. In the debate surrounding the digital economy, tension stems from the varying levels of appetite for liberalization among advanced and developing economies. As the consensus-building model continues to lose steam, it is imperative that Japan maximizes the benefits of a multistakeholder approach and arrives at a comprehensive inventory of policy prescriptions to drive its initiatives forward. But to be effective on the international stage, advocating for such a multistakeholder approach must be rooted in a whole-of-Japanese-society approach.

Evaluating the outcomes of the G20 summit in 2019, the President of Genron, Yasushi Kudo, made the general observation that the Abe government must invest the same level of enthusiasm into raising awareness and igniting support for its proposals among the local Japanese population as it was doing on the international stage (*Genron-NPO* 2019). Kudo's observation reflects the potential disconnect between Japan's local and international efforts — a stark reality that must be faced by any government attempting to hug the global limelight in advocating for a specific issue.

However, in the case of Japan, the prospects for closing the gap between local and international efforts are quite promising. Despite some shortcomings, Japan was able to carve out a collaborative and inclusive environment which encompasses various stakeholders — government, the private sector, academia, and civil society organizations — that will support its bid to establish an international consensus on global data governance.

Since Japan is one of the world's most highly industrialized economies, as Minister Seko from METI pointed out, its manufacturing sector can play a vital role in demonstrating the positive effects of adopting the DFFT framework (*METI-Journal* 2019). In 2018, METI launched a pilot project to establish a system that enables the exchange of data among different companies such as Fanuc Corp, DMG Mori Co., Mitsubishi Electric Corp., and Hitachi Ltd. Seko argued that by maximizing the high-quality data from Japanese manufacturing companies, firms can benefit from the accumulation and distribution of large datasets across borders (*METI-Journal* 2019). If lessons can be learned from the pilot project, Seko is optimistic that efforts to share and distribute data will usher in the era of smart manufacturing, while encouraging progress in other industries across borders (*METI-Journal* 2019).

Likewise, at the B20 Tokyo Summit, the Japanese Business Federation, also known as Keidanren, endorsed the need to develop the next generation data governance framework. The B20 conference, which gathered leading companies from across Japan and G20 member-states, reached a consensus on the promotion of international interoperability standards across jurisdictions and the free flow of data beyond borders. The group also voiced their support for expediting the process during the highly anticipated WTO trade negotiations on e-commerce to achieve a high-standard outcome in an open, inclusive, and participatory setting (*B-20* 2019). A parallel group called the T20, or Think20, a consortium of leading thinktanks based in Japan and other G20 members, compiled a list of research-based policy recommendations to achieve harmonization in data flow (*RIETI Highlight* 2019).

By orchestrating an inclusive and collaborative approach to policy-making that transcends the domestic and international audience, Japan utilized an arena in which it can demonstrate and test the viability of adopting DFFT. The outcomes of a multistakeholder approach illustrate how policy harmonization can be achieved across industries and geographies, and how it may be possible to mitigate the rise of a digital bloc economic system.

Finding common ground: DFFT and the ASEAN Digital Data Governance Framework

Japan has the opportunity to find common ground with emerging data governance regimes in Southeast Asia through the Association of Southeast Asian Nations (ASEAN) Digital Data Governance Framework. At the 25th International Conference on the Future of Asia, Prime Minister Abe called on ASEAN to support Japan's promotion of DFFT in the upcoming WTO meeting. Abe highlighted ASEAN's dynamism as a key driver in building a favorable supply chain which permits the flow of goods and emphasized its growing contribution to the global economy. Drawing on so-called ASEAN centrality, Abe was keen to leverage ASEAN's collective vision to embark on a major transformation at the WTO to reflect the digitalization of the world economy as the basis for cooperation (Abe 2019b). In a further collaborative effort, Japan invited Singapore, Vietnam, and Thailand to attend the G20 summit and witness the launch of the Osaka Track (MOFA 2018). This provided an opportunity for Japan to work more closely with the three ASEAN member-states in amplifying policy interoperability that is already integrated with existing mechanisms promoted via the Asia Pacific Economic Cooperation and the CPTPP.

As one of its dialogue partners, Japan has been very active in supporting the digital transformation of Southeast Asia through the realization of the ASEAN Economic Community. With the launch of its Framework on Digital Data Governance, ASEAN is determined to seize opportunities provided by its growing digital economic boom. The framework will facilitate cross-border data flow, harmonize legal and regulatory frameworks, and strengthen cybersecurity. With the framework in place, Japan and ASEAN can start to find a common approach toward data flow.

Complementing cybersecurity with data governance

Japan is regarded in Southeast Asia as the "most trusted major power" (Mun *et al.* 2020). According to the 2020 State of Southeast Asia Survey Report, 61.2% of respondents in the region are confident that Japan will "do the right thing." Likewise, Japan was hailed as the "quintessential smart power" and the leader of the liberal order in Asia based on the Lowy Institute's Asia Power Index in 2019 (*Lowy Institute* 2019). Japan could capitalize on these positive perceptions to position itself as the trusted partner in collaboration with Southeast Asian states on data governance. After all, Japan has been supporting ASEAN's indigenous efforts to realize its potential as a digital economic powerhouse. Japan has a track record in the realm of cybersecurity and has made efforts to support ASEAN's digital economy. Notable initiatives in this area include the establishment of the ASEAN–Japan Cybersecurity Capacity Building Centre (AJCCBC) in 2018. Through Japanese-led programs, the AJCCBC upgraded the capabilities of government organizations' cybersecurity workforce and drafted the incident response framework. Both elements were essential to the establishment of the ASEAN Computer Emergency Response Team (CERT) tasked with accomplishing the ASEAN ICT Master Plan 2020 (Bhunia 2018). Based on this engagement, it would therefore be feasible for Japan and ASEAN member-states to set up a technical working group on data governance that would complement their past and current engagements in cybersecurity to create a trusted digital economy.

Crafting a targeted approach to policy interoperability

Japan's efforts to attract greater support for DFFT within ASEAN may face an uphill battle. As previously mentioned, Indonesia walked away from signing the Osaka Declaration, while Thailand and Vietnam are more inclined to support legislation that encourages data localization. Notwithstanding the CPTPP provisions on e-commerce and the digital economy that are aligned with the DFFT principles, and to which Singapore and Vietnam have signed up, Japan must be willing to engage with Southeast Asia and emphasize the need for policy interoperability. Such engagement must be premised on a comprehensive policy deliberation between ASEAN and Japan to explore compatibility mechanisms rather than a blanket approach that embraces data sovereignty. In this dialogue, Japan and ASEAN could explore the adoption of mutual recognition agreements on the cross-border flow of high-value data in critical industries that include financial services, manufacturing, and healthcare. Stocktaking appropriate policies will mitigate discriminatory approaches toward foreign and local business enterprises, especially Japanese companies operating in the region.

Furthermore, Japan must also recognize the differences in maturity of the Southeast Asian countries' digital economies. The extreme unevenness of these states' capacity to participate in digital trade and e-commerce should remind Japanese policymakers to work alongside their Southeast Asian counterparts in promoting best practice and self-regulatory policies, as well as bridging any gaps through capacity-building initiatives. Recognizing this divide will enable Japan to craft targeted policy engagements that encourage Southeast Asian states to move toward a participatory discussion on data governance.

Conclusion

Japan's bold ambition to write the rules of the Fourth Industrial Revolution is underpinned by its role as an intermediary and coalition-builder in rule-making. As geopolitical and ideological conflict accelerates the fragmentation of the global consensus, Japan has remained steadfast in advancing the continuing role of multilateral institutions, while making up for their limitations by engaging in multistakeholder platforms to speed up results and facilitate decision making. By pursuing this two-pronged approach, Japan reinforces its convening power to buttress the declining global governance in cooperation with like-minded partners. Due to the uncertainty that currently besets the international policymaking landscape, Japan will most likely continue to follow central and peripheral routes — multilateral and multistakeholder. It will democratize the process through the participation of a multitude of voices while respecting the varying appetites of nation-states for e-commerce and digital trade, particularly in Southeast Asia. Furthermore, Japan can leverage its intermediary role to encourage multinational ICT companies to recognize their *de facto* roles in the rule-making process in the 21st century digital economy. The scale and speed of technological disruptions are outpacing the legal and regulatory frameworks of governments. Through its convening power, Japan can facilitate dialogue between IT giants and governments to overcome barriers that lead to siloed policymaking. In this context, the two-pronged strategy of complementing multilateralism with a multistakeholder approach is a practical way of facilitating the realization of mutually beneficial outcomes.

References

Abe, Shinzo. 2019a. Defeatism about Japan is Now Defeated. *WEF*, January 23. https://www.weforum.org/agenda/2019/01/abe-speech-transcript/.

Abe, Shinzo. 2019b. A Japan Moving Forward, and the Future Being Built Together with Asia. *Speeches and Statements by the Prime Minister*, May 30. https://japan.kantei.go.jp/98_abe/statement/201905/_00002.html.

B-20. 2019. B-20 Tokyo Summit Report. March 14–15, p. 32. https://www.keidanren.or.jp/en/policy/2019/020_Report.pdf.

Basu, Arindrajit and Justin Sherman. 2020. Key Global Takeaways from India's Revised Personal Data Protection Bill. *Lawfareblog*, January 23. https://www.lawfareblog.com/key-global-takeaways-indias-revised-personal-data-protection-bill.

Basu, Arindrajit. 2020. The Retreat of the Data Localization Brigade: India, Indonesia, and Vietnam. *The Diplomat*, January 10. https://thediplomat.com/2020/01/the-retreat-of-the-data-localization-brigade-india-indonesia-and-vietnam/.

Bhunia, Priyankar. 2018. ASEAN–Japan Cybersecurity Capacity Building Centre to be Launched in Thailand in June 2018. *Open Gov Asia*, March 31. https://www.opengovasia.com/asean-japan-cybersecurity-capacity-building-centre-to-be-launched-in-thailand-in-june-2018/.

G20. 2019. Osaka Declaration on the Digital Economy. June 28. http://www.g20.utoronto.ca/2019/osaka_declaration_on_digital_economy_e.pdf.

Genron-NPO. 2019. Outcome of the 2019 G20 Osaka Summit. July 19. http://www.genron-npo.net/en/issues/archives/5498.html.

Japan Times. 2020. Japan Should Feel the Temperature at Davos. January 30. https://www.japantimes.co.jp/opinion/2020/01/30/editorials/japan-feel-temperature-davos/.

Kania, Elsa, Samm Sacks, Paul Triolo, and Graham Webster. 2017. China's Strategic Thinking on Building Power in Cyberspace. *New America*, September 25. https://www.newamerica.org/cybersecurity-initiative/blog/chinas-strategic-thinking-building-power-cyberspace/.

Kodama, Kazuo. 2019. Global Economics 2.0: Data-Driven, AI-Powered, Ecommerce-Forced, Human Centric? *EU–Japan*, June 18. https://www.eu.emb-japan.go.jp/files/000490347.pdf.

Liu, Jinhe. 2018. China's Data Localization. *Chinese Journal of Communication* 13 (1): 84–103. https://doi.org/10.1080/17544750.2019.1649289.

Livingston, Scott. 2017. Data Localisation in China and Other APEC Jurisdictions, *SSRN*. https://papers.ssrn.com/sol3/papers.cfm?abstract_id=2895610.

Lowy Institute. 2019. Lowy Institute Asia Power Index. May 29. https://power. lowyinstitute.org/downloads/Lowy-Institute-Asia-Power-Index-2019-Key-Findings.pdf.

Manantan, Mark. 2020a. Huawei's Quest for Self-Reliance. *East Asia Forum*, February 14. https://www.eastasiaforum.org/2020/02/14/huaweis-quest-for-self-reliance/.

Manantan, Mark. 2020b. Prospects for Trilateral Cooperation: The Philippines, Australia, and Japan. *Asia Pacific Pathways to Progress*, May 13. https:// appfi.ph/images/2020/Research/Trilateral_Cooperation_Manantan.pdf.

METI-Journal. 2019. Minister to Take the Helm in Realizing, Promoting Free Flow of Data. August 6. https://meti-journal.japantimes.co.jp/2019-06-08/2/.

METI-Journal. 2019a. Minister to Take the Helm in Realizing, Promoting Free Flow of Data. August 6. https://meti-journal.japantimes.co.jp/2019-06-08/2/.

METI-Journal. 2019b. Governance Innovation. December 26. https://www.meti. go.jp/english/press/2019/pdf/191226001.pdf.

Mizuho. 2019. Mizuho Economic Outlook and Analysis. July 2. https://www. mizuho-ri.co.jp/publication/research/pdf/eo/MEA190726.pdf.

MOFA. 2018. Announcement of the G20 Osaka Summit Invited Guest Countries and International Organizations. *Press Releases*, December 18. https://www. mofa.go.jp/press/release/press4e_002275.html.

Mun, Tang Siew, Hoang Thi Ha, Anuthida Saelaow Qian, Glen Ong, and Pham Thi Phuong Thao. 2020. *The State of Southeast Asia: 2020 Survey Report.* Singapore: ASEAN Studies Centre, ISEAS-Yusof Ishak Institute. https:// www.iseas.edu.sg/images/pdf/TheStateofSEASurveyReport_2020.pdf.

RIETI Highlight. 2019. Trade, Investment and Globalization. p. 34. https://www. rieti.go.jp/en/about/Highlight_75/Highlight_75.pdf.

Sacs, Samm. 2018. Beijing Wants to Rewrite the Rules of the Internet. *The Atlantic*, June 18. https://www.theatlantic.com/international/archive/ 2018/06/zte-huawei-china-trump-trade-cyber/563033/.

Chapter 9

Enabling Human Values in Foreign Policy: The Transformation of Taiwan's New Southbound Policy

Alan Hao Yang and Jeremy Huai-Che Chiang

Introduction

Can foreign policy embody human values? Or does it only reflect the values and interests of political and social elites? These questions are not only the focus of academic debates (Pratt 2001; Baglione 2008; Gaskarth 2013; Bayram 2016) but also public concerns across the world (Souva 2005; Schoen 2007). In the past, foreign policy was seen as the exclusive territory of the political elites, designed to uphold state interests and enhance international influence of a specific country (Headley and Reitzig 2012; Murray *et al.* 1999; Roberts 2009). In recent years, however, domestic factors are increasingly being incorporated and highlighted as key elements in foreign policy making.

In some cases, foreign policymaking seems to fulfill domestic appeals, either from within or from the society of the targeted countries. The major powers, in particular, often claim that their foreign policies are based on prevailing values for the purpose of legitimizing their influence by avoiding accusations of hegemony (Chandler 2007).

The United States, for example, instills its foreign policy with the specific features of democracy and human rights, thereby strengthening the link between American interests and universal values. As the State

Department reiterates its rationale of diplomacy in action, "promoting freedom and democracy and protecting human rights around the world are central to U.S. foreign policy" (Bureau of Democracy, 2018).

Another example is Japan's "heart-to-heart" diplomacy developed in the late 1970s. The then Fukuda Doctrine was aimed at reversing Japan's international image of militarism and reinventing closer ties with Southeast Asian countries by providing development assistance and facilitating regional growth (Lam 2007).

A recent case is China's "good neighbor" diplomacy. As China's economic and political power continues to develop, Beijing has also begun to expands its influence starting from its immediate neighboring countries (The State Council, the People's Republic of China 2015). It offers abundant economic resources and incentives through the Belt and Road Initiative (BRI), highlighting China's development model and its governance experience, and forming another kind of ideological value, that of proactive growth (Swaine 2015).

Foreign policy centered on human values is neither the prerogative of the major powers nor is it a normative proposition endorsed by the United Nations and other international organizations. This chapter argues that there are at least two connotations of human values. In terms of normative definition, human values embody the universal values of the equal economic rights, social welfare, and political rights that ensure the sustainability of human survival. Each country should be responsible for ensuring equality, openness, and freedom for its people., In operational terms, governments of all countries should prioritize policy instruments and arrangements which uphold and practice human values while safeguarding their national interests.

Foreign policy featured with human values plays an even more important role for small countries in terms of protecting their strategic interests and ensuring state survival. For example, global climate change is threatening the very existence of the Pacific island states (Howes *et al.* 2018). By all means, the Pacific island states prioritize the importance of collective action and collaboration in their foreign policies in tackling with climate risks and hazards, to defend sustainable development and environmental security. The purpose of which, of course, is to ensure the state survival and the welfare of the people in the name of safeguarding human values that are threatened by environmental degradation. Similar to its Pacific counterparts, Taiwan is an island country vulnerable to natural disasters and external political inference. It is worthwhile to explore how

Taiwan utilizes its new foreign policy undertakings and efforts to secure its survival while contributing to the regional community. Since 2016, Taiwan unfolded the New Southbound Policy (NSP) as envisaged by President Ing-wen Tsai as its "regional strategy for Asia" (Office of the President 2017). The NSP is also at the core of Tainan's Indo-Pacific strategy. The NSP is featured with its people-centered agenda deeply imbued with human values for domestic development and regional growth. This chapter highlights how the NSP responds to prevailing human values by developing social connectivity between Taiwan and its neighbors in Southeast Asia. It begins with the introduction of the NSP in securing the state survival of Taiwan. Then on, it addresses the people-centered agenda of the NSP and highlight its blueprint for transcending political constraints set on Taiwan, and for facilitating human values upheld and throughout the region.

The NSP and Taiwan's state survival

The strategic rationale underlying the NSP is to link Taiwan to the ASEAN-led regional integration process and regional communities (Yang 2016). The implementation of the NSP highlights Taiwan's strategic importance and contribution to facilitate development and growth in Asia.

Compared with previous efforts made by Taiwan government since the 1990s, the NSP's strategic thrust emphasizes people-to-people exchanges and a people-centered agenda for regional and national development in Southeast, South Asian countries, Australia, and New Zealand. It is a strategic move echoing the regional community-building process initiated by ASEAN and embraced by its dialogue partners in accordance with the prevailing values of the United Nations (Wu 2018). Moreover, the NSP is implemented in line with Taiwan's own national growth and social transformation projects.

There are three reasons to address how the NSP would facilitate Taiwan's state survival.

First, Taiwan is facing imminent economic and social transformation within the region. In terms of ensuring economic growth, it is imperative that Taiwan's domestic industries strengthen their ties with regional production networks. The NSP is aimed at securing the economic interests and welfare of Taiwanese people in the region by setting up and upgrading institutional arrangements in trade, investment, and related fields. Moreover, institutional connectivity between Taiwan and Southeast Asia needs to move beyond economic issues toward technology, education, public health, and agriculture. And in terms of social development, the number of immigrants and foreign workers in Taiwan has been increasing since the 1990s, most of whom come from Southeast Asia (Shaw 2017). Currently, there account for 3% of Taiwan's population, with over 600,000 people from Southeast Asia, increasingly transforming how Taiwanese perceive themselves and their relationship with the region (Chiang and Yang 2018). The need for taking good care of their rights and welfare is in great demand. By safeguarding human rights and labor rights of migrant workers and ensuring fair access to education and social welfare for "new immigrants" living in Taiwan, the government would be demonstrating its determination to address human values in relation to the value of development in Asia.

Second, the NSP can be seen as Taiwan's strategic move to support the ASEAN-led regional community building masterplan. As ASEAN has been developing a people-centered regional community for more than five decades, its governments and societies are prioritizing human values in regional development upon its three pillars: the ASEAN Political Community, the ASEAN Economic Community, and the ASEAN Social Community (Mahbubani and Sng 2017; Natalegawa 2018). Over the past two decades, Taiwan has devoted itself to promoting political development, accelerating economic prosperity, and facilitating social stability by highlighting the dignity of its people, improving quality of life, and fostering a vibrant civil society. The NSP is a crucial bridge in the development of regional prosperity among Taiwan and like-minded stakeholders.

Finally, Taiwan needs to respond diplomatic restrictions imposed by China through developing new pragmatic partnerships with its Asian neighbors. This challenge will not be easily resolved anytime soon in the near future, as China still firmly maintains its aggressive claims on Taiwan. This antagonism toward Taiwan is also being increasingly enhanced by the upsurge and state-support of reckless nationalism among its citizens. For a long time, Beijing has tried to frame Cross-Strait relations in an arbitrary manner (Bloomberg News 2018), treating the values of Taiwanese people with disdain and restricting this island country from being normally integrated as a part of the international society (Horton 2017; Kyodo News 2018). One recent example of this is China's intervention to exclude Taiwan from the World Health Assembly (WHA), which has deprived Taiwanese people of sharing valuable experience in public health with the world and disrupting the Asian and global epidemic prevention system. China's opposition to Taiwan's developmental role in the region is a loss for everyone but itself. If Taiwan is prevented from defending its people's rights or from participating in international organizations, the human values of its people and those of citizens of other countries will be endangered.

These factors demonstrate how Taiwan needs to prioritize human values in its foreign policy posture to secure its state survival. In this regard, the NSP can develop common interests and values, and strive for more regional links and international ties. This also makes the NSP more relevant to the people both in Taiwan and Asia.

The NSP: A people-centered foreign policy

The Democratic Progressive Party (DPP) as the ruling party in Taiwan since 2016 prioritized the NSP as its flagship foreign policy stance along with its people-centered agenda (Hsiao and Yang 2022). The NSP-related initiatives envisaged an ever-closer relationship between Taiwan and Southeast Asia and South Asia through heightened awareness of regional community. Its purpose is to reinforce Taiwan's "warm power" contributing to economic integration and social stability of Asia (Public Television Service Foundation 2018).

As its diplomatic allies have severed their ties with Taipei under the political pressure and economic inducement from China, Taiwan only has 17 diplomatic allies out of more than 200 countries in the world, none of which are in Asia. In addition to defending its relationship with allies, this island country's foreign policy needs to actively engage in different fronts. The people-centered rationale of the NSP reflects the changing mentality of Taiwan's foreign policy making. It is Taiwan's continuous effort that relocates itself in Asia by upholding human values in regional development agendas.

For Taiwan, emphasizing the people-centered development agenda can highlight its experiences and resources in promoting sustainable development and inclusive growth manifesting as human values shared by Taiwan and its Asian neighbors. Since 2016, Taiwan reinvigorated these experiences and resources into the substantial content of the NSP from four issue-areas (economic collaboration, people-to-people exchanges, resource sharing, and regional links) to five flagship programs, that is, *industrial innovation and cooperation, industrial talent development, medical and public health cooperation, regional agricultural development*, and setting up regional and national platforms and forums such as the "Yushan Forum: Asian Dialogue for Innovation and Progress." The five flagship programs have so fa produced encouraging results (Hsiao and Yang 2022). The flagship program on *industrial innovation and cooperation* is designed to strengthen regional ties on industrial innovation between Taiwan and its Asian counterparts in the field of green energy and technology, industrial network, and smart machinery. The focus of cooperation is not only on facilitating commodity trade of technological collaboration, but also on consolidating institutional linkage with regional counterparts. For example, as the NSP emphasizes the importance of India and South Asia, the Indian cabinet approved the signing of a Bilateral Investment Agreement between India and Taiwan in October 2018, which will increase investment flows between both sides and facilitate better environment for investment in both countries (Press Information Bureau 2018).

In terms of *industrial talents cultivation*, Taiwan plans to establish institutional platforms for bi-directional exchanges and then strengthen its multi-faceted engagement in Asia. In addition, the Taiwan government and its civil society are paying extensive attention to Southeast Asian and South Asian residents in localities with its empowerment and capacity building projects. They can together become important linkages and stakeholders for Taiwan and Asia to make progress. Since 2016, increasing numbers of students from Southeast Asia and South Asia to study in universities and colleges in Taiwan. In 2019, Taiwan aims to receive and train 58,000 young talents in higher education from the region (Focus Taiwan News Channel 2018).

With regard to *medical and public health cooperation*, Taiwan is implementing the "One County One Center" (1C1C) project, linking up the national hub of hospital collaboration in the Philippines, Vietnam, Thailand, Malaysia, Indonesia, and India with Taiwan's counterpart hospitals for the purpose of upgrading collaboration in public health, medical services, and in establishing transnational disease prevention network. Moreover, facilitated by the Ministry of Health and Welfare, the New Southbound Market Healthcare Union will prioritize its ties with local hospital and medical service network in Southeast Asia (Taiwan News 2018).

In the area of *regional agriculture*, the NSP focuses on common interests in agricultural industry, sustainable development, and local empowerment in rural area. One successful example of "Agricultural

Demonstration Farm (ADF)" is set in Karawang in Indonesia with a specific focus on facilitating irrigation, rice cultivation, horticulture, smart agriculture, and farmer training, while also securing food security through bilateral and regional undertakings (Chairunnisa 2018). Not only in Indonesia, the Philippines is also partnering with Taiwan through joint venture agreement in setting up the ADF at localities to produce high-value crops (Hou and Yeh 2018).

Finally, Taiwan pledges to organize new regional dialogues for sharing ideas and practices of regional development. The Yushan Forum, Taiwan initiated and annually held, is one of the key mechanisms to promote warm power diplomacy and seek for more participation from regional stakeholders. In 2018, this Taiwan-initiated regional platform hosted by the Taiwan-Asia Exchange Foundation (TAEF) attracted more than 1,000 participants from Taiwan and neighboring countries. There were 51 representatives from 17 countries, including international leaders such as Nobel Peace Prize laureates Frederik Willem de Klerk and Kailash Satyarthi to address the human values and people-centered development agenda for regional prosperity (Yang and Chiang 2018).

In Taiwan, the people-centered agenda and practice of the NSP enjoys solid support from within. It is encouraging that according to public opinion surveys conducted by MOFA in 2016 and 2017, the NSP enjoyed supports from the majority of Taiwanese people. In 2016, 71% of respondents said they were "satisfied" with the policy, while 80% said they were "supportive" of it (Taiwan Today Agencies 2017).

Highlighting people-centered regional and global values

Taiwan's President Ing-wen Tsai emphasizes strengthening "values-based diplomacy" with "like-minded" international partners as a way to secure its survival niche (Tiezzi 2018). The NSP is her flagship foreign policy initiative to promote its values-based diplomacy in Asia and with like-minded partners.

As the NSP is to promote the regional identity and human values shared by the Taiwanese people and the region, rather than merely exporting a so-called "Taiwan model" to neighboring countries. Its "soft branding" looks at reinforcing solid partnerships between Taiwan and regional stakeholders in tacking development challenges. In other words, Taiwan is seeking to develop regional recognition that will eventually lead to more regional collaboration. The prevailing regional and global values are also the values that are being promoted by Taiwan. To this end, Taiwan can contribute to the modalities of good governance and share its practice on how these challenges can be addressed common interests can be shaped. The process of sharing and cultivating partnerships facilitates linkages between human and regional values.

At a regional level, since ASEAN began its community-building process in the late 1990s, it has sought to promote a people-centered agenda by underlining the importance of human values in regional integration (Morada 2008). For instance, the ASEAN Economic Community (AEC) plans to accelerate regional economic growth by creating a single production base and an integrated market. The economic benefits of this undertaking will be shared with the people of ASEAN. The ASEAN Political Security Community (APSC) is aimed at creating a stable environment for political development that will protect the rights and interests of its people. The ASEAN Social and Cultural Community (ASCC) is being developed in response to the new transnational challenges, regional connectivity and economic integration. Its purpose is to encourage social transformation and foster multicultural values.

Taiwan has been aware of the community-building process in ASEAN for the past two decades. It is therefore keen to utilize the NSP to catch up and be included in the process of the ongoing regionalization. Now that ASEAN members are embracing the idea of ASEAN Connectivity, with the purpose of establishing transnational connections among institutions, infrastructures, and people, Taiwan is eager to share its experience in developing soft infrastructure and good governance as well as participating in physical infrastructure projects.

With regard to the APSC, Taiwan is firmly in favor of securing regional peace and stability, and hopes to promote this with values of good governance. Taiwan's responses to the AEC and the ASCC are embodied in the NSP's five flagship programs as well as in the potential policy areas such as e-commerce, infrastructure, and tourism.

At a global level, these efforts also show that Taiwan's NSP is moving toward the practice of value diplomacy corresponding to the Sustainable Development Goals upheld by the United Nations (see Figure 1). The flagship program on industrial innovation and cooperation, for example, addresses six SDGs out of seventeen goals, such as "affordable and clean energy," "decent work and economic growth," "industry innovation and infrastructure," "reduced inequalities," "responsible consumption and production," "climate action," and "partnership for the goals." In effect,

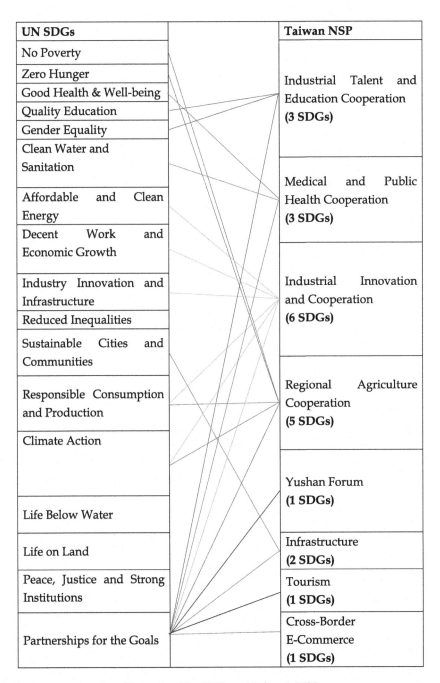

Figure 1: The SDGs and Taiwan's NSP

13 out of 17 SDGs are addressed by the NSP's flagship programs as well as its potential policy engagement areas. In this regard, the NSP not only ensures Taiwan's national interests, but more importantly, implements the vision of regional and global co-prosperity with human values through bilateral and multilateral engagement.

In defense of regional and global human values, Taiwan's NSP has at least three significant features: material sharing, capacity upgrading, and identity making.

First, at the material level, the promotion of the NSP represents Taiwan's provision of material resources and support toward its neighbors, and cooperation with their local communities in building production bases or securing common development needs. Taiwan does not aim to act alone, but instead seeks to work in tandem with local efforts. In countries or localities with insufficient development opportunities in Asia, Taiwan is working together with local partners in providing equal educational opportunities for people, building facilities such as water pumping stations, and developing specific local assistance programs. Material sharing by Taiwan can contribute in freeing people from the threat of hunger, and provide them the opportunity to access sufficient food and clothing.

Second, in other Asian countries or societies that have already attained foundations for further development, Taiwan's NSP focuses more on promoting or enhancing the development capabilities of its partners. This is the idea and practice of "from mere possessing to attaining excellence." Through the sharing of resources and experiences of development, the NSP facilitates the government and people of partner countries in adopting a sustainable and balanced inclusive growth model, translating the results of bilateral cooperation into a reference for the government and people's self-improvement.

From the perspective of education and talent cultivation cooperation, this is not just about providing school hardware, but to introduce the supplementary concepts of education and empowerment, so that more talents may be developed for local needs. A good example is the Taiwan–Indonesia joint project in ADF is the Karawang mentioned earlier. This is not a trailblazing mission to open new farmlands, but instead aims to upgrade agricultural practices and irrigation systems, and promote the development of "Smart Agriculture." This project is embodied in the spirit that people should not be left in hunger and destitution, but should have a better, more sustainable livelihood in which adequate food and clothing should not be a distant dream.

Third, in addition to the advancement of material and capabilities, the NSP strives to enable the establishment of a regional community identity, which will be embedded within and supported through the deeper mutual understanding and interaction between people in the region. These people-to-people exchanges are not limited to political and social elites, or to only businessmen and young leaders. By intimate interaction and dialogue, and by sharing common concerns, embracing common interests and executing common endeavors, social actors from different backgrounds and nationalities in the region become part of other living world experience. Through intensive cooperation, Taiwan and the people of neighboring countries can jointly advance the goal of "from good to common prosperity". This is not only a value upheld by Taiwan and neighboring countries, but also commonly shared by the world.

Linking societies and people as a regional community

The NSP is not a short-term policy initiative; rather, it is a long-term self-reform of Taiwan. It proceeds with a specific blueprint of "in-ward looking" regional engagement in promoting human values through public and private partnership. Its sustainability requires the engagement of various stakeholders and partnerships through new synergies. For Taiwan, the particularity of the NSP is related to the nature of Taiwan's immigrant society. While developing its "regional strategy for Asia," Taiwan needs to prioritize the welfare and rights of Southeast Asian communities in Taiwan. It would be an encouraging model of enabling human values in foreign policy for countries in Asia.

We believe that there are at least two modalities of domestic efforts to localize the people-centered NSP in Taiwan society: one is the efforts made by the Taiwan's public sector, and the other is the capacity building projects and social engagements initiated by civil society. The former has mostly ensured the basic rights of migrant communities of Southeast Asia in Taiwan, while the later focuses on the enhancement of their welfare and consolidates mutual understanding among people in Taiwan and the region.

It is true that public sectors in Taiwan have been devoted to ensuring the basic rights and interests of immigrant in Taiwan. Some further steps are made by Taiwan government through the implementation of the NSP. In 2018, there are 696,000 migrant workers in Taiwan, of which 260,000 are from Indonesia, 210,000 from Vietnam, and 150,000 from the Philippines. Taiwan government has been committed to providing basic protection for migrant workers, as well as ensuring labor rights, and adopting equal standards of minimum wage for both domestic and migrant workers.

In this regard, Taiwan's National Immigration Agency (NIA) has increased its capacity in protecting the labor rights and securing the interests of migrant workers from the guaranteeing basic minimum wage and promoting the Respite Care Service for special domestic caregivers. For years, there is a number of migrant workers in Taiwan who had fled out of factories for different reasons, called by governments in the past as "runaway migrant workers." The NIA has recently adjusted the term "runaway migrant workers" with "foreign workers lost in contact." It not only shows the changing mentality of bureaucrats but also shows Taiwan's respect for the basic human rights and human values of its economic partners.

In the seaports of Taiwan, due to the population shift to urban cities and insufficient labor resources, migrant workers are in great demand in the fishing industry. The labor rights of fishermen have not been properly taken care of, especially in cases of overseas employment, which has become a concern for Taiwan government and civil society. In Yilan, Yilan Migrant Fisherman Union (YMFU) was set up in 2013 with specific focus on protecting and ensuring labor rights and basic rights of Indonesian and Pilipino migrant fishermen. The YMFU has long been committed to the care of fishermen and provides training courses. Its Secretary-General, Allison Lee, with her contribution, was awarded as "Hero Acting to End Modern Slavery Award" from the U.S. State Department in 2017 (Everington 2017).

For decades, many migrant fishermen from Indonesia have been working for the local village of Donggang Township, a famous port in southern Taiwan. They raised a total of NTD 7 million to set up a Donggang Mosque which has become a religious center for Indonesian migrant fishermen there, valued and respected by local people. Taiwan's NIA also assists in recruiting resources for the Mosque in providing facilities or computer classroom to facilitate capacity building program for migrant workers.

In addition to, upgrading and capacity building programs, more efforts are made by Taiwan's social enterprises. One-Forty, one of the leading NGOs working on capacity building program for migrant workers in Taiwan, pledges to establish a "Business School for Migrant Workers" with free courses, including classes for Chinese language, savings, business, and photography on the weekend. Those who are trained during their stay in Taiwan — initially beginning with only 10 students, now has increased to 400 every year — have successfully operated businesses after returning to their home countries. Moreover, One-Forty is offering online courses for more than 22,000 subscribers. Labor workers are helped by newly acquired talents, subsequently, then become civilian ambassadors of Taiwan when they return to Indonesia, the Philippines, and Vietnam.

The exchanges and understanding between Taiwan and Asian neighbors should not be limited to the areas of economic, commerce, investment, or migration issues. In particular, bilateral exchanges on cultures and arts would be meaningfully to contribute to deeper social understanding of Taiwan and Asian societies. For example, Vietnam National Institute of Culture and Arts Studies (VICAS) under Vietnam's Ministry of Culture, Sport, and Tourism worked with Taiwan-Asia Exchange Foundation (TAEF) and National Culture and Art Foundation (NCAF) in developing cultural leaders and artists exchange in late 2018. A delegation of contemporary artists, as the first group of VICAS for bilateral exchange, was invited to Taiwan for in-depth visit and dialogues with local counterparts. They not only learned that the development of contemporary art in Taiwan has been deeply influenced by its historical legacy, political development, economic and social transformation and also believe that the display of art is the best projection of Taiwan's civil society and human values. Through the exchange of art, it can better overcome the obstacles of languages and foster a genuine community for Taiwan and Vietnam.

Conclusion

Human values are the positive driving force for the advancement of national and regional development. Taiwan seeks to defend and ensure human values in partnership with regional stakeholders with the same goals that regional governments and civil societies aspire to. Human values should not be represented as negative quantitative indicators, or a social credibility waiting to be deducted (Hatton 2015), nor should they be mere slogans used by the government to sustain the regime. They should be people-oriented, not people-targeted.

It is not easy for any country to enable human values in its foreign policy. As some major powers utilize "sharp power" (Walker and Ludwig 2017) to impose their ideology on others, what they are promoting is pursuing hegemony over other countries, rather than promoting human values for all. When it is practiced by small states, diplomacy with human values is more likely to be ignored or brought into question because these small powers have insufficient resources or lacks commitment. But Taiwan is not such a case.

Taiwan is a small state that has endured decades of political constraints imposed on it by China. These constraints have limited the island's ability to contribute to the international community. However, Taiwan has also undergone a long period of economic transition and social transformation. Based on Taiwan's record of good governance, people-centered political development, and foreign policy transformation, the NSP is able to contribute to the promotion of human values and the realization of regional community in Asia. While President Tsai's predecessor focused too much on Taiwan's relations with China, the current administration has worked vigorously to relocate Taiwan into the ongoing dynamism in Asia. This new value-based NSP bases itself on the humanistic aspirations that are shared by most Taiwanese politicians from both sides of the aisle. While as a democratic country, Taiwan inevitably experiences electoral power transitions, its people and leaders should be aware that Taiwan's human values and progressive achievements, not only its military and economic capacities, are key to its own state survival. It should strive to share its resources and experiences for the betterment of its surrounding neighbors.

Taiwan's execution of its NSP is not without its own set of challenges. While China's aggression is a constant background factor, the hesitance of other regional countries to expand relations with Taiwan due to their fear of upsetting China may also limit the success of the NSP. In light of that, Taiwan should not proceed with unilateral actions, but instead treat carefully the cautious feelings of its neighbors, and strive to carve out innovative collaboration linkages that may contribute to stability and development in the region. Taiwan must maintain an active role while avoid being too high-profile, so that it may not cause the unease of its partners.

And on the other hand, the Taiwanese government needs to communicate its policy objectives to its people with more clarity, to inform the public the necessity of comprehensive engagement with neighboring countries and not only focusing on trade and investment. While economic cooperation is important and one of the key concerns of the Taiwanese public, people-to-people relations must also be emphasized so that the NSP may continue to progress organically into the future after the policy's execution, not only in the public sector but also among the civil societies within the region.

The execution of the NSP may be challenging, but it is the right path to take if one envisions a region embedded in human values, with Taiwan playing an active role in this evolution. Taiwan's NSP embodies a people-centered and people-oriented agenda for regional development, one which utilizes its economic and social resources to develop new regional economic network and social partnership. Only by emphasizing human values and the prosperity of the entire regional community, can we persuade Taiwan's international partners to actively support Taiwan's existence and contribution, thus ensuring Taiwan's role as a key link in global development.

References

Baglione, L. A. 2008. Emphasizing Principles for a Moral Foreign Policy. *American Behavioral Scientist* 51(9): 1303–1321.

Bayram, A. B. 2016. Values and Prosocial Behaviour in the Global Context: Why Values Predict Public Support for Foreign Development Assistance to Developing Countries. *Journal of Human Values* 22(2): 93–106.

Bloomberg News. 2018. U.S. Airlines Alter Websites to Meet China's Demand on Taiwan's Name. *Bloomberg.* p. 168. https://www.bloomberg.com/news/articles/2018-07-25/u-s-airlines-alter-websites-to-meet-china-demand-on-taiwan-name.

Bureau of Democracy, Human Rights, and Labor, the United States. Department of State. p. 166. https://www.state.gov/j/drl/index.htm.

Chairunnisa, Shafira. 2018. RI Set to Reap Rewards to Taiwan's NSP. *Jakarta Post.* http://www.thejakartapost.com/news/2018/07/11/ri-set-reap-rewards-taiwan-s-nsp.html.

Chandler, D. 2007. Hollow Hegemony: Theorising the Shift from Interest-Based to Value-Based International Policy-Making. *Millennium* 35(3): 703–723.

Chiang, J. and A. H. Yang 2018. A Nation Reborn? Taiwan's Belated Recognition of Its Southeast Asian Heritage. *The Diplomat.* https://thediplomat.com/2018/09/a-nation-reborn-taiwans-belated-recognition-of-its-southeast-asian-heritage/.

Everington, Keoni. 2017. Taiwanese Hailed as "Hero" by U.S. State Department. *Taiwan News.* https://www.taiwannews.com.tw/en/news/3198441.

Focus Taiwan News Channel. 2018. Taiwan Universities See Rise in Number of Southeast Asian Students. *Focus Taiwan News Channel*. http://focustaiwan. tw/news/aftr/201810050024.aspx.

Gaskarth, J. 2013. Interpreting Ethical Foreign Policy: Traditions and Dilemmas for Policymakers. *The British Journal of Politics and International Relations* 15(2): 192–209.

Hatton, C. 2015. China "Social Credit": Beijing Sets Up Huge System. *BBC News*. https://www.bbc.com/news/world-asia-china-34592186.

Headley, J. and A. Reitzig. 2012. Does Foreign Policy Represent the Views of the Public? Assessing Public and Elite Opinion on New Zealand's Foreign Policy. *Australian Journal of International Affairs* 66(1): 70–89.

Horton, C. 2017. Blocked by China, Taiwan Presses to Join U.N. Agency's Meeting. *The New York Times*. p. 168. from:https://www.nytimes.com/2017/05/08/world/asia/taiwan-world-health-china-.html.

Hou, E. and J. Yeh. 2018. New Southbound Policy Bearing Fruit: Philippines Envoy. *Focus Taiwan News Channel*. http://focustaiwan.tw/news/afav/201808050003.aspx.

Howes, E. L., S. Birchenough, and S. Lincoln. 2018. Effects of Climate Change Relevant to the Pacific Islands. *Pacific Marine Climate Change Report Card Science Review* (2018): 1–19.

Hsiao, Hsin-Huang and Yang, A.H. 2022. The New Southbound Policy: Startegizing Taiwan's Warm Power Practice. Taipei: Taiwan-Asia Exchange Foundation.

Kyodo News. 2018. China Says Taiwan Not Invited to U.N. Health Meeting. *ABS-CBN News*. p. 168. https://news.abs-cbn.com/overseas/05/07/18/china-says-taiwan-not-invited-to-un-health-meeting.

Lam, P. E. 2007. Japan's Quest for "Soft Power": Attraction and Limitation. *East Asia* 24(4): 349–363.

Mahbubani, K. and J. Sng. 2017. *The ASEAN Miracle: A Catalyst for Peace.* Singapore: The National University of Singapore Press.

Morada, N. M. 2008. ASEAN at 40: Prospects for Community Building in Southeast Asia. *Asia-Pacific Review* 15(1): 36–55.

Murray, S. K., J. A. Cowden, and B. M. Russett. 1999. The Convergence of American Elites' Domestic Beliefs with Their Foreign Policy Beliefs. *International Interaction* 25(2): 153–180.

Natalegawa, M. 2018. *Does ASEAN Matter? A View from Within.* Singapore: ISEAS.

Office of the President. 2017. President Tsai Holds 2017 Year-End Press Conference. *Office of the President, the Republic of China.* https://english.president.gov.tw/News/5313.

Pratt, C. 2001. Ethical Values and Canadian Foreign Policy: Two Case Studies. *International Journal* 56(1): 37–53.

Press Information Bureau. 2018. Cabinet approves signing of Bilateral Investment Agreement between India Taipei Association in Taipei and the Taipei

Economic and Cultural Center in India. Government of India, Cabinet. http://
pib.nic.in/newsite/printRelease.aspx?relid=184328&fbclid=IwAR1ZzjVbhF
OSGX2wPpFCX5WE21Wo5XBl8gARLNnKs8ubKgBGUJVAwll42hU.
Public Television Service Foundation. 2018. Warm Power against China's
Pressure: Foreign Ministry. *Public Television Service Foundation.* https://
news.pts.org.tw/article/410093.
Roberts, P. 2009. The Transatlantic American Foreign Policy Elite: Its Evolution
in Generational Perspective. *Journal of Transatlantic Studies* 7(2):
163–183.
Schoen, H. 2007. Personality Traits and Foreign Policy Attitudes in German
Public Opinion. *Journal of Conflict Resolution* 51(3): 408–430.
Shaw, I. 2017. Taiwan's Southward Turn Aligns with Demographic Reality.
Global Taiwan Brief 2(29). http://globaltaiwan.org/2017/07/26-gtb-2-29/.
Souva, M. 2005. Foreign Policy Determinants: Comparing Realist and Domestic-
Political Models of Foreign Policy. *Conflict Management and Peace Science*
22(2): 149–163.
Swaine, M. D. 2015. Chinese Views and Commentary on the One Belt, One Road
Initiative. *China Leadership Monitor* 47(2): 3–27.
Taiwan News. 2018. Taiwan Forms Healthcare Union of 17 Hospitals Targeting
Southeast Asian Countries. *Taiwan News.* https://www.taiwannews.com.tw/
en/news/3466044.
Taiwan Today Agencies. 2017. Poll Finds Overwhelming Support in Taiwan
for New Southbound Policy. *Taiwan Today.* https://taiwantoday.tw/news.
php?unit=2,6,10,15,18&post=120306.
The State Council of the People's Republic of China. 2015. Chronology of
China's Belt and Road Initiative. English.Gov.Cn. http://english.gov.cn/
news/top_news/2015/04/20/content_281475092566326.htm.
Tiezzi, S. 2018. Facing Chinese Pressure, Taiwan's President Tsai Seeks
"Survival Niche." *The Diplomat.* https://thediplomat.com/2018/10/facing-
chinese-pressure-taiwans-president-tsai-seeks-survival-niche/.
Walker, C. and J. Ludwig. 2017. From 'Soft Power' to 'Sharp Power': Rising
Authoritarian Influence in the Democratic World. *Sharp Power: Rising
Authoritarian Influence.* National Endowment of Democracy. https://www.
ned.org/sharp-power-rising-authoritarian-influence-forum-report/
Wu, J. 2018. Taiwan Can Help the UN Achieve Its Goals. *The Diplomat.* https://
thediplomat.com/2018/09/taiwan-can-help-the-un-achieve-its-goals/.
Yang, A. H. 2016. "Contextualizing Taiwan's New Southbound Policy in ASEAN
Community: The Need to Prioritize Mutual Interests." *Prospect Journal* 16: 25–48.
Yang, A. H. and J. Chiang. 2018. Taiwan is Retaking the Initiative With Its
New Southbound Policy. *The Diplomat.* https://thediplomat.com/2018/10/
taiwan-is-retaking-the-initiative-with-its-new-southbound-policy.

Part III
Regional Consideration

Chapter 10

Navigating the Regional Geo-Economic Climate and Fostering Economic Transformation: Considerations for Malaysia

Ivy Kwek

Introduction

Southeast Asia is fast becoming one of the most contested regions in the battle for strategic superiority and economic dominance. While in the past, strategic control was predicated on military strength, economic power is increasingly becoming the form of statecraft used to exert control, particularly by the great powers seeking to achieve their geopolitical goals. The line between economic interests and strategic objectives has been blurred, leading to the coining of the term "geo-economics." Whereas "geopolitics" is often used to refer to the "the links between geography, state territoriality, and world power politics," geo-economics "concerns a nation's pursuit of strong economic performance and sustainable economic competitiveness," with the two being strongly intertwined (Yu 2017).

In Southeast Asia, the rise of China as a dominant economic force has caused concern that it might use its economic muscle to arm-twist the smaller countries in the region into deference, especially in relation to the long-standing territorial disputes in the South China Sea. A precedent for this was observed when some smaller countries in the European Union (EU) with strong economic ties with China backed down from criticizing Beijing on human rights issues (Leonard *et al.* 2019). Although Southeast Asia welcomes Chinese investments, concern over the sustainability of some of the projects and the risk of a "debt trap" has caused some to rethink and renegotiate their partnerships.

The United States' categorization of China as a strategic competitor also ushered in a new era of great power rivalry which has now spilled over into the economic sphere, as can be seen from the U.S.–China trade war. Increasingly, great power competition is also manifested in Southeast Asia with a race for investments, creating what Kuik (2021) has characterized as a "twin-chessboard" situation. In 2017, the Trump administration launched the Free and Open Indo-Pacific (FOIP) Strategy, reviving the term "Indo-Pacific" to describe the vast region which embraces what used to be known as the Asia-Pacific (including East and Southeast Asia) and South Asia. The forerunners of the "Indo-Pacific" vision — the United States, Japan, Australia, and India — also spearheaded the Quadrilateral Dialogue (QUAD) mechanism. Although in the past, partners of the United States in the region, such as Japan and India, have trod lightly in order not to displease China, they have been more forthcoming in QUAD cooperation in recent years.

Now, more countries are using the term Indo-Pacific and developing strategies for engagement in the region, albeit with different iterations of the vision. This includes France, Germany, the Netherlands, and the EU as a whole. The Association of Southeast Asian Nations (ASEAN) has also published the ASEAN Outlook on the Indo-Pacific (ASEAN 2019), seen as an attempt to offer a moderate and inclusive vision for the region.

The central theme in these geopolitical shifts is undoubtedly China. Indeed, China presents both an opportunity and a risk for regional countries. Middle powers and smaller countries want to do business with China, but at the same time they are wary of China's efforts to expand its diplomatic influence, military strength, and economic prowess in the region.

Malaysia, as a key member of ASEAN, is not immune to these global trends. Malaysia has an open economy that relies on export-oriented growth, and its industries, particularly in the manufacturing sector, have benefited greatly from foreign investment. This relatively open approach, coupled with a developmental state, led to economic success in the 1990s, to the extent that Malaysia was considered one of the four "Asian Tigers."

Malaysia has always maintained a neutral, friends-to-all posture and has avoided choosing sides in the U.S.–China strategic competition. So far, it has been quite successful in compartmentalizing its security challenges and economic relations. However, if the great powers persist in their competitive approach to economic relations, most notably in the form of techno-nationalism, it is feared that smaller states might soon be compelled to take sides. This will hamper Malaysia in its effort to transform itself into a high-income country, with high-value industry and high paying jobs, through foreign direct investment (FDI) and trade.

Economically, Malaysia is facing mounting competition from countries that offer more competitive labor costs and more abundant natural resources. While it has been successful in transforming itself from low- to a middle-income country, it is now languishing in the middle-income trap and urgently needs to transform into a high-income nation.

The COVID-19 pandemic has increased the need for economic reform in Malaysia, just as it has changed much of the calculus of regional cooperation. Malaysia's net foreign investment fell 56%, from 31.7 billion ringgit in 2019 to 13.9 billion ringgit (US$3.43 billion) in 2020, while its GDP contracted by 5.6% over the same period — the country's worst economic performance since the Asian financial crisis of 1997 (Sipalan 2021).

COVID-19 and geopolitical tension have also caused a rethink on supply chain resilience in the region, particularly where strategic and essential goods are concerned. In particular, disruptions to supply chains due to the negative supply shocks and positive/negative demand shocks have motivated some to nearshore or reshore production, and the U.S.–China decoupling as well as the unpredictability of Chinese strategic attitudes have caused some to adopt the China+1 model.

More consideration is needed to safeguard Malaysia's interests in this new geo-economic climate, and at the same time overcome the inertia that is preventing it from transforming its economy.

Research Questions and Structure of the Chapter

In this chapter, I will attempt to answer the following questions. How dependent is Malaysia on foreign investment, and to what extent is the significance of its foreign investment caused Malaysia to be beholden by its investors? Will Malaysia be able to withstand the impact of the growing strategic competition between the United States and China in the geo-economic realm? What role might Malaysia play in the regional economic integration?

The chapter is divided into four sections. In the first, I will explore Malaysia's economic development from a historical perspective and demonstrate the impact of FDI and global trade on the Malaysian economy. In the second, I examine Malaysia's perception of "economic security" and its efforts to demonstrate its agency as a small state in handling what is deemed not to accord with its wider interests. The third section consists of a discussion of Malaysia's involvement in regional economic arrangements, notably the Belt and Road Initiative (BRI), the Regional Comprehensive Economic Partnership (RCEP), and the Comprehensive and Progressive Agreement for Trans-Pacific Partnership (CPTPP), and offers an analysis of the benefits and implications of this involvement for Malaysia, taking into consideration the complexity of the country's political and social fabric. In the final section, I offer some suggestions on how Malaysia can avoid the pitfalls that it might face as a small state in the midst of intensified strategic competition, and how it can enhance its economic security while carrying out much needed economic reform.

Malaysia's Economic Development and Foreign Direct Investment — The Historical Context

Malaysia is a middle-income country that has benefited from being an open economy. Having gained independence in 1957, the young nation enjoyed great success as it adopted an export-oriented economic model. Given that the country was blessed with an abundance of natural resources, in particular tin and rubber, its primary sector accounted for 45% of Malaysia's total exports in the year of independence. As the two commodities dwindled, palm oil production was encouraged and incentivized to the extent that Malaysia became the world's largest producer of palm oil in the early 1970s.

Malaysia's transformation from an agrarian to a manufacturing-based economy has been touted as an economic success. By 2019, the share of agriculture in Malaysia's GDP had dropped to around 7%, while the share of the manufacturing sector grew from 10% in 1960 to 22% in 2019 (Figure 1) (World Bank Database).

FDI played a huge role in spurring economic growth in Malaysia, which had one of the region's fastest growing economies before the Asian

Figure 1: Contribution of Agriculture, Forestry, and Fisheries to Malaysia's GDP (%), 1960–2015

Source: World Bank Database. https://data.worldbank.org/indicator/NV.AGR.TOTL.ZS? locations=MY (accessed 31 July 2021).

financial crisis in 1998. The state played an important role in this through its industrial policy. After Malaysia gained independence from the United Kingdom in 1957, concerted efforts were made to attract FDI and enable import-substituting industrialization (ISI), particularly by developing the country's infrastructure and offering credit facilities, with British companies being among the first to seize the opportunities offered (Gomez and Jomo 1997). Beginning in the 1960s, Malaysia started to pursue export-oriented industrialization, attracting FDI through the provision of free trade zones, infrastructure, incentives, and other supportive interventions contained in the Investment Incentives Act of 1968. Meanwhile, ISI continued, aided by a high level of tariff protection for local firms as well as the adoption of the New Economic Policy (NEP) in 1971, which aimed to uplift the socioeconomic status of the native Malays (or *Bumiputera,* sons of the soil) via a series of affirmative action policies.

By the 1980s, the advanced heavy industrialization policy launched during the tenure of Dr. Mahathir Mohamed, Malaysia's longest serving prime minister, led to several initiatives, most notably the production of Malaysia's first national car, the Proton, via the establishment of the Heavy Industries Corporation of Malaysia (HICOM) in collaboration with

Japanese companies. Unfortunately, the economic successes under Mahathir's premiership were marred by crony capitalism and hampered by high-profile losses and failures (Figures 2 and 3).

In 1982, Mahathir also launched the Look East Policy under which East Asia, particularly Japan, was looked upon as a role model because of its economic success and cultural finesse. Indeed, Malaysia benefitted from the Japan-led "Flying Geese Model," and Mahathir hoped that the Japanese model, including Japan's discipline and culture of hard work, could be replicated in Malaysia. Japanese investment in Malaysia soared in the mid-1980s, encouraged by a drastic appreciation of the yen against the U.S. dollar as well as the deregulation of foreign equity ownership provided through the Promotion of Investment Act (1986).

While Japan's economic success was a pull factor, the Look East Policy also marked a shift in attitudes and an attempt to diversify Malaysia's economic partnerships away from the developed countries of the West. It coincided with the 1981 "buy British last" campaign, launched after Mahathir took offense at several British policies on Malaysia and criticism of his premiership. These policies included the withdrawal of tuition subsidies for Malaysian students studying in Britain (many of whom were sponsored by the government) and criticism of the New Economic Policy (Leifer 1994). Internationally, Mahathir was also a frontrunner in the push for "Asian values."

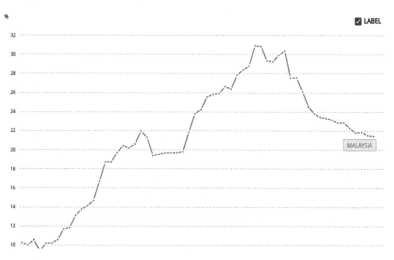

Figure 2: Contribution of Manufacturing Sector to GDP, Malaysia (%)

Source: World Bank Database. https://data.worldbank.org/indicator/NV.IND.MANF.ZS?contextual=default&end=2020&locations=MY&start=2000&view=chart (accessed July 31, 2021).

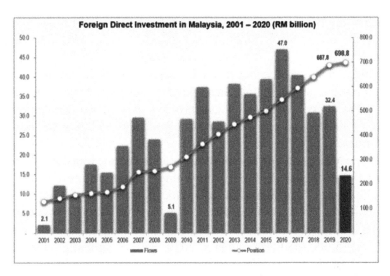

Figure 3: Foreign Direct Investment in Malaysia, Flows and Position, 2001–2020, RM Billion

Note: 1 USD = myR4.16 (June 2021).

Source: Department of Statistics, Malaysia. https://www.dosm.gov.my/v1/index.php?r=column/cthemeByCat&cat=322&bul_id=WjJ6NU94Z3haUHEzcUxMaEdVbVVBQT09&menu_id=azJjRWpYL0VBYU90TVhpclByWjdMQT09 (accessed July 31, 2021).

The economic boom led to Mahathir's introduction in 1991 of "Vision 2020" which aspired to see Malaysia becoming a developed nation by that date. However, the Asian financial crisis in 1997 hit Malaysia hard, causing a near meltdown of the economy. The crisis was a wake-up call, exposing the vulnerability of Malaysia's currency and economy to external factors. In response, Malaysia opted for an unconventional approach, going against International Monetary Fund (IMF) advice and pegging the ringgit to the U.S. dollar, and managed to achieve a V-shaped recovery within a year, recording a 6.1% growth rate in 1999 (Lee and Tham 2007).

Unfortunately, despite this recovery, as Menon (2014) shows, Malaysia did not succeed in regaining the confidence of international investors in the years following the crisis, although it did maintain its edge in international trade (especially in agricultural commodities).

The period following the financial crisis coincided with the opening up and rapid growth of the Chinese economy, and China soon superseded Japan as the major investor in the region. Economic partnership between China and Malaysia gained pace in 2013 with President Xi Jinping's launch of the BRI, an ambitious plan to connect Asia and Europe via land and sea. Fourteen memoranda of understanding with China were signed during the premiership of Najib Razak, and Chinese FDI was at an all-time high. Some of the big-ticket Chinese projects Malaysia attracted included the East Coast Rail Link, Bandar Malaysia, Malacca Gateway, and Forest City. However, these projects have been contentious in terms of their price tag, financing method, and spillover to the local economies.

Prime Minister Najib also pushed for an economic transformation that would propel Malaysia toward becoming a high-income country. The New Economic Model and the economic transformation program were formulated in 2010, with the target of lifting Malaysia's gross national income (GNI) per capita from US$6,700 (23,700 ringgit) in 2009 to more than US$15,000 (48,000 ringgit) in 2020, with an annual growth rate of 6%. Unfortunately, the prime minister became mired in a corruption scandal which eventually led to the incumbent coalition losing the election in 2018 — the first such loss in Malaysia's history.

During the campaign for Malaysia's 14th general election, the opposition parties raised concerns about the viability of some of the Chinese projects and the risks they posed to national security and social cohesion. In particular, the Forest City project was described as having the potential to become a "foreign enclave" if Chinese immigrants were allowed to move into it *en masse*. There were concerns that it would hurt local small and medium-sized enterprises (SMEs) which might lose out in competition with Chinese companies, with the risk that Chinese companies would dominate the entire supply chain (Todd and Slattery 2018). When the opposition won the election, the new government managed to renegotiate the price of the East Coast Rail Link to 44 billion ringgit (US$10.6 billion), down from the initial 65 billion ringgit (US$15.6 billion) (Lim 2018).

The Malaysian economy has performed well over the past 60 years, despite the volatility of oil and commodity prices in the 1970s and 1980s, the Asian financial crisis of the 1990s, and the global financial crisis in the 2000s. By East Asian standards, however, Malaysia's record is "respectable but not stellar" (Hill *et al.* 2012). Many domestic factors were at play too, including crony capitalism and the politicization of the New Economic Policy as well as the unwillingness of political elites to tackle institutional reform and transparency issues in governance.

Even though Malaysia has grown in terms of GDP and GDP per capita, it has fallen short of achieving the Vision 2020 goals that have

Figure 4: Malaysia's GDP Growth Per Capita (Annual %) 1961–2020

Source: World Bank Database. https://data.worldbank.org/indicator/NY.GDP.PCAP. KD.ZG?locations=MY (accessed July 31, 2021).

guided Malaysia's development for the last three decades or so. Ironically, 2020 saw Malaysia beset not only by a pandemic-induced economic downturn but also unprecedented political instability that culminated in the collapse of an administration that had only been in power since 2018. Faced with mounting global and domestic challenges, Malaysia has a lot of work to do (Figure 4).

FDI, Trade, and the Concept of Economic Security in Malaysia

As can be seen from the previous section, FDI and trade have been major factors in Malaysia's economic growth. External risks have been taken into consideration as a trade-off for greater gains, although Malaysia has always been aware of the danger of overexposure to global markets. Even though it is not explicitly discussed, economic security is arguably at the back of its policymakers' minds.

Economic security is a relatively new concept to Malaysia. The National Security Policy (NSP) 2019 listed "economic integrity" as one of the core values, and this was defined as "the country [having] a sustainable and resilient economy that can weather any internal or external economic threat." The policy also listed two strategies related to upholding economic integrity, namely:

(1) To cultivate economic resilience by strengthening national economic fundamentals to face global economic competition as well as maintain the legitimacy of the government to manage the economy of the country without foreign influence (Strategy 11).

(2) To bridge the socioeconomic gap by increasing job opportunities for citizens, improving income equality among communities, and transforming rural areas so as to raise the people's well-being (Strategy 8) (National Security Council, Malaysia 2019).

Unfortunately, the NSP neither elaborates on how this will be achieved nor has it been visibly harmonized with other government documents.

Granted that economic security has a wide range of definitions, in this chapter I will confine my discussion to foreign investment and trade, and Malaysia's ability to withstand geo-economic pressures.

Malaysia has thus far managed to maintain a healthy domestic direct investment (DDI) to FDI ratio as well as a diversity of FDI sources. In 2020, foreign investment (worth 64.2 billion ringgit) accounted for 39.1% of total approved investments (164 billion ringgit) (Malaysia Investment Development Authority 2021). China is the biggest investor at 18.1 billion ringgit, followed by Singapore (10 billion ringgit), the Netherlands (7 billion ringgit), and the United States (4.3 billion ringgit) (Figure 5; Table 1).

International trade has consistently accounted for over 100% of Malaysia's GDP since 1998, reaching 131.1% in 2017. Malaysia's total trade in April 2021 recorded the strongest growth since 1998 with a surge of 43.2%, reaching 190.8 billion ringgit, compared to the April 2020 figure of 133.2 billion ringgit. Exports remained at a higher level, increasing by 63.0% over the previous year to 105.6 billion ringgit. Imports in April 2021 were valued at 85.1 billion ringgit, a 24.4% increase year-on-year. Malaysia continued to record a trade surplus which that year was worth 20.5 billion ringgit (Department of Statistics, Malaysia 2021).

China has been Malaysia's largest trading partner for 12 consecutive years since 2009. In 2016, China also became Malaysia's largest investor,

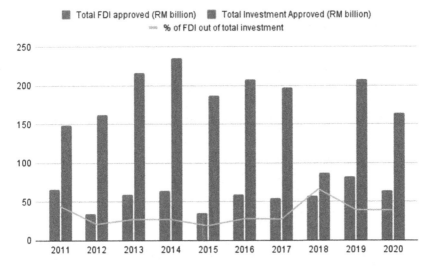

Figure 5:   Approved Investments in Malaysia, 2011–2020

Source: Mida reports, author's own calculations.

contributing investments worth US$1.6 billion (17.5% of the country's total FDI inflow) (Liu and Lim 2019), and was the largest source of FDI for the manufacturing sector for 5 consecutive years. In 2020, the volume of Malaysia's bilateral trade with China grew by 4.2%, Chinese investment in Malaysia's manufacturing sector grew by 10.3%, and Malaysia's exports to China were at a historical high (Ouyang 2021).

Malaysia's geographic advantage and central location in Asia has made it an important partner in China's BRI. Estimated to be worth US$1 trillion, this infrastructure development initiative has the potential to transform the region. Since 2013, Malaysia has attracted and negotiated several big Chinese projects, notably the East Coast Rail Link (ECRL), Bandar Malaysia, the Malaysia–China Kuantan Industrial Park (the sister park of China-Malaysia Qinzhou Industrial Park in Guangxi province), and the now-defunct Melaka Gateway project (Strangio 2020). In 2018, Malaysia was estimated to receive US$98 billion in capital inflows from BRI-related projects (Yan 2018).

For China, the BRI serves several purposes. For one, it secures a reliable maritime route for its exports, thus helping to resolve China's "Malacca Strait dilemma." The ECRL is particularly significant, as it also provides an alternative route to the narrow waterways. Secondly, by

Table 1: Top 5 FDI Source Countries from 2018–2020 (Information from 2017 and before are not available)

Year	Top 1 Investor	Amount (RM billion)	Top 2 Investor	Amount (RM billion)	Top 3 Investor	Amount (RM billion)	Top 4 Investor	Amount (RM billion)	Top 5 Investor	Amount (RM billion)	Total (RM billion)	Total FDI Approved	% of Top 5 out of total
2018	China	19.7	Indonesia	9	Netherlands	8.3	Japan	4.1	USA	3.2	44.3	58.0	76.4
2019	USA	26.8	China	15.7	Japan	12.1	Singapore	6.4	Taiwan	5.3	66.3	82.4	80.5
2020	China	18.1	Singapore	10	Netherlands	7	USA	4.3	Hong Kong	3.5	42.9	64.2	66.8

Source: MIDA Reports, author's own tabulation.

improving infrastructure in Southeast Asia, the BRI enhances China's connectivity and speeds up economic integration with its neighbors. There are, however, some domestic factors at play here. The BRI is essentially a response to the excess production capacity of China's industries (Yu 2017). Jones and Zeng (2019) also argue that the perception of the BRI as a revisionist power's geopolitical offensive overestimates the Chinese leaders' capacity to create and implement such a grand strategy. They conclude that it is rather a collection of loose, bottom-up policy initiatives which accommodate diverse interests within the party-state apparatus. Meanwhile, Liu and Lim (2019) highlight the critical role Southeast Asia plays in the BRI, stressing that "unlike other national plans ... that fall within the domestic political economy of China, its operation and success (or failure) depends fundamentally upon the engagement with and response from countries alongside the BRI nations" (Liu and Lim 2019, p. 217).

In response to the BRI, several countries have been stepping up efforts to provide investment alternatives in the region. In 2018, the United States passed the Better Utilization of Investment Leading to Development (BUILD) Act, which created the U.S. International Development Finance Corporation (USIDFC) that promised to double the U.S. government's development financing capacity to US$60 billion, and the Asia Reassurance Initiative Act (ARIA) which aims to invest US$150 million in the Indo-Pacific region each year from 2019 to 2023. The following year, the United States launched the Blue Dot Network, which is described as "a multi-stakeholder initiative, [that] promotes infrastructure projects around the world that meet high standards of transparency, sustainability, and developmental impact" (USIDFC 2020).

Other QUAD countries also launched various initiatives, including, in 2015, Japan's Partnership for Quality Infrastructure, which Prime Minister Shinzo Abe pledged to collaborate and provide approximately US$110 billion for "quality infrastructure investment" in Asia over the following 5 years. In 2016, Japan expanded the scope of the partnership with the injection of around US$200 billion. India launched the Indo-Pacific Ocean Initiative, and three of the QUAD countries — Australia, Japan, and India — launched the Supply Chain Resilience Initiative (Panda 2021). Meanwhile, Taiwan and South Korea also respectively rolled out the New Southbound Policy and the New Southern Policy, both of which involve investing more in the region.

Of all the QUAD members, Japan has often been touted as a counterbalance to China in Southeast Asia, given that it is arguably the most integrated economically in the region. Contrary to general perception, a Fitch Solutions survey published in 2019 showed that Japan is the biggest investor in infrastructure in Southeast Asia, where it has outstanding projects valued at US$367 billion, whereas China's projects are valued US$255 billion (Mourdoukoutas 2019).

Beyond strategic calculations, there is also a realization in Japan that it needs to stay engaged in Southeast Asia and reduce reliance on China. With Japan's declining population, its companies need to reach out to be profitable. Japanese investment in ASEAN peaked in 1992 and has now fallen to less than half that level. Interestingly, Japan's FDI in ASEAN has surpassed its investment in China by a wide margin in the years since 2008. Japanese investment in Malaysia in the period 2008–2017 registered a 225% increase over the preceding 10 years (Kikuchi and Unzaki 2019).

Likewise, Taiwan's New Southbound Policy is also driven by the strategic thinking of the Democratic Progressive Party (DPP) administration which recognizes the need to reduce Taiwan's reliance on China, although the policy is often contested by its political opponents. Ngeow (2017) has argued that although the New Southbound Policy is, on the face of it, aimed at strengthening Taiwan's relations with Southeast Asia, "in reality it has always been associated as a policy tool to counterbalance China–Taiwan economic integration, along with other strategic benefits, such as enlarging Taiwan's 'international space' and increasing Taiwan's relevance and leverage in Southeast Asia" (p. 97).

Evidently, Southeast Asia is an attractive destination for FDI. While it is true that China is increasingly a prominent economic actor in the region, talk of Chinese domination tends to under-emphasize the role of other investors and the agency of host countries. Other than concerns over China's increasing dominance in Southeast Asia, reducing economic reliance on China is also among the factors driving East Asian countries to strengthen their cooperation with Southeast Asia. While not explicitly based on hedging considerations, Malaysia's foreign investment profile has remained healthy. The "twin-chessboard" competition, while potentially precarious, also offers more options for Southeast Asia and Malaysia and can help improve the quality of FDI.

Malaysia and Regional Trade Integration

Malaysia has participated in the mega trade deals of recent years, such as RCEP and the CPTPP. Those two deals in particular are often characterized as being related to U.S.–China competition, but the reality is more nuanced. RCEP, negotiations for which were started in 2012, was signed in 2020. Even after India's last minute withdrawal, this is still the world's largest free trade deal, covering 29% of global GDP and 30% (2.3 billion) of the world's population. Meanwhile the CPTPP represents 500 million people and 13.5% of global GDP (Government of Canada 2020). Apart from RCEP and CPTPP, Malaysia has signed seven bilateral free trade agreements (FTAs) and seven regional FTAs which cover about 66.7% of Malaysia's total trade (Ministry of International Trade and Industry, Malaysia 2020).

However, the strategic significance of such deals seems to over-shadow their economic importance for Malaysia. Despite its well-publicized benefits, some doubt whether RCEP offers Malaysia any real economic advantages, given that it is in effect an amalgamation of an existing "noodle bowl" of trade agreements, with little ambition in terms of tariff elimination or standard-setting (Dieter 2020). Additionally, Malaysia faces competition from lower-cost RCEP signatories, such as Vietnam and Indonesia (Azhar 2020). RCEP is expected to benefit local industries by lowering barriers and opening markets, but there are con-cerns about the harm imported goods will inflict on the local market given that the access is reciprocal.

Even though Malaysia has signed CPTPP, it has not ratified it to date. While the proponents of the trade deal believe that ratifying it is in line with the government's reform agenda, especially on procurement prac-tices and raising labor and environmental standards, and that it will instill confidence among investors and send a strong signal to the world that Malaysia is open for business (Ong 2021), others have voiced concerns that the CPTPP might over-liberalize the economy. In particular, Malaysia is concerned about the issue of intellectual property rights, the require-ment for a level playing field between state-owned enterprises and foreign investors, and investor-state dispute settlement (ISDS) (Loh 2020). Some of the commitments require a broader institutional reform which might affect the continuation of race-based preferential policies. K. S. Jomo, a prominent economist and former assistant secretary-general for economic development at the United Nations who is an ardent opponent of the CPTPP, point blank called the trade pact a fraud that would cause more harm than good to Malaysia (Jomo 2020).

Malaysia's concerns are perhaps epitomized by the discourse of free versus fair trade brought up by the minister of international trade and investment Azmin Ali when he was asked about Malaysia's timeline for ratifying the CPTPP (Shankar 2020). Mahathir expressed a similar concern during his trip to China in 2018 (Needham 2018). More than a decade earlier, in a speech delivered in 2002 at the 20th anniversary of the Look East Policy in Japan, Mahathir expressed his concern that Malaysia is too trade dependent, as its trade volume at that time was almost twice as big as its GDP. He also had a bone to pick with the West and the IMF which, according to him, exerted economic pressure on Asian countries to open up and float their currencies during the Asian financial crisis. He then went on to lecture Japan about taking more of a leadership role in the East instead of merely trying to emulate the West.

A decade earlier, Mahathir proposed the establishment of the East Asian Economic Caucus as a counterweight to the Asia Pacific Economic Cooperation (APEC) forum, to be led by Japan. This, however, did not sit well with Japan due to its exclusion of the Western countries. The grouping subsequently turned into ASEAN+3, consisting of the 10 ASEAN countries plus China, Japan, and Korea — an initial attempt to include Taiwan was dropped due to a protest from China.

Granted that much of this anti-West sentiment is due to Mahathir's leadership style and personal grudges, it does go to show how Malaysia's trepidation about economic dominance by great powers has led it to gravitate toward regionalism. This partially explains Malaysia's decision to follow through with the discussions on the two trade deals.

Even though RCEP is seen as a victory for China, and indeed China stands to gain economically and strategically from RCEP, the process was actually initiated and driven by ASEAN (Intan 2020). It was proposed by ASEAN after China and Japan failed to reach a consensus on the two competing proposals — the East Asia Free Trade Agreement initiated by ASEAN+3 and the Comprehensive Economic Partnership in East Asia driven by the East Asia Summit (Lee 2021). Indeed, RCEP has been touted as a triumph for ASEAN's middle power diplomacy (Petri and Plummer 2020).

The U.S. withdrawal has not deterred other countries from continuing with the trade deal which has now become CPTPP. The CPTPP differs from RCEP and is touted as one of the most important trade deals. It involves more far-reaching liberalization than other deals and eliminates tariffs on nearly 96% of products in intra-regional trade, whereas RCEP will likely cover 90% (Lim 2021). Other economies continue to express an interest in joining the CPTPP, including the United Kingdom,

Indonesia, Korea, the Philippines, Taiwan, Thailand, and even, at one point, China. Japan's leadership here needs to be recognized as it is proving to be an important factor in sustaining the pact and maintaining the liberalization and regulatory standards (Hipert 2021). It demonstrates the ability of middle powers to exert influence — ASEAN in the case of RCEP, Japan in the case of the CPTPP. Indeed, joining trade deals is not just about economic gains; it also has diplomatic, strategic, and security implications. Japan is also a member of RCEP, which gives it an additional advantage in taking a leadership role in the regional trade order.

Economic integration is also at the top of the agenda for Malaysia, with the ASEAN Economic Community as its main pillar, while the ASEAN+3 mechanism enables ASEAN to engage with East Asia at the same time as maintaining ASEAN centrality. Just as the rise of China increased the importance of East Asia in the 1990s, the increasingly complex geo-economic situation has increased the need to maintain a rules-based economic order in the region. Interestingly, the withdrawal of the United States from the CPTPP and India from RCEP has inadvertently stimulated a stronger East Asian integration and delayed the Indo-Pacific integration envisioned by the deals' main drivers.

The Way Forward

Malaysia had an early move advantage in the 1970s with macroeconomic stability, policy credibility, openness, and excellent infrastructure, but now it is struggling to catch up with its neighbors in transforming itself into a high income country due to a lack of economic reform (Hill *et al.* 2012). While Malaysia was initially able to attract FDI, it is clear that it can no longer compete with countries such as Indonesia and Vietnam in terms of the cost of doing business.

What Malaysia needs to do is maintain its economic sovereignty in the face of increasing geo-economic competition, transform its economy to stay competitive and transition to a high income country, and, post-COVID-19, to find a good exit strategy to build the economy back better — that is, more sustainable, inclusive, and resilient.

In order to do this, Malaysia, first of all, needs to be more selective when it comes to foreign investment. It should reorient its incentives packages to enable a move away from labor-intensive FDI. This can be done by adopting a carrot and stick approach — investing in building in-house R&D capacity to help industries move up the value chain and making cheap migrant labor, as often as not underpaid and badly treated, less readily available. Good quality FDI should also have a positive spill-over effect on local SMEs, which make up 98.5% of Malaysia's manufacturing sector, as well as creating high-paying jobs. The sustainability of the FDI must also be a main consideration. The Isa-Shima principles, introduced by the G7 in 2016, provide a coherent and organized framework for bridging the global infrastructure gap and can serve as a starting point for guidelines to ensure sustainable infrastructure investment (Ministry of Foreign Affairs, Japan n.d.).

The Industry4WD plan launched in 2020 acknowledged Malaysia's move away from a destination for cheap labor manufacturing and recognized that it must now keep up with global technological trends in order to stay competitive. In particular, the plan acknowledges the shift in the global economic order resulting from the rise of China and changes in global supply chain dynamics, the need for Malaysia to keep up with technology advancement and convergence, and the knowledge and skills required for the future (Ministry of International Trade and Industry, Malaysia 2018). With the tagline ACT — short for "Attract, Create, Transform" — it aims to transform Malaysia's manufacturing landscape, which accounted for 22% of Malaysia's GDP between 2015 and 2020.

Malaysia has also launched the Digital Economy Blueprint and the National Automotive Policy. The automotive industry contributes about 40 billion ringgit, or 4% of Malaysia's GDP, and employs close to 700,000 people. A new Services Sector Blueprint and a National Policy Framework for Industrial Revolution 4.0 are also reportedly in the pipeline.

Secondly, Malaysia should adopt a "mission-oriented" approach (as expounded by the prominent economist Mariana Mazzucato) to FDI (Mazzucato 2015), integrating its FDI strategy with its innovation policy to create a virtuous cycle in which innovation creates exports, exports attract FDI, and this spurs further innovation (Donahue and McDearman 2015). Lessons can also be drawn from the experience of Japan, Korea, and Taiwan, countries which concluded technology transfer agreements with their foreign joint venture (JV) partners (Bernama 2021). The role of the Technology Depository Agency, an entity established by the Ministry of Finance, Malaysia, in 2002 to support the technology development needs of local industry, should be strengthened.

At least three sectors warrant serious examination. They are:

- *Green industries*: The green economy has been listed as a key area of economic growth since Malaysia signed up to a cut of 45% in its green-house gas emissions by 2030 in the 2015 Paris Agreement. The National Green Technology Policy identified four focuses, namely, energy, building, waste management, and transportation. The government has introduced incentives such as the Green Technology Financing Scheme 2.0 to spur the adoption of renewable energy technology in Malaysia (*Malay Mail* 2020). Notably, Malaysia is also the fourth largest producer of photovoltaic cells in the world and the largest exporter of these to the United States.

- *Digitalization*: The digital economy accounted for an estimated 19.1% of Malaysia's GDP in 2019. The Malaysia Digital Economy Blueprint aims to increase the sector's contribution to GDP to 22.6% and create 500,000 jobs by 2025, ensuring Malaysia's place at the forefront of the digital economy as well as overcoming the digital divide. However, the trend toward technology decoupling between the United States and China — with President Biden emphasizing an alliance of "techno-democracies" and China pursuing its Digital Silk Road (DSR) — might complicate things (Harjani 2021). Malaysia has signed a formal agreement with China on the DSR, and China's Alibaba Cloud has operated local data centers in Malaysia since 2017.

- *Semiconductors*: Microchips now hold the key to an increasingly digitized global economy. Malaysia is the world's seventh biggest supplier of chips, although it lacks cutting-edge technology and concentrates on outsourced assembly and testing and the manufacture of advanced testing equipment (Liew 2020). SilTerra, which was formed in 1995 and is owned by the sovereign wealth fund Khazanah, is one of the few semiconductor wafer pure-play foundries in the country. More R&D should be invested in this sector.

Third, Malaysia should prepare for the U.S.–China decoupling that has been accelerated by COVID-19. The global uncertainty also offers opportunities. Southeast Asia is seen as an alternative to China, with the China+1 model, and more companies are looking to spread out the risk. The Malaysia Investment Development Authority (MIDA) reported that Malaysia saw "noteworthy investment inflow" due to investment diversion caused by the U.S.–China trade war.

In the long run, however, great power competition is likely to be detrimental to Malaysia. This competition is set to intensify under the Biden administration, as can be seen from some of the steps it has already taken, including convening a QUAD summit. The course seems to have been set for technology decoupling in the near future, with the United States taking protectionist measures to strengthen the resilience of its supply chain (White House 2021), which will have a huge impact on Southeast Asia.

Geopolitical uncertainties have caused countries to nearshore and reshore their production. In the case of semiconductors, the Chinese government has committed US$120 billion to propping up its domestic semiconductor manufacturing with the goal of producing 70% of all chips needed for local consumption under the Made in China 2035 Plan. The United States is also investing in developing foundries for advanced semiconductors locally, with an investment by Taiwan's TSMC (Ioannu 2020). Malaysia needs to build resilience into its supply chains by growing its key industries in such a way as to move up the global value chain.

Finally, Malaysia needs to adopt a more holistic approach to economic security and sovereignty. Malaysia has hitherto been able to separate its economic relations from its security concerns, particularly with regard to its territorial disputes with China, but this is a difficult tightrope to walk on. Malaysia must be prepared for stiffer competition and at the same time preserve its economic sovereignty so that it can occupy a favorable strategic position *vis-à-vis* external powers. A whole-of-government approach to policy making with inter-ministerial involvement is needed to facilitate this.

Conclusion

Malaysia has an open economy combined with an interventionist developmental state approach. Various internal and external factors have caused it to underperform, but it has fared well in uplifting the living standards of its population and achieving middle-income status, and it has avoided being beholden to any of the major powers. Economic sovereignty, while not explicitly stated, has been part of the Malaysian psyche since the early days of independence. Malaysia has been able to take advantage of the FDI trend by leveraging its location and its relations with regional countries, experiencing moderate success in translating this into economic growth.

Now, Malaysia is at a crossroads. It urgently needs to transform its economy in an era of increasing global instability caused by great power competition. Other challenges include the rise of China, geo-economic shifts, and an unpredictable post-COVID recovery. However, this could be a moment of opportunity when Malaysia can recalibrate its FDI policy to focus on attracting investment in niche areas and encourage domestic innovation, both of which will reinforce efforts to increase economic resilience.

FDI and trade will continue to be important aspects of Malaysia's economy, but it is no longer feasible for Malaysia to rely on an FDI-led growth strategy. That said, this chapter has shown that Malaysia has agency, and it should take advantage of current geo-economic trends to attract the right kind of FDI and strengthen its position.

Regionalization is likely to become more important. From the experience of RCEP and the CPTPP, it is clear that middle powers are playing an important role in keeping multilateralism alive. In addition to the United States and China, the other Asian economies — Japan, South Korea, and Taiwan — have a role in upholding the rules-based economic order. An ASEAN-led mechanism might not be the strongest, but it offers a way of navigating between a U.S.-led alliance and a Chinese-dominated geo-economy.

There are of course dangers in "over-securitizing" an economy. In some instances, it could be used to rationalize protectionism or preferential treatment for one country over another for no more than strategic reasons. But there is no denying that geo-economics has become a main feature of the contestation between the great powers, and economic power has become increasingly weaponized. As a small state, Malaysia has in the past been moderately successful in navigating geopolitics and the trend toward globalization. It must now take bold steps to deal with new challenges.

References

ASEAN. 2019. ASEAN Outlook on Indo-Pacific. https://asean.org/storage/2019/06/ASEAN-Outlook-on-the-Indo-Pacific_FINAL_22062019.pdf.

Azhar, Kamarul. 2020. RCEP Benefits Malaysia but Watch Out for Competition from Vietnam, Indonesia. *The Edge*, December 3. https://www.

theedgemarkets.com/article/rcep-benefits-malaysia-watch-out-competition-vietnam-indonesia.

Bernama. 2021. Focus on FI Quality, not Quantity, Says UM Economist. *Free Malaysia Today*, May 9. https://www.freemalaysiatoday.com/category/business/2021/05/09/focus-on-fdi-quality-not-quantity-says-um-economist/.

Department of Statistics, Malaysia. 2021. *Malaysia Trade Statistics Bulletin*, May 28. https://www.dosm.gov.my/v1/index.php?r=column/cthemeByCat&cat=139&bul_id=RElFN1d1SzQwa0J4c21TWVNlcTd5Zz09&menu_id=az JjRWpYL0VBYU90TVhpclByWjdMQT09.

Dieter, Heribert. 2020. End of the Spaghetti Bowl: RCEP Does not Create an Asia-Pacific Trade Bloc. *Asia Global Online*, November 19. https://www.asiaglobalonline.hku.hk/end-spaghetti-bowl-rcep-does-not-create-asia-pacific-trade-bloc.

Donahue, Ryan and Brad McDearman. 2015. Metro Areas Merge Export and FDI Strategies. *Brookings Institution*, December 29. https://www.brookings.edu/blog/the-avenue/2015/12/29/metro-areas-merge-export-and-fdi-strategies/.

Gomez, Edmund Terence, and K. S. Jomo. 1997. *Malaysia's Political Economy: Politics, Patronage and Profits*. Cambridge: Cambridge University Press.

Government of Canada. Updated December 21, 2020. CPTPP Explained. https://www.international.gc.ca/trade-commerce/trade-agreements-accords-commerciaux/agr-acc/cptpp-ptpgp/cptpp_explained-ptpgp_apercu.aspx?lang=eng.

Harjani, Manoj. 2021. Is Southeast Asia Ready for a US-China Tech Decoupling? *The Interpreter* (Lowy Institute), May 31. https://www.lowyinstitute.org/the-interpreter/southeast-asia-ready-us-china-tech-decoupling.

Hill, Hal, Tham S. Yean, and Ragayah H. M. Zin. 2012. Malaysia: A Success Story Stuck in the Middle? *The World Economy* 35(12): 1687–1711. https://doi.org/10.1111/twec.12005.

Hipert, Hanns Günther. 2021. New Trade Agreements in Asia. SWP Comment, April. https://www.swp-berlin.org/publications/products/comments/2021 C25_TradeAgreementsAsia.pdf.

Intan, Rocky. 2020. What RCEP Can Tell Us about Geopolitics in Asia. *The Interpreter* (Lowy Institute), December 1. https://www.lowyinstitute.org/the-interpreter/what-rcep-can-tell-us-about-geopolitics-asia.

Ioannou, Lori. 2020. A Brewing US–China Tech Cold War Rattles the Semiconductor Industry. CNBC, September 18. https://www.cnbc.com/2020/09/18/a-brewing-us-china-tech-cold-war-rattles-the-semiconductor-industry.html.

Jomo, K. S. 2020. Why Is Malaysia Still Committed to the CPTPP Fraud? *Malaysiakini*, August 7. https://www.malaysiakini.com/news/537678.

Jones, Lee and Jinghan Zeng. 2019. Understanding China's 'Belt and Road Initiative': Beyond 'Grand Strategy' to a State Transformation Analysis. *Third World Quarterly* 40(8): 1415–1439.

Kikuchi, Tomoo and Sayaka Unzaki. 2019. Japanese Infrastructure Investment in Southeast Asia. S. Rajaratnam School of International Studies, Singapore. https://www.rsis.edu.sg/wp-content/uploads/2019/05/PR190503_Japanese-Infrastructure-Investmentin-in-SEA.pdf.

Kuik, Cheng-Chwee. 2021. The Twin Chessboards of US–China Rivalry: Impact on the Geostrategic Supply and Demand in Post-pandemic Asia. *Asian Perspective* 45(1): 157–176. https://doi.org/10.1353/apr.0.0010.

Lee, Jaehyon. 2021. Diplomatic and Security Implications of the Regional Comprehensive Economic Partnership. The Asian Institute for Policy Studies, March 15. http://en.asaninst.org/contents/diplomatic-and-security-implications-of-the-regional-comprehensive-economic-partnership-rcep/#3.

Lee, Poh Ping and Siew Yean Tham. 2007. Malaysia Ten Years After the Asian Financial Crisis. *Asian Survey* 47(6): 915–929.

Leifer, Michael. 1994. Anglo-Malaysian Alienation Revisited. *The Round Table* 83(331): 347–359.

Leonard, Mark, Jean Pisani-Ferry, Elina Ribakova, Jeremy Shapiro, and Guntram B. Wolff. 2019. Redefining Europe's Economic Sovereignty. Policy Contribution No. 9, European Council on Foreign Relations. https://www.bruegel.org/wp-content/uploads/2019/06/PC-09_2019_final-1.pdf.

Liew, Jia Teng. 2020. Cover Story: Where Are Malaysia Players in the Semiconductor Value Chain? *The Edge*, October 15. https://www.theedgemarkets.com/article/cover-story-where-are-malaysian-players-semiconductor-value-chain.

Lim, Guanie. 2018. Resolving the Malacca Dilemma: Malaysia's Role in the Belt and Road Initiative. In *Securing the Belt and Road Initiative*, edited by Alessandro Arduino and Xue Gong. Singapore: Palgrave Macmillan. https://doi.org/10.1007/978-981-10-7116-4_5.

Lim, Justin. 2021. FMM Urges Govt to Expedite Ratification Process for RCEP and CPTPP to Aid Recovery. *The Edge*, April 16. https://www.theedgemarkets.com/article/fmm-urges-govt-expedite-ratification-process-rcep-and-cptpp-aid-recovery.

Liu, Hong and Guanie Lim. 2019. The Political Economy of a Rising China in Southeast Asia: Malaysia's Response to the Belt and Road Initiative. *Journal of Contemporary China* 28(116): 216–231.

Loh, Jason. 2020. CPTPP: Good that Malaysia Is Cautious? *The ASEAN Post*, November 21. https://theaseanpost.com/article/cptpp-good-malaysia-cautious.

Malay Mail. 2020. Minister: Malaysia Set to Maximise Green Industry, Renewable Energy Potential in 2020. January 3. https://www.malaymail.

com/news/malaysia/2020/01/03/minister-malaysia-set-to-maximise-green-industry-renewable-energy-potential/1824394.

Malaysia Investment Development Authority (MIDA). 2021. Malaysia Investment Performance Report 2020: Geared for Recovery. https://www.mida.gov.my/wp-content/uploads/2021/03/MIDA-IPR-2020_FINAL_March4.pdf.

Mazzucato, Mariana. 2015. Mission-Oriented Finance for Innovation: New Ideas for Investment-Led Growth. Institute for New Economic Thinking, March 19. https://www.ineteconomics.org/perspectives/blog/mission-oriented-finance-for-innovation-new-ideas-for-investment-led-growth.

Menon, Jayant. 2014. Growth Without Private Investment: What Happened in Malaysia and Can It Be Fixed? *Journal of the Asia Pacific Economy* 19(2): 247–271. https://link.springer.com/chapter/10.1007/978-981-10-7116-4_5#CR34.

Ministry of Foreign Affairs, Japan. n.d. G7 Ise-Shima Principles for Promoting Quality Infrastructure Investment. https://www.mofa.go.jp/files/000160272.pdf.

Ministry of International Trade and Industry Malaysia. Last updated November 27, 2020. Malaysia's Free Trade Agreements. https://fta.miti.gov.my/index.php/pages/view/4?mid=23.

Ministry of International Trade and Industry, Malaysia. 2018. Industry4WD: National Policy on IR4.0. https://www.miti.gov.my/miti/resources/National%20Policy%20on%20Industry%204.0/Industry4WRD_Final.pdf.

Mourdoukoutas, Panos. 2019. Japan, not China, Is the Biggest Investor in Southeast Asia's Infrastructure. *Forbes*, June 26. https://www.forbes.com/sites/panosmourdoukoutas/2019/06/26/japan-beats-china-in-the-philippines-singapore-and-vietnam/?sh=52cb3f1839d8.

National Security Council, Malaysia. 2019. National Security Policy. https://www.mkn.gov.my/web/wp-content/uploads/sites/3/2019/08/English-National_Security_Policy.pdf.

Needham, Kirsty. 2018. Mahathir Calls for 'Fair Trade' in China, Warns of 'New Colonialism'. *Sydney Morning Herald*, August 20. https://www.smh.com.au/world/asia/mahathir-calls-for-fair-trade-in-china-warns-of-new-colonialism-20180820-p4zymq.html.

Ngeow, Chow Bing. 2017. Taiwan's Go South Policy: 'Déjà vu' All Over Again? *Contemporary Southeast Asia* (ISEAS-Yusof Ishak Institute) 39 (1): 96–126. https://www.jstor.org/stable/44683886.

Ong, Kiang Ming. 2021. Ratify the RCEP and CPTPP to Increase FDI and External Trade. *The Edge*, April 12. https://www.theedgemarkets.com/article/ong-kian-mings-statement-rcep-cptpp.

Ouyang, Yujing. 2021. Sailing Towards a Brighter Future: Commemorating the 47th Anniversary of China–Malaysia Diplomatic Relations. Embassy of the

People's Republic of China in Malaysia, May 31. http://my.china-embassy. org/eng/sgxw/t1879945.htm.

Panda, Jagannath. 2021. Decoupling and Diversification: China, the Belt and Road, and the Supply Chain Resilience Initiative. *AsiaGlobal Online,* June 2. https://www.asiaglobalonline.hku.hk/decoupling-and-diversification-china-belt-and-road-and-supply-chain-resilience-initiative.

Petri, Peter A. and Michael Plummer. 2020. RCEP: A New Trade Agreement that Will Shape Global Economics and Politics. *Brookings Institution,* November 16. https://www.brookings.edu/blog/order-from-chaos/2020/11/16/ rcep-a-new-trade-agreement-that-will-shape-global-economics-and-politics/.

Shankar, Arjuna Chandran. 2020. Azmin: Malaysia to Address Sensitive Issues before Deciding on CPTPP Ratification. *The Edge,* September 1. https:// www.theedgemarkets.com/article/azmin-malaysia-address-sensitive-issues-deciding-cptpp-ratification.

Sipalan, Joseph. 2021. Malaysia Says FDI Inflows Dropped 56% in 2020 to $3.4bln. *Reuters,* March 2. https://ww.reuters.com/article/malaysia-economy-investment-idINL3N2L014I.

Strangio, Sebastian. 2020. In Malaysia, a Gargantuan Chinese-Backed Development Bites the Dust. *The Diplomat,* November 19. https://the diplomat.com/2020/11/in-malaysia-a-gargantuan-chinese-backed-development-bites-the-dust/.

Todd, Laurence and Meghan Slattery. 2018. Impacts of Investment from China in Malaysia on the Local Economy. Policy Ideas No. 54, Institute of Democracy and Economic Affairs (IDEAS). https://www.ideas.org.my/ wp-content/uploads/2021/04/P154-China_FDI_V2.pdf.

USIDFC (U.S. International Development Finance Corporation). 2020. Blue Dot Network Steering Committee Holds First Meeting. Press release, January 31. https://www.dfc.gov/media/press-releases/blue-dot-network-steering-committee-holds-first-meeting.

World Bank. 2021. Agriculture, forestry, and fishing, value added (% of GDP) - Malaysia. World Bank Database. https://data.worldbank.org/indicator/ NV.AGR.TOTL.ZS?locations=MY.

White House. 2021. Building Resilient Supply Chains, Revitalizing American Manufacturing and Fostering Broad-Based Growth: 100-Day Reviews under Executive Order 14017, June.

Yan, Jinny. 2018. The Belt and Road Initiative in Southeast Asia. In *China's Belt and Road Initiative (BRI) and Southeast Asia,* 4–9. CIMB ASEAN Research Institute (CARI). https://www.lse.ac.uk/ideas/Assets/Documents/reports/ LSE-IDEAS-China-SEA-BRI.pdf.

Yu, Hong. 2017. Motivation Behind China's 'One Belt, One Road' Initiatives and Establishment of the Asian Infrastructure Investment Bank. *Journal of Contemporary China* 26(105): 353–368.

Chapter 11

Malaysia's Political Contestations in the COVID-19 Era and Their Economic Impacts: An Assessment

Karl Chee Leong Lee

Introduction

This chapter examines Malaysia's political contestations in the COVID-19 era and their impacts on the domestic economy. Prior to the pandemic, which started with the country's first reported case on January 25, 2020 (*Borneo Post* 2020a), identity politics and the centralization of federal powers had continued to besiege the Malaysian political scene despite the historic general election of May 2018 that saw the end of the 61-year rule of Barisan Nasional (BN) and put Pakatan Harapan (PH) into power. Beleaguered by identity politics after its rise to power, the PH administration collapsed on February 24, 2020, after only 22 months, following the resignation of former Prime Minister, Mahathir Mohamad and the departure of Parti Pribumi Bersatu Malaysia (Bersatu) as well as another group of lawmakers from the ruling coalition (Chew 2019; Lim 2020b). The PH government was succeeded by the Malay/Muslim-centric multiracial coalition known as Perikatan Nasional (PN), led by Prime Minister Muhyiddin Yassin, comprised of Bersatu, UMNO (the United Malay National Organisation), Parti Islam Se-Malaysia (PAS), and other BN component parties that represented Malaysia's minority races. This shift in the ruling configuration was so drastic that one leading political

211

scientist characterized it as "the return of Malaysia's identity politics" (Chin 2020c).

Despite the fact that decentralization was one of PH's campaign pledges, the centralization of federal powers continued unabated (Pakatan Harapan 2020). During the PH government's 22 months in power, the decentralization agenda experienced a bumpy road, as tangible measures to devolve federal powers to state governments and even local councils did not cross the starting line. To the disappointment of civil society in the likes of Aliran (Loh 2018) and prominent intellectuals, including Woo Wing Thye and Tricia Yeoh (Woo 2019; Yeoh 2019), who had hoped that the PH government would carry out its decentralization agenda, there was barely any progress, apart from the attempt to amend the Constitution Bill in 2019 to restore the status of Sabah and Sarawak (East Malaysia) as equal partners of West Malaysia (or Peninsular Malaysia). But even that attempt failed to gain a two-thirds majority in the parliament when the then opposition bloc abstained from voting on the bill (Aziz 2019).

As for the issue of local elections, they were resisted even by former Prime Minister Mahathir who openly disagreed with PH's campaign pledge to revive local council elections throughout the country (Kannan and Mohd Noor 2018). In fact, the then Mahathir-led PH administration continued the federal patronage practices of the BN era, in spite of voters expecting a transparent and accountable government after the 2018 general election. The Muhyiddin-led PN government has been criticized for the same practice (Gomez 2019, 2020). As highlighted by James Chin, any decentralization of powers is likely to disrupt the patronage network which federal parties use to control local political forces (Ng 2020; Augustin 2020). As with BN administrations of the past, the "politicization" of Malaysian federalism between federal and state governments (Jomo and Wee 2002) came to the fore again when the state governments (especially the opposition-held states) became mired in a political contest with Putrajaya (the federal capital) on the implementation of COVID-19 recovery plans. This political contestation will be explored later in this chapter.

Given these two long-standing foundations of Malaysian politics, this chapter will explore the political contestations that occurred during the height of COVID-19 pandemic — defined as the period to which Malaysia recorded its first COVID-19 case in February 2020 until the start of mass inoculation in May 2021. First and foremost, it looks at the two forms of political contestation, namely, national identity contestation and federal-state authority contestation, that have their origins in enduring identity politics and centralized federalism. In addition, I shall assess how the economic impacts of the two forms of political contestation made it difficult for the Malaysian economy to recover from the pandemic. The chapter concludes by presenting a number of scenarios that may emerge from the political struggles and gauging to what extent they will affect Malaysia's economy in the medium term.

National Identity Contestation

The first form of political contestation is the national identity contestation between PN and the opposition bloc at the federal level. While such contestation is independent of the COVID-19 pandemic itself, the fact that regime change occurred in such a difficult period allowed the contestation to develop unimpeded. With their different political compositions and governance ideologies, the PN and the PH-dominated opposition bloc have been Malaysia's two main political rivals since the change of government that occurred in the early stage of the pandemic. Whereas the former is a Malay/Muslim-centric multiracial coalition centered on an ethno-religious governance ideology (Chin 2020c), the latter is in the process of forging an East–West Malaysian multiracial coalition with Parti Warisan Sabah (or Warisan) and Mahathir's faction to unseat the PN coalition. Since PH is the dominant opposition bloc, it is foreseeable that its liberal-leaning posture will color any potential coalition of the three opposition parties. That said, with no solution in sight in the short term, national identity contestation is likely to compound the economic difficulties caused by COVID-19 by injecting prolonged political instability into the equation.

Unexpected political setting after change of government

While there has been no formal disclosure concerning the rationale behind the initiation of the change of government during the COVID-19 pandemic instead of earlier, any observer of Malaysian politics would be aware that the attempt was triggered by the contentious transition issue involving Mahathir and Anwar and the rancorous identity politics that placed Bersatu in a passive and difficult position within the larger multi-cultural coalition of PH. In what is known as the "Sheraton Move" by the Malaysian media (Tan 2020c; Hew 2020), Bersatu (aligned with Muhyiddin) and Azmin's camp of the then Parti Keadilan Rakyat (PKR) had reportedly been plotting regime change with BN and PAS leaders just after the news of six political party leaders having an audience with the Yang di-Pertuan Agong (Malaysian King) came out on the afternoon of February 23, 2020 (*The Star* 2020b; *The Edge Markets* 2020).

That said, the whole grand coalition plan did not turn out exactly as the leaders of the Sheraton Move expected. Instead, a political setting in which both sides of the political divide were locked in a symmetrical contest ensued, following two consecutive developments unforeseen by the Sheraton Move leaders. Unwilling to cooperate with UMNO *en bloc*, Mahathir swiftly resigned from his post, marking the end of the entire PH cabinet (Ho 2020; Poveira and Yusof 2020). At the same time, being a strong supporter of Mahathir, Shafie Apdal (Warisan's leader and Sabah's chief minister) also pulled out of the coalition after the former decided not to join the PN government and to continue as part of the opposition bloc instead (Fong 2020a).

After Muhyiddin Yassin was chosen as PN's candidate for prime minister and sworn in on March 1, 2020 (*Free Malaysia Today* 2020b), the ruling coalition was faced with an immediate and long-term predicament. Without the support of Mahathir's faction and Warisan, PN's control of the Dewan Rakyat (House of Representatives) was based on its razor-thin majority of parliamentary seats. As of August 15, 2020, the PN bloc had a majority of 2 instead of 17 — with the component parties now including UMNO, PAS, other BN parties, Gabungan Parti Sarawak (GPS), Parti Bersatu Sabah (PBS), Parti Bersatu Rakyat Sabah (PBRS), and Homeland Solidarity Party (STAR), with one independent member of parliament (MP). As outlined in Table 1, the total number of parliamentary seats held by the PN coalition was 113 while the opposition (PH, Warisan, Mahathir faction) controlled the remaining 109 seats. Far from establishing a strong federal government from the grand partnership of all Malay political parties, the PN coalition was now confronted with the strongest opposition in Malaysian history and risked having a hung parliament if any of its MPs defected to the opposition bloc. Furthermore, the PN government would have to face a lot of difficulties in getting important bills (including the national budget bill) passed in the parliament.

Table 1: Composition of Parliamentary Seats in Dewan Rakyat (As of August 15, 2020)

Political Parties	Number of Parliamentary Seats
Perikatan Nasional (PN)	*113*
Bersatu	31
BN Coalition (UMNO, MCA, MIC & PBRS)*	43
PAS	18
GPS Coalition	18
PBS	1
STAR	1
Independent	1
Opposition	*109*
PH (PKR, DAP & AMANAH)**	91
Mahathir Faction (Independent)	6
Warisan	9
UPKO***	1
PSB***	2

Notes: *Malaysian Chinese Association (MCA); Malaysian Indian Congress (MIC). **Democratic Action Party (DAP); Parti Amanah Negara (AMANAH). ***United Progressive Kinabalu Organisation (UPKO); Parti Sarawak Bersatu (PSB).
Source: Parliament of Malaysia.

Battle for the centrist electorate

The overarching political resistance, however, went beyond these scenarios in the parliament. Unlike in the past when the ruling coalition was a dominant force, the current composition of the Malaysian Parliament has emboldened the ruling PN and the opposition (PH-majority) blocs to battle with each other for the support of the electorate. In addition to consolidating their electoral bases, both sides of the political divide are also looking to strengthen their appeal among centrist voters throughout the country. This is indeed what has been happening on the ground ever since the establishment of the PN government in late February 2020. Each distinguished by its political composition and governance ideology, the ruling coalition and the opposition bloc are mired in contestation at the federal level.

Differences in Political Composition. The most obvious difference between the two blocs concerns the composition of their coalitions.

As alluded to by the president of PAS, Hadi Awang, the PN government is a "Malay-Muslim unity" government that is different from the purportedly "non-Muslim dominant" PH administration (Welsh 2020b; *Malaysiakini* 2020a).[1] As such, the political composition of the whole coalition reflects its Malay/Muslim-centric multiracial representation that is derived from its electoral base in the mainly Malay conservative urban, suburban, and rural areas of West Malaysia.[2] As for the opposition bloc dominated by PH, its political composition is relatively multiracial, with significant non-Malay/non-Muslim representation from West Malaysia, and a smaller group of East Malaysian MPs (or parliamentary seats). In contrast to PN, the PH coalition's electoral base mainly consists of liberal-leaning voters in racially and religiously diverse urban and suburban areas of both West and East Malaysia.

As shown in Table 2, the whole coalition is dominated by the three Malay-Muslim parties — altogether, Malay-Muslims made up 69.0% of PN's total of 78 MPs, whereas the non-Malay/non-Muslim (West Malaysia) and East Malaysian parties have 3 (2.7%) and 32 (28.3%) seats, respectively.[3] In contrast, the PH-Warisan-UPKO coalition had a relatively diverse composition prior to the Sheraton Move that saw its ouster from power: 44.6% were Malay-Muslim MPs from West Malaysia, 33.8% were non-Malay/non-Muslim MPs (West Malaysia), and 21.6% came from East Malaysia (Official Portal of Parliament of Malaysia

---

[1] Although UMNO and PAS have non-Muslim members, their influence in these parties is negligible. Similarly, Bersatu's latest move to admit non-Malays as associate members is reminiscent of the PAS supporters wing, and they will find it extremely challenging adjusting to the party's overall Malay-centric agenda.

[2] Sarawak GPS is not included in this calculation as it claims not to be a part of PN, but rather a PN-friendly coalition of political parties in the East Malaysian state that cooperated with PN to ensure the political stability of Malaysia. As such, GPS Sarawak is not involved in the construction of PN ideology. Also, as a coalition that succumbed to East Malaysian sub-nationalist sentiment, GPS Sarawak did not subscribe to the Malay-Muslim identity politics that colored the political scene in West Malaysia. For more information, see (*Dayak Daily* 2020).

[3] Since East Malaysia has its own sub-nationalist sentiment that transcends race and religion, it is considered as a single bloc rather than being divided into Malay-Muslim and non-Malay/Muslim as in the case of West Malaysia. As such, the number of East Malaysian MPs and cabinet members consists of all MPs from the two states of Sabah and Sarawak.

Table 2: Political Composition of PN and Opposition Bloc in Dewan Rakyat and Cabinet (As of August 15, 2020)

Members	Dewan Rakyat	Cabinet
Ruling PN	*113*	*32*
Malay (West Malaysia)	78	24
Non-Malay (West Malaysia)	3	2
East Malaysia	32	6
Opposition Bloc	*109*	—
Malay (West Malaysia)	47	—
Non-Malay (West Malaysia)	46	—
East Malaysian	16	—

Source: Cabinet of Malaysia and Parliament of Malaysia.

2020a).[4] Even after the Sheraton Move that saw thirty of its MPs (mostly West Malaysian Malays) defecting, PH still preserved the largely diverse composition it had when it formed the Malaysian government in May 2018. As of August 15, 2020, the opposition bloc consisted of 47 (43.1%) West Malaysian Malay-Muslims, 46 (42.2%) West Malaysian non-Malay/non-Muslims, and 16 (14.7%) East Malaysian MPs (Portal Rasmi Parlimen Malaysia 2020). At the same time, the PN cabinet was made up of 24 Malay-Muslims from West Malaysia and only 2 non-Malays/non-Muslims — compared to the 14 Malay-Muslims (West Malaysia) and 7 non-Malay/Muslim ministers (West Malaysia) in the previous PH government (see Table 2 and Cabinet of Malaysia 2020; Awang Pawi 2018).[5] The only similarity is that both the PN and PH governments attached high importance to the East Malaysian states of Sabah and Sarawak, with the former appointing six ministers from that part of Malaysia and the latter appointing four (Cabinet of Malaysia Website 2020; Awang Pawi 2018).

---

[4]Before the Sheraton Move, PH-Warisan had 62 Malay MPs and 47 non-Malay MPs from West Malaysia, and a total of 30 MPs elected in East Malaysia.

[5]The important portfolios of finance, defense, and home affairs were taken by Malay-Muslims, another strong indication that it does not intend to repeat the controversial appointment of a Chinese minister-in-charge of the Finance Ministry as in the previous PH administration.

To sum up, there is a clear difference in terms of political composition between PN and the opposition bloc. Whereas the former is a Malay/Muslim-centric multiracial coalition, the latter is a strong multiracial coalition with a relatively diverse political composition. At the same time, the Malay/Muslim-centric political composition of the PN coalition and the cabinet also appealed to Malay centrist voters in West Malaysia who might have voted for PH in the previous general election. Arguably, this will be the electoral battleground which the opposition bloc (including PH and the Mahathir faction) are hoping to preserve and expand before the next election as well. That said, PH is also looking to expand into East Malaysia due to its strong multiracial composition, an advantage that the Mahathir faction does not possess and one which makes Warisan a natural partner for the coalition (Lee 2020; *Bernama* 2020b; *The Star* 2020a).[6]

Different Governance Ideologies. The other difference between the two sides of the political divide lies in their governance ideologies. As with their political composition, PN and the opposition bloc relied on their ideology to expand their appeal among centrist voters. For PN, its position on various issues reflects its national ideology, centered upon (ethno-religious) Malay-Muslim governance, while multiculturalism remains the governing ideology binding together the constituent political parties of the opposition bloc, including the dominant PH. Altogether, there are four potent issues that stand at the forefront of such differences.

The first issue is the call for the banning of alcohol throughout Malaysia. For PN, the problem of road deaths resulting from drink driving should be resolved through strict measures derived from its Malay/Muslim-centric governance ideology. Thus, it is unsurprising to hear calls for an alcohol ban from PAS leaders, while UMNO Youth have demanded central control of alcohol sales and consumption to tackle the drink driving problem (*Malay Mail* 2020; *Malaysiakini* 2020e). In response to these calls, PH leaders steadfastly upheld the right of non-Muslims to drink

---

[6]On August 7, 2020, five members of the Mahathir faction announced the establishment of a new independent political party, the principles of which, according to the former prime minister, are rooted in racial moderation and anti-corruption. Five days later, the party was unveiled as Parti Pejuang Tanahair (Pejuang) and it is expected to compete with Bersatu, UMNO, and PAS in the Malay suburban and rural areas of West Malaysia. The other member of the Mahathir faction, Syed Saddiq, was expected to establish a new youth-centric and multiracial political party.

while at the same time criticizing UMNO's suggestion as being an encroachment on state autonomy in the area of alcohol regulation (*The Malaysian Insight* 2020a; Suhaimi 2020). Even after strong opposition from the Chinese- and Sarawak-based organizations as well as opposition leaders, the PN government made a rather assertive decision on the issue, albeit a more acceptable one for these opposing voices — they suspended new applications for alcohol licenses until new guidelines are drawn up and revision of the laws is completed (Aruno *et al.* 2020; *Borneo Post* 2020b; Suhaimi 2020; Hassan 2020; Tan 2020a).

The second issue is official recognition of the United Examination Certificate (UEC), a qualification held by graduates of Chinese-medium schools in Malaysia. This is a source of anger among a big segment of Malay voters against the PH administration (especially the DAP) on account of its strong commitment to recognition of this non-national academic qualification (*Malaysiakini* 2020b). Both UMNO and PAS continued to oppose such a move based on ethno-nationalist grounds. For those two parties, and for Bersatu, recognition of the UEC amounts to denigration of the status of the Malay language as the national language of the country (Kaos and Timbuong 2018; *The Star* 2018; Fuad 2018). With the establishment of the PN government, PH's campaign promise to recognize the UEC was shelved altogether — especially after Prime Minister Muhyiddin himself clarified for the first time that his government did not intend to grant recognition following news reports that he might do so in the future (*New Straits Times* 2020b; *Malaysiakini* 2020c). As expected, certain PH leaders, such as Ronnie Liu, continued to pressure Muhyiddin to carry out the coalition's pledge on UEC recognition, as the latter had been one of the senior leaders who approved it in the 2018 general election (Mohd. Amin 2020).

The third issue is the amendment of the Shariah Courts (Criminal Jurisdiction) Act (or Act 355) which PAS has long wanted to debate in parliament. In a move that is bound to consolidate its support among Muslims in West Malaysia, PAS continued to push for the right time to promote the shariah law amendment despite being aware that this would cause great concern among non-Muslims (*The Malaysian Insight* 2020b; Periasamy 2019). From the opposition side, PH's West Malaysia-centric multicultural stance was the dominant ideology behind its stand against the tabling of the shariah law amendment in 2017. While DAP opposed amendment, citing its violation of the Federal Constitution, PKR leader, Anwar Ibrahim, consistently insisted that non-Muslims be included in the parliamentary debate on Act 355 before any vote (Mok 2017; Robertson 2018). Like the alcohol ban and UEC recognition, the amendment of Act 355 is yet another issue on which PN and PH differ in line with their respective governance ideologies.

The last issue is the electoral battle between contrasting governance ideologies that would break out in the case of a snap general election. As highlighted by the Malaysian analyst Tony Paridi Bagang, the PN coalition will become a formidable force if the three Malay parties are able to resolve the seat allocation impediment among themselves (Dzulkifly and Chan 2020). Should this happen, it is expected that PN will contest the election as a Malay/Muslim-centric multiracial coalition that will also include the non-Malay parties of West Malaysia as well as the independent GPS in East Malaysia. While Muhyiddin can bank on his current popularity, earned by leading the country out of the COVID-19 pandemic, and his personal appeal as a low-key and listening management figure (Welsh 2020a), it is his coalition's Malay/Muslim-centric governance ideology that will be the overarching factor in winning over not only conservative Malay-Muslim voters but also that community's centrist voters in West Malaysia.

As for the opposition bloc, an expanded East-West Malaysian multicultural ideology (from PH's West Malaysian-centric multiculturalism) is the way forward according to PH strategists such as Liew Chin Tong, who are pushing for the coalition to tap both the Sabah and Sarawak electorates as "kingmakers" in any change of government at the federal level (Liew 2020). A proposal supported by Mahathir himself — the possibility that Sabah's chief minister, Shafie Apdal, could be the prime ministerial candidate of the opposition bloc — cannot be dismissed, as it has the preliminary backing of both DAP and Amanah (*Malaysiakini* 2020d). Should Shafie enhance his leadership credibility through the upcoming Sabah election and should DAP and Amanah be able to get endorsement for such an unprecedented proposal from Anwar Ibrahim and PKR (Welsh 2020c; Chin 2020a), it is expected that the opposition bloc would then be equipped with the overarching East-West Malaysian multicultural governance ideology capable of appealing not only to its main liberal electoral base in West Malaysia but also to centrist voters in East Malaysia (Sabah and Sarawak).

From the above discussion of the four potent issues, it is obvious that the two sides of the political divide are contesting with each other in line with their respective governance ideologies. Like their differences in political composition, the differences in relation to governance ideology between PN and the opposition reflect their respective identities. While the ruling PN coalition is attempting to expand its electoral appeal to Malay-Muslim centrist voters through its Malay/Muslim-centric governance ideology, the opposition is also aiming to appeal to East-West Malaysia's centrist electoral base with a different governing ideology. Beyond seeking consolidation of its liberal electorate through PH's West Malaysian-centric multicultural governance ideology on the three issues of an alcohol ban, UEC recognition, and the amendment of Act 355, the opposition bloc is looking to venture into the centrist electoral base of East Malaysia. With the help of other multicultural opposition parties, such as Warisan, UPKO, the Mahathir faction, and even PSB, the PH coalition is trying to develop its East–West Malaysian multicultural governance ideology for the upcoming electoral battle nationwide.

Economic impact

The prolonged political instability caused by these polarizing national identity contestations has had a detrimental impact on the Malaysian economy, exacerbating the economic recession triggered by the COVID-19 pandemic. Unlike the PH government which was only confronted with the economic fallout of the U.S.–China trade war (Sipalan and Latiff 2019),[7] PN has had much more to deal with. It came to power at the height of the pandemic and was successful in stemming its second wave. But the PN government has a more difficult challenge ahead in responding to the economic recession produced by the nationwide movement control order (MCO) that saw most economic activity halted for a period of three months.

Malaysia had experienced political instability as far back as the PH administration of May 2018–February 2020. Following its rise to power, the PH government enthusiastically promoted the "New Malaysia" vision that rested on racial and religious equality and inclusiveness. From the attempted ratification of the International Convention on the Elimination of All Forms of Racial Discrimination (ICERD) and recognition of the

---

[7]After the optimistic growth forecasts of its first year in office, the PH government faced economic headwinds in its second year. For more information about the PH administration's reforms and economic growth during its first year, see (Lee 2019, pp. 32–33).

UEC, the PH administration's policy implementation was based on its West Malaysian-centric multicultural governance ideology, which of course provoked opposition along ethno-religious lines.

As reported by Wai Weng Hew, Ikatan Muslimin Malaysia (ISMA) and the allies of the Perlis state Mufti, Dr. Mohd. Asri Zainul Abidin (or Dr. Maza), were among the groups persuading urban middle-class Malay-Muslims to oppose PH on the basis that the "DAP-led" coalition government was a threat to Malay-Muslim rights (Hew 2020). The anti-ICERD rally and anti-UEC protest were the two outcomes that showcased the mobilization power of Ummah — a coalition of Malay-Muslim nongovernmental organizations (NGOs) of which ISMA is a component. The same avenues provided opportunities for both UMNO and PAS leaders to press the PH administration to halt or delay these two policies (Zain 2018; Fuad 2020; Ariff 2018). Throughout PH's 22 months in power, ethno-religious opposition voices and movements became so apparent and incontestable that one of its component parties, Bersatu, decided to break away from the coalition and join UMNO and PAS to form a new Malay/Muslim-centric government.

The current PN government will face the same predicament, given that UMNO, Bersatu, and PAS are confident of having solid support from a large segment of the Malay-Muslim electorate in West Malaysia. From the call for an alcohol ban, outright denial of UEC recognition, the amendment of Act 355, and probable propagation of Malay/Muslim-centric governance ideology in the event of a snap federal election (as explained in the last sub-section), it is clear that PN, and especially UMNO and PAS, are increasingly prepared to push for ethno-religious policies that will appeal more to its wider Malay-Muslim electorate.

As shown by the opposition to these three issues recently and in the past, ethno-religious policies remain contentious for business associations and liberal-leaning groups from both West and East Malaysia. These include Sarawak-based associations of pub, bistro, and café owners as well as the Federation of Chinese Associations Malaysia (Hua Zong) which steadfastly opposed the PAS call for an alcohol ban; the United Chinese School Committees' Association of Malaysia (Dong Zong) and Hua Zong, both of which continued to seek government recognition of the UEC; and the NGO group, BEBAS, which has been critical of the amendment of Act 355 since the days of the Najib administration (*Borneo Post* 2020b; Pfordten *et al.* 2020; *Malaysiakini* 2020c; Zainuddin 2017). For sure, there will be no shortage of opposition from these groups to the implementation of other Malay/Muslim-centric policies that are perceived as encroaching on (or not safeguarding) their rights in the future. If there is a lack of inclusive consultation with these groups on these policies, the PN administration may even find itself confronting the kind of public protests and rallies experienced by the previous PH government.

Needless to say, any such eventuality will result in prolonged political instability following the earlier abrupt change of regime in the middle of the COVID-19 pandemic. As the finance minister, Tengku Zafrul Aziz, has said, Malaysia is currently facing the worst economic recession in its history, with a short-term fall in GDP and rising unemployment (Landau 2020). The prolonged political instability will only serve to create more risk for the country's economy that was expected by the World Bank to contract by 3.1% in 2020 (World Bank 2020).[8] Both Fitch and Standard and Poor's revised their outlook on Malaysia from stable to negative in April and June 2020, respectively, due to the deterioration in economic growth (business activities and export earnings) and the tighter fiscal space resulting from the pandemic-induced MCO (Fitch Ratings 2020; Standard and Poor's 2020). Those assessments did not take account of the prolonged political instability likely to result from the national identity contestations between the two sides of the political divide. Observers of Malaysian politics and economy and ratings agencies, therefore, should be alert to this in the coming months.

Federal-State Authority Contestation

The second form of political contestation is federal-state authority contestation, especially between the PN federal government and state governments controlled by PH or the Warisan-PH-UPKO coalition. Unlike the contestation over national ideology which is independent of the COVID-19 pandemic, this form of contestation is a political battle induced by the global pandemic. It became evident in the issue of the implementation of the Conditional MCO (CMCO) throughout the country, as certain state governments modified the COVID-19 recovery

---

[8] Malaysia's central bank, Bank Negara, estimated Malaysia's GDP to be between −3.5% and −5.5% in 2020. For more information see Idris (2020).

order to suit their sub-national situations.[9] These discrepancies between the federal and state governments disrupted the inter-state supply chain of goods and services, thus increasing the extent of losses among businesses during the pandemic. This was a short-term economic impact of federal-state authority contestation.

Modification of CMCO by state governments

On May 1, 2020, Prime Minister Muhyiddin announced the reopening of the Malaysian economy in a national address made in conjunction with the Labour Day celebrations. The CMCO was the first COVID-19 recovery order, and it allowed most activities, especially economic activities, to resume throughout the nation. With the exception of team sports, religious gatherings, face-to-face learning in educational institutions, and interstate travel (even for the Muslim religious holiday/Eid celebrations), all other activities were to be permitted from May 4, 2020, onwards. This was an economically-motivated decision (as Muhyiddin himself admitted), as the cessation of most economic activities under the MCO had resulted in a daily economic loss of US$572.4 million (2.4 billion ringgit) (*Bernama* 2020c; Palansamy 2020).

That said, the announcement caught the state governments by surprise as there had been no warning by Putrajaya that the MCO was about to be replaced by the CMCO. In these circumstances, Prime Minister Muhyiddin's announcement triggered a federal-state authority contestation that saw the federal government mired in conflict with the state governments, especially those controlled by the opposition. Soon after the federal announcement, seven states rolled out their modified CMCO measures that were devised in line with their sub-national situations. While the prime minister's CMCO announcement was swiftly gazetted into federal law by Putrajaya, the PN-ruled states of Sarawak and Pahang emphasized their compliance with the federal government's order (Lim 2020a; Awang 2020),

---

[9]There were also sporadic spats between certain state governments and the federal government over the implementation of the Recovery MCO (RMCO) from June 10, 2020, onwards. However, these are excluded from this chapter as they did not spark any tangible federal-state authority contestation as the three states involved either complied with the RMCO after reporting no new outbreak clusters during the CMCO period (the case of Penang) or acted within their autonomous areas of jurisdiction under the Federal Constitution (the cases of Sabah and Sarawak).

whereas the opposition-controlled states of Penang, Selangor, Negeri Sembilan, Sabah, and Kedah took a different line.

The first of the opposition-controlled states to diverge from the federal CMCO decision was Kedah.[10] Following Sarawak's announcement that it would comply, the then first minister of Kedah, Mukhriz Mahathir, announced that his state would postpone implementation of the CMCO until the state's Security Working Committee had studied the measures and made its decision (*Bernama* 2020d). Kedah did eventually implement the CMCO on May 4 as announced by the federal government, although it made certain modifications designed to reduce the spread of disease, such as not allowing the reopening of recreational parks or dining-in at restaurants (*New Straits Times* 2020a).

The other opposition-controlled states of Selangor, Negeri Sembilan, Sabah, and Penang also modified the CMCO measures either moderately or drastically. Like Kedah, the state governments of Selangor, Sabah, and Negeri Sembilan opted for minor modifications — the former only allowing open-air sports and recreational activities while Negeri Sembilan maintained its total ban on those activities throughout the state (Nazari 2020; Jalil 2020). Both states, however, continued the ban on dining-in, only allowing takeaway delivery or drive through (Nazari 2020). In Sabah, Chief Minister Shafie Apdal adjusted his earlier decision not to comply with the federal government's CMCO and rolled out a phase-by-phase recovery plan for the state (Mohsen 2020). Like Selangor and Negeri Sembilan, North Borneo opted for minor modifications of the CMCO, and its version was comprised of three phases: the resumed operation of the construction, maintenance, and forestry sectors from May 8, 2020; food, agriculture, manufacturing, and logistics from May 9; and finally, tourism, recreation, and cultural and nature-related activities on May 10 (*Bernama* 2020g, 2020h, 2020f).

Of the opposition-controlled states, Penang was the only one that drastically modified the federal CMCO. Not only did it not implement the order on May 4, 2020 (like Sabah), it modified the CMCO in line with its Penang Gradual Recovery Strategy (PGRS). Under this strategy, all sectors of the economy had to go through three phases: preparation, familiarization, and opening. Four days (May 4–7) were devoted to preparation

---

[10]The Kedah government here refers to the former Mukhriz administration (or PH+ government) which was ousted by the PN coalition on May 12. Mukhriz is Mahathir's son and a member of the Mahathir faction in the Parliament.

according to the federal CMCO's standard operating procedures (SOPs); another five days (May 8–12) were allowed for familiarization; and the full opening of all sectors was to take place from May 13 (Chow 2020). Instead of drawing up a state-level recovery plan based on different sectors of the economy as implemented in Kedah, Selangor, Negeri Sembilan, and Sabah, Penang adopted a comprehensive "soft landing" approach that cut across all sectors, allowing for a gradual resumption of economic activities. As emphasized in the state's PGRS, the MCO would end on May 13, rather than May 4, the date announced by Prime Minister Muhyiddin in his Labour Day speech (Chow 2020; *Bernama* 2020c). Penang, therefore, modified Putrajaya's CMCO quite drastically and opened the economy in a gradual manner that took into consideration the risk of another wave of COVID-19 as well as its own economic recovery needs.

Competing claims of legal authority

With so many states expressing skepticism about the CMCO measures so soon after their announcement, the federal government issued a strong caution to the state governments. Senior minister and Minister of International Trade and Industry (MITI), Azmin Ali, framed the federal government's CMCO implementation plans in accordance with the Prevention and Control of Infectious Diseases Act 1988 (or Act 342). This gave Putrajaya lawful authority over the states to ensure that they implemented the recovery order starting on May 4, 2020 (*Borneo Post* 2020c). Azmin warned the state governments that the CMCO had legal force and they risked legal action being taken against them by businesses should they refuse to implement it (*Borneo Post* 2020c).

This show of legal authority by the federal government, however, failed to dissuade the state governments from arguing their case. Penang's chief minister, Chow Kon Yeow, explained that the state's PGRS allowed for the gradual implementation of the CMCO and even expressed readiness to face any lawsuits from businessmen who were dissatisfied with the state's modification of the order (Trisha 2020). His counterpart in Sabah, Shafie, also emphasized that the state governments were responsible for implementing the CMCO and that the federal government should have consulted the states before announcing the recovery order on May 1 (Fong 2020b).

However, it was the Selangor government that responded to Azmin's statement by pointing out that the states had concurrent legal authority with the federal government in the implementation of the CMCO within their territories. While stating that state governments had the legal right not to fully comply with all the federal CMCO measures, Selangor's chief minister, Amirudin Shari, described his state's modifications of the federal recovery order as being lawful under Malaysia's Federal Constitution (*The Star* 2020b).[11] As one of the state's executive councilors, Teng Chang Khim, pointed out, Paragraph 4 of the Ninth Schedule of the Constitution placed public health, sanitation, and prevention of diseases on the list of subjects under concurrent jurisdiction (*The Star* 2020b). This gave the state governments authority to modify the CMCO measures as long as they did not reject them completely. Rather, the states' modifications should be understood as a tightening of the federal measures and, as legal expert Derek Fernandez put it, it was a question of the degree of implementation rather than a matter of not implementing the CMCO at all (*Bernama* 2020a; Fernandez 2020).

From the modification of the CMCO across seven states in Malaysia, we can see that PN-controlled states were involved in federal-state authority contestation as well as opposition-controlled ones. What is different is the extent of the contestation: Sarawak and Pahang, states held by the ruling coalition, introduced slight modifications in line with their local situation and highlighted their general compliance with the federal CMCO to avoid conflict with the ruling PN coalition in Putrajaya. As for the opposition-controlled states, all but Penang introduced moderate modifications of the CMCO. These states included Selangor, Negeri Sembilan, Sabah, and Kedah (which was at that time administered by the Mukhriz administration). Penang introduced drastic modifications in line with its PGRS, and it was the only state to do so in the early days of the recovery order. All of these opposition-held state governments ended up in conflict with the federal government which claimed sole legal authority to implement the CMCO. These states refuted Putrajaya's legal authority claim, with Selangor taking the clearest stance, insisting that state governments have concurrent legal authority with the federal government to

---

[11]As state governments control the local municipal councils (or local governments) in Malaysia, they would be the ones ensuring the CMCO measures were complied with by businesses on the ground.

implement the CMCO measures under Paragraph 4 of the Ninth Schedule of the Federal Constitution.

Economic impact

The federal-state authority contestation had a direct impact on the Malaysian economy. While the discrepancies in the implementation of the Recovery MCO (RMCO) between the federal and state governments did not have a significant impact on Malaysia's economy, as most businesses had opened by then, this was not the case for the CMCO. As it was the first step toward full economic recovery from the pandemic, the federal-state conflict over the CMCO led to an abrupt disruption of the inter-state supply chain of goods and services throughout the country. After the 47-day-long MCO that halted most economic activities and disrupted the entire supply chain, the Malaysian business community was eager to get back to work and avoid more losses from the COVID-19 pandemic. Keen to prevent a similar crisis that saw agricultural producers and fishermen dumping their produce and suffering huge business losses as a result of the MCO's travel restrictions (Ng and Wahid 2020; Wahid and Ng 2020),[12] the larger business community was steadfast in its determination to avoid another round of inter-state supply chain disruption.

The first to respond to the federal-state conflict over the implementation of the CMCO was the Federation of Malaysian Manufacturers (FMM), who called for the state governments to implement the CMCO on the federal government's designated date of May 4, 2020. This would have freed-up economic activities throughout the country, regardless of whether a state was controlled by the ruling party or the opposition. According to this influential organization, only through consistent implementation of the CMCO throughout Malaysia could disruption of the interstate supply chain (including employees) be avoided, paving the way for industries to restart operations effectively (*Free Malaysia Today* 2020a).

A total of 59 chambers of commerce and industry associations joined the call 2 days after the FMM's initial gesture. A day after the CMCO was

---

[12]The closure of markets in the cities and the logistics companies' lack of foreign workers had affected the transportation of vegetables as well as the operations of warehouse facilities for fish.

supposed to come into force, Malaysia's most powerful business groups jointly lobbied for the state governments to follow the federal government's lead and allow most economic activities to resume in their states. Once again, they argued that it would be difficult for businesses to restart their operations if there was disruption to the supply chain in some states (Shankar 2020).[13] Furthermore, the 59 business groups highlighted the high stakes involved — potential collapse of the whole economy and job losses if companies were not allowed to resume their operations as early as possible (Shankar 2020).

After 47 days of the MCO that halted most economic activity in the country, any delay to the full resumption of the economy would increase the extent of most businesses' losses. And this delay and disruption was caused by a politically-inspired contestation between the PN federal government and the opposition-controlled state governments. With some of the states — such as Penang, Selangor, and Sabah — insisting on modifying the CMCO, it was clear that resumption of economic activities throughout the country was still a challenging goal. Although the delay in reopening was not as long as the business groups had feared, it still added to Malaysia's economic losses which during the MCO period amounted to US$572.4 million (2.4 billion ringgit) per day (Muhamad 2020).

Conclusion

In the Malaysian case, political contestations during the COVID-19 pandemic had some short-term economic impacts. At the federal level, the contestation over national identity between the ruling PN and the opposition bloc generated prolonged political instability on top of the pandemic-induced economic recession in 2020. This kind of economic impact rooted in politics threatens the stable economic environment foreign investors need for their businesses to prosper. Furthermore, the federal-state authority contestation that erupted over the reopening of the economy disrupted the inter-state supply chain of goods and services. The delay in the full resumption of economic activities added to the losses most businesses had suffered under the MCO.

---

[13] The chambers of commerce included local businessmen and foreign investors operating in Malaysia.

Going forward, there are two dynamics that will likely affect political contestation in Malaysia. The most immediate one is the upcoming Sabah state election in which the caretaker chief minister, Shafie Apdal, and the Warisan-PH-UPKO coalition are pitted against a confluence of political forces from both opposition parties in the state as well as the PN. Due to the balance of political power between PN and the opposition bloc at the federal level, this Sabah election will be the most important election in the state's history. As highlighted by Bridget Welsh, a win for the Warisan-PH-UPKO coalition would boost Shafie's political standing as a strong and decisive leader and the federal opposition bloc's prime-minister-in-waiting (Welsh 2020c). The only impediments are Anwar's stance on Shafie's potential nomination as the prime ministerial candidate for the opposition (including PH) and whether PKR is willing to cooperate or even support the latter in his bid for the premiership. As for PN, victory for Shafie in the state election would not augur well for Muhyiddin's credibility as the national leader given that the leader of the failed political coup in Sabah, Musa Aman, had previously linked the federal government with his attempt to form a new government in the East Malaysian state (*Bernama* 2020e). A state election win for Muhyiddin might increase the likelihood of an early snap election at the federal level.

The other political dynamic is the mounting pressure from UMNO for Muhyiddin to call an early snap federal election and distribute contested seats among the three Malay parties, especially in West Malaysia. While such internal politicking was less overt during the early months of the PN government, it has certainly become more apparent following former prime minister Najib Razak's conviction in one of the corruption cases against him. Three days after he was given a twelve-year sentence in July 2020 (Latiff 2020), UMNO's president, Zahid Hamidi, announced that his party would not formally join the PN coalition. Zahid unexpectedly revealed that Bersatu intended to join Muafakat Nasional (MN) — another coalition set up by UMNO and PAS to unite Malay-Muslims in West Malaysia (Tan 2020b).[14] As described by one political observer, Awang Azman Awang Pawi, UMNO's resistance to the registration of the PN coalition should be construed as a warning to Muhyiddin and an indication that MN will likely delay any negotiation with Bersatu over electoral seats until parliament is dissolved (Chin 2020b). The other option, of

---

[14]As revealed by Prime Minister Muhyiddin, Bersatu eventually applied to join MN on August 15, 2020. For more information, see (Rahim 2020).

course, is to continue supporting Muhyiddin as prime minister but at the same time make him and Bersatu beholden to UMNO under the MN umbrella. That would also lead to a snap federal election, as the probability of a Malay/Muslim-centric coalition victory in most West Malaysian seats is high (Loheswar 2020).

Both the Sabah state election and UMNO's increasing pressure on Muhyiddin point to a snap federal election. A huge victory for PN in such an election would not necessarily translate into an asymmetrical division of political power between the two sides. With PH-administered states (Selangor, Penang, and Negeri Sembilan) having resolved not to dissolve their state assemblies in tandem with any snap federal election (Ar 2020), PH will retain its political bases regardless of any losses at the federal level. Such a situation would also apply in Sabah if Shafie and his political coalition manage to hold on to power in the upcoming state election. Moreover, there is no guarantee that the Muhyiddin-led administration (whether under the banner of PN or MN) can replicate its success in handling COVID-19 and remain popular even after a snap federal election. As the opposition, PH, Warisan, and the other political parties will continue to contest the ruling coalition at both national and sub-national levels. In other words, national identity and federal-state authority contestations between both sides of the political divide will likely continue even after any snap federal election.

References

Ar, Zurairi. 2020. Pakatan Says Its State Govts Won't Be Dissolved Should Snap Polls Be Called. *Malay Mail*, July 6, 2020. https://www.malaymail.com/news/malaysia/2020/07/06/pakatan-says-its-state-govts-wont-be-dissolved-should-snap-polls-be-called/1881908 (accessed August 5, 2020).

Ariff, Syed Umar. 2018. Anti ICERD Rally Organisers Claim They Have Met Their Target. *New Straits Times*, December 8, 2018. https://www.nst.com.my/news/nation/2018/12/438643/anti-icerd-rally-organisers-claim-they-have-met-their-target (accessed July 31, 2020).

Aruno, C., Hanis Zainal, and R. Aravinthan. 2020. Govt Urged to Promote Awareness on Drink Driving. *The Star*, May 30, 2020. https://www.thestar.com.my/news/nation/2020/05/30/govt-urged-to-promote-awareness-on-drink-driving (accessed July 28, 2020).

Augustin, Robin. 2020. Zuraida's Position Precarious, Says Analyst. *Free Malaysia Today*, July 17, 2020. https://www.freemalaysiatoday.com/category/

nation/2020/07/17/zuraidas-position-precarious-says-analyst/ (accessed July 26, 2020).

Awang Pawi, Awang Azman. 2018. Kabinet Tampilkan Demografi Kaum (Cabinet Showcases Racial Demography). *Berita Harian (Daily News)*, July 3, 2018. https://www.bharian.com.my/kolumnis/2018/07/444363/kabinet-tampilkan-demografi-kaum (accessed July 28, 2020).

Awang, Asrol. 2020. Pahang Setuju Laksana PKPB (Pahang Agrees to Implement CMCO). *Harian Metro (Metro Daily)*, May 8, 2020. https://www.hmetro.com.my/mutakhir/2020/05/576085/pahang-setuju-laksana-pkpb (accessed August 2, 2020).

Aziz, Adam. 2019. No Two-Thirds Majority for Bill to Make Sabah, Sarawak Equal Partners. *The Edge Markets*, April 9, 2019. https://www.theedgemarkets.com/article/no-twothirds-majority-bill-make-sabah-sarawak-equal-partners (accessed July 26, 2020).

Bernama. 2020a. Can State Govts Choose to Defy MCO? Lawyers Explain. *Bernama,* May 5, 2020. https://www.malaymail.com/news/malaysia/2020/05/05/can-state-govts-choose-to-defy-cmco-lawyers-explain/1863398 (accessed August 2, 2020).

Bernama. 2020b. Dr Mahathir's New Party Now Known as Pejuang. *Bernama,* August 12, 2020. https://www.bernama.com/en/politics/news.php?id=1869675 (accessed August 19, 2020).

Bernama. 2020c. Essence of Conditional Movement Control Order. *Bernama,* May 1, 2020. https://web.archive.org/web/20200502065534/https://www.bernama.com/en/general/news.php?id=1837487 (accessed August 2, 2020).

Bernama. 2020d. Kedah Defers Implementation of CMCO — Mukhriz. *Bernama,* May 2, 2020. https://www.bernama.com/en/general/news_covid-19.php?id=1837879 (accessed August 2, 2020).

Bernama. 2020e. Musa Aman Claims to Have Simple Majority to Form Sabah Government. *Bernama,* July 29, 2020. https://www.theedgemarkets.com/article/musa-aman-claims-have-simple-majorityform-sabah-govt (accessed August 5, 2020).

Bernama. 2020f. PKPB: Sabah Benarkan Beberapa Lagi Sektor Beroperasi Berperingkat (CMCO: Sabah Allows a Few More Sectors Operating in Phases). *Bernama,* May 10, 2020. https://www.bharian.com.my/berita/nasional/2020/05/687439/pkpb-sabah-benarkan-beberapa-lagi-sektor-beroperasi-berperingkat (accessed August 2, 2020).

Bernama. 2020g. PKPB: Sabah Benarkan Sektor Pembinaan, Penyelengaraan, Perhutanan Beroperasi Mulai Hari Ini (CMCO: Sabah Allows Construction, Maintenance and Forestry Sectors to Operate Starting Today). *Bernama,* May 8, 2020. https://www.bernama.com/bm/am/news_covid-19.php?id=1839718 (accessed August 2, 2020).

Bernama. 2020h. PKPB: Sektor Peruncitan, Makanan, Pengangkutan Awam Beroperasi Mulai Hari Ini di Sabah (CMCO: Retail, Food and Public Transport Sectors to Operate in Sabah Today Onwards). *Bernama,* May 9, 2020. http://www.buletinsabah.com/2020/05/pkpb-sektor-peruncitan-makanan.html (accessed August 2, 2020).

Borneo Post. 2020a. First Coronavirus Cases in Malaysia: 3 Chinese Nationals Confirmed Infected, Quarantined in Sungai Buloh Hospital. *Borneo Post,* January 25, 2020. https://www.theborneopost.com/2020/01/25/first-corona-virus-cases-in-malaysia-3-chinese-nationalsconfirmed-infected-quarantined-in-sungai-buloh-hospital/ (accessed July 26, 2020).

Borneo Post. 2020b. People Generally Against PAS' Suggestion on Alcohol Ban. *Borneo Post,* May 28, 2020. https://www.theborneopost.com/2020/05/28/people-generally-againstpas-suggestion-on-alcohol-ban/ (accessed July 28, 2020).

Borneo Post. 2020c. States Have No 'Lawful Authority' to Stop Businesses under CMCO, Says Azmin. *Borneo Post,* May 4, 2020. https://www.theborneopost.com/2020/05/04/states-have-no-lawful-authority-tostop-businesses-under-cmco-says-azmin/ (accessed August 2, 2020).

Cabinet of Malaysia. 2020. Ahli-Ahli Jemaah Menteri (Cabinet Ministers). Cabinet of Malaysia Website. Last modified August 6, 2020. http://www.kabinet.gov.my/bkpp/index.php/anggota-pentadbiran/menteri (accessed August 7, 2020).

Chew, Amy. 2019. Malaysia's Dangerous Racial and Religious Trajectory. *The Interpreter,* September 25, 2019. https://www.lowyinstitute.org/the-interpreter/malaysia-s-dangerous-racial-and-religious-trajectory (accessed July 26, 2020).

Chin, Emmanuel Santa Maria. 2020a. After Dr M, Amanah and DAP Say Shafie-for-PM Proposal Needs to Clear Party and Pakatan Top Council First. *Malay Mail,* June 27, 2020. https://www.malaymail.com/news/malay2020/06/27/after-dr-m-amanah-and-dap-say-shafie-for-pm-proposal-needs-to-clear-party-a/1879423 (accessed July 31, 2020).

Chin, Emmanuel Santa Maria. 2020b. Analysts: Umno's Perikatan 'Snub' More to Do with Strengthening Party, Muafakat's Position Ahead of GE15 Seat Negotiations than Najib's SRC Conviction. *Malay Mail,* August 1, 2020. https://www.malaymail.com/news/malaysia/2020/08/01/analysts-umnos-perikatan-snub-more-to-do-with-strengthening-party-muafakats/1890043 (accessed August 5, 2020).

Chin, James. March 2020c. Race and Religion in Command: Malaysia Returns to Identity Politics. *Global Asia* 15(1): 48–53.

Chow, Kon Yeow. 2020. Media Statement by the Chief Minister of Penang on 3 May 2020 at Komtar, George Town. Invest Penang Website. Last modified May 3, 2020. https://investpenang.gov.my/wp-content/uploads/2020/05/20200503_CKY_MCO47_EkonomiOpen_English-rs-rev.pdf (accessed August 2, 2020).

Dayak Daily. 2020. GPS Supports Muhyiddin but Not Part of PN Coalition. *Dayak Daily*, May 17, 2020. https://dayakdaily.com/gps-supports-muhyiddin-but-not-part-of-pncoalition/ (accessed July 28, 2020).

Dzulkifly, Danial and Julia Chan. 2020. Analysts: If Perikatan Can Sort Out Bersatu, It May Be a Formidable Force Once Snap Polls Called. *Malay Mail*, June 13, 2020. https://www.malaymail.com/news/malaysia/2020/06/13/analysts-if-perikatan-can-sort-out-bersatu-itmay-be-formidable-forceonce/1874985 (accessed July 30, 2020).

Fernandez, Derek. 2020. Why States Have No Power to Modify Putrajaya's MCO. *Free Malaysia Today*, May 5, 2020. https://www.freemalaysiatoday.com/category/opinion/2020/05/05/whystates-have-no-power-to-modify-putrajayas-mco/ (accessed August 2, 2020).

Fitch Ratings. 2020. Fitch Revises Malaysia Outlook to Negative, Affirms at 'A-'. Fitch Ratings Website. Last modified August 9, 2020. https://www.fitchratings.com/research/sovereigns/fitch-revises-malaysia-outlook-to-negative-affirms-at-a-09-04-2020 (accessed August 1, 2020).

Fong, Durie Rainer. 2020a. Nothing Personal, Sabah CM Tells Putrajaya on Non-Compliance with CMCO. *Free Malaysia Today*, May 5, 2020. https://www.freemalaysiatoday.com/category/nation/2020/05/05/nothing-personal-sabah-cm-tells-putrajaya-on-non-compliance-with-cmco/ (accessed August 2, 2020).

Fong, Durie Rainer. 2020b. Kami Sokong Dr M, tapi akan Kerjasama dengan Kerajaan Muhyiddin (We Support Dr M but Will Cooperate with Muhyiddin Government). *Free Malaysia Today*, March 5, 2020. https://www.freemalaysiatoday.com/category/bahasa/2020/03/05/kami-sokong-dr-m-tapiakan-kerjasama-dengan-kerajaan-muhyiddin-kata-shafie/ (accessed July 27, 2020).

Free Malaysia Today. 2020a. All Businesses Must Resume at Same Time, FMM Tells State Govts. *Free Malaysia Today*, May 3, 2020. https://www.freemalaysiatoday.com/category/nation/2020/05/03/all-businesses-must-resume-at-same-time-fmm-tells-state-govts/ (accessed August 4, 2020).

Free Malaysia Today. 2020b. It's Official, Muhyiddin Sworn in as PM8. *Free Malaysia Today*, March 1, 2020. https://www.freemalaysiatoday.com/category/nation/2020/03/01/itsofficial-muhyiddin-sworn-in-as-pm8/ (accessed July 27, 2020).

Fuad, Faris. 2018. Rais Suggests Government Integrates UEC into Mainstream Education System. *New Straits Times*, July 28, 2018. https://www.nst.com.my/news/nation/2018/07/395479/rais-suggests-government-integrates-uec-mainstreameducation-system (accessed July 29, 2020).

Fuad, Faris. 2020. 2,000 Umat Islam Banjiri Himpunan Kebangkitan Ummah (2,000 Muslims Flooded the Rise of Islam Brotherhood Gathering). *Berita Harian (Daily News)*, July 28, 2020. https://www.bharian.com.my/berita/nasional/2018/07/454865/2000-umat-islambanjiri-himpunan-kebangkitan-ummah (accessed July 31, 2020).

Gomez, Edmund Terrence. 2019. Patronage-based Business as Usual in 'New Malaysia'. *East Asia Forum*, May 8, 2019. https://www.eastasiaforum.org/2019/05/08/patronage-based-business-as-usual-in-new-malaysia/ (accessed July 26, 2020).

Gomez, Edmund Terrence. 2020. How Muhyiddin Consolidates Power through GLC Appointments. *Malaysiakini*, April 11, 2020. https://www.malaysiakini.com/news/520044 (accessed July 26, 2020).

Hassan, Hazlin. 2020. Drunk Driving a Racial, Religious Weapon in Malaysian Politics. *The Straits Times*, May 30, 2020. https://www.straitstimes.com/asia/se-asia/drink-driving-a-racial-religious-weapon-in-malaysian-politics (accessed July 28, 2020).

Hew, Wai Weng. 2020. Manufacturing Malay Unity and the Downfall of Pakatan Harapan. *New Mandala*, June 8, 2020. https://www.newmandala.org/manufacturing-malay-unity-and-the-downfall-of-pakatan-harapan/ (accessed July 27, 2020).

Ho, Wah Foon. 2020. Malaysia's Dr Mahathir Quits as Premier. *The Star*, February 24, 2020. https://www.thestar.com.my/news/regional/2020/02/24/malaysias-drmahathir-quits-as-premier (accessed July 27, 2020).

Idris, Ahmad Naqib. 2020. BNM Revises 2020 GDP Forecast to between −3.5% and −5.5% amid Unprecedented MCO Length. *The Edge Markets*, August 14, 2020. https://www.theedgemarkets.com/article/bnm-2020-gdp-forecast-revised-between-35-and-55 (accessed August 1, 2020).

Jalil, Mohd. Amin. 2020. PKPB: Hanya Sektor Tertentu Boleh Beroperasi di NS (CMCO: Only Certain Sectors are Allowed to Operate). *Berita Harian (Daily News)*, May 3, 2020. https://www.bharian.com.my/berita/wilayah/2020/05/684574/pkpb-hanya-sektortertentu-boleh-beroperasi-di-ns (accessed August 2, 2020).

Jomo, K.S. and Hui Wee Chong. November 2002. The Political Economy of Malaysian Federalism: Economic Development, Public Policy and Conflict Containment. UNU-WIDER Discussion Paper, No. 113, pp. 1–48.

Kannan, Hashini Kavishtri and Mohd Husni Mohd Noor. 2018. Dr M Says 'No' to Local Council Elections. *New Straits Times*, December 10, 2018. https://www.nst.com.my/news/nation/2018/12/439143/dr-m-says-no-local-council-elections (accessed July 26, 2020).

Kaos Jr, Joseph and Jo Timbuong. 2018. Uphold BM, No to UEC, Says PAS. *The Star*, September 2018. https://www.thestar.com.my/news/nation/2018/09/16/pas-no-to-uec-recognition (accessed July 29, 2020).

Landau, Esther. 2020. Malaysia Facing Worst Economic Recession in its History. *New Straits Times*, May 2, 2020. https://www.nst.com.my/news/nation/2020/05/589338/malaysia-facing-worst-economic-recession-itshis (accessed August 1, 2020).

Latiff, Rozanna. 2020. Malaysia's Najib Sentenced to Over a Decade in Jail in 1MDB Trial. *Reuters*, July 28, 2020. https://www.reuters.com/article/

usmalaysia-politics-najib/malaysias-najib-sentenced-to-over-a-decade-in-jailin-1mdb-trial-idUSKCN24T042 (accessed August 5, 2020).

Lee, Annabelle. 2020. Mahathir Announces 'Independent' Malay Party, Not Tied to Harapan or BN. *Malaysiakini*, August 7, 2020. https://www.malaysiakini.com/news/537765 (accessed August 19, 2020).

Lee, Cassey. 2019. Economic Reforms in the Aftermath of Regime Change in Malaysia. ISEAS Economics Working Paper, No. 9, pp. 1–43.

Liew, Chin Tong. 2020. The Great Reset (Part 1) — Resetting Malaysian Politics. Liew Chin Tong Website. Last modified July 3, 2020. https://liewchintong.com/2020/07/03/the-great-reset-part-1-resetting-malaysianpolitics/ (accessed July 30, 2020).

Lim, How Pim. 2020a. Sarawak will not Implement Condition MCO on May 4. *Borneo Post*, May 2, 2020. https://www.theborneopost.com/2020/05/02/sarawak-will-not-implementconditional-mco-on-may-4/ (accessed August 2, 2020).

Lim, Ida. 2020b. Dr M Resigns as PM. *Malay Mail*, February 24, 2020. https://www.malaymail.com/news/malaysia/2020/02/24/dr-m-resigns-aspm/1840368 (accessed July 26, 2020).

Loh, Francis. 2018. Centralised Federalism in Malaysia: Urgent Need to Decentralise. Aliran Website. Last modified June 20, 2018. https://aliran.com/aliran-csi/centralised-federalism-in-malaysia-urgent-need-todecentralise/ (accessed July 26, 2020).

Loheswar, R. 2020. As Muhyiddin Seeks Mandate to Lead Malaysia, Will Perikatan Back Him as PM? *Malay Mail*, June 25, 2020. https://www.malaymail.com/news/malaysia/2020/06/25/as-muhyiddin-seeksmandate-to-lead-malaysia-will-perikatan-back-him-as-pm/1878614 (accessed August 5, 2020).

Malay Mail. 2020. PAS Calls on Govt to Suspend Alcohol Sales, Production to Prevent Drunk Driving in Malaysia. *Malay Mail*, May 26, 2020. https://www.malaymail.com/news/malaysia/2020/05/26/pas-calls-on-govt-to-suspend-alcohol-salesproduction-to-prevent-drunk-driv/1869726 (accessed July 28, 2020).

Malaysiakini. 2020a. Hadi: PAS Open to 'Pakatan Nasional' Gov't to Unite Malay-Muslim Power. *Malaysiakini*, February 7, 2020. https://www.malaysiakini.com/news/509945 (accessed July 28, 2020).

Malaysiakini. 2020b. Nga: DAP will Not Hesitate to Leave Gov't if UEC Not Recognised. *Malaysiakini*, January 29, 2020. https://www.malaysiakini.com/news/508784 (accessed July 29, 2020).

Malaysiakini. 2020c. PM Hopes for Government Recognition of UEC, Says Huazong. *Malaysiakini*, July 17, 2020. https://www.malaysiakini.com/news/534931 (accessed July 29, 2020).

Malaysiakini. 2020d. Shafie as PM and Anwar, Mukhriz as Dpms Backed by Amanah, DAP Leaders — Dr M. *Malaysiakini*, June 27, 2020. https://www.malaysiakini.com/news/532047 (accessed July 30, 2020).

Malaysiakini. 2020e. Umno Youth Wants Federal Law to Regulate Sales and Consumption. *Malaysiakini*, May 2, 2020. https://www.malaysiakini.com/news/527452 (accessed July 28, 2020).

Mohd. Amin, Khairil Anwar. 2020. Muhyiddin Harus Kota Janji Iktiraf UEC (Muhyiddin Should Keep His Promise for UEC Recognition). *Sinar Harian (Daily Light)*, July 18, 2020. https://www.sinarharian.com.my/article/92696/BERITA/Nasional/Muhyiddin-harus-kota-janji-iktiraf-UECDAP (accessed July 29, 2020).

Mohsen, Amar Shah. 2020. Sabah Too Will Not Implement CMCO. *The Sun Daily*, May 3, 2020. https://www.thesundaily.my/home/sabah-too-will-notimplement-cmco-HY2364779 (accessed August 2, 2020).

Mok, Opalyn. 2017. Guan Eng: BN Components Must Bear Full Responsibility Over RUU355 Tabling. *Malay Mail*, April 7, 2017. https://www.malaymail.com/news/malaysia/2017/04/07/guan-eng-bn-componentsmust-bear-full-responsibility-over-ruu355-tabling/1351579 (accessed July 29, 2020).

Muhamad, Hasimi. 2020. Malaysia Loses RM 2.4 Billion A Day Throughout MCO — Prime Minister. *Astro Awani*, May 1, 2020. http://english.astroawani.com/malaysia-news/malaysia-loses-rm2-4-billion-daythroughout-mco-prime-minister-241019 (accessed August 4, 2020).

Nazari, Tasneem. 2020. Selangor Announces a Modified Version of CMCO for Reopening for Economy. *The Rakyat Post*, May 3, 2020. https://www.therakyatpost.com/2020/05/03/selangor-announces-a-modified-versionof-cmco-for-reopening-of-economy/ (accessed August 2, 2020).

New Straits Times. 2020a. CMCO: Selangor, Kedah to Comply with SOP. *New Straits Times*, May 6, 2020. https://www.nst.com.my/news/nation/2020/05/590277/cmco-selangor-kedah-comply-sop (accessed August 2, 2020).

New Straits Times. 2020b. PM Denies Claim Gov't Will Recognise UEC. *New Straits Times*, July 19, 2020. https://www.nst.com.my/news/nation/2020/07/609804/pm-denies-claimgovt-will-recognise-uec (accessed July 29, 2020).

Ng, Xiang Yi and Ramieza Wahid. 2020. Cameron Highlands Farmers Dump Hundreds of Tonnes of Vegetables. *Malaysiakini*, March 25, 2020. https://www.malaysiakini.com/news/516704 (accessed August 4, 2020).

Ng, Xiang Yi. 2020. UMNO, PAS Oppose Zuraida's Local Government Election Plan. *Malaysiakini*, July 15, 2020. https://www.malaysiakini.com/news/534567 (accessed July 26, 2020).

Pakatan Harapan (PH). 2020. Buku Harapan. https://kempen.s3.amazonaws.com/manifesto/Manifesto_text/Manifesto_PH_EN.pdf (accessed July 26, 2020).

Palansamy, Yiswaree. 2020. PM: Almost All Economic Sectors Can Reopen May 4, Subject to Conditions. *Malay Mail*, May 1, 2020. https://www.malaymail. com/news/malaysia/2020/05/01/pm-almost-all-economicsectors-businesses-can-reopen-may-4-subject-to-condi/1861989 (accessed August 2, 2020).

Parliament of Malaysia. 2020a. Ahli Dewan (Members of House of Representatives). Parliament of Malaysia Website. https://www.parlimen. gov.my/ahli-dewan.html?uweb=dr& (last accessed August 8, 2020).

Parliament of Malaysia. 2020b. Sitting Arrangement of Members of House of Representatives. Parliament of Malaysia Website. Last modified February 21, 2020. https://www.parlimen.gov.my/tempat-duduk-ahli-dr. html?uweb=dr&lang=en (accessed July 28, 2020).

Periasamy, M. 2019. Kaum India Tidak Perlu Bimbang Dengan RUU 355 (Indians Should Not Worried of the Act 355). *Astro Awani*, December 8, 2019. http://www.astroawani.com/berita-malaysia/kaum-india-tidak-perlu-bimbang-denganruu-355-224758 (accessed July 29, 2020).

Pfordten, Diyana, C. Aruno, and R. Aravinthan. 2020. Dong Zong Hopes to Meet PM to Discuss UEC Issue. *The Star*, July 24, 2020. https://www.thestar.com. my/news/nation/2020/07/24/dong-zong-hopes-to-meet-pm-to-discuss-uec-issue (accessed August 1, 2020).

Poveira, Adib and Ayisy Yusof. 2020. Mahathir Does Not Share Muhyiddin's Views on Umno Cooperation. *New Straits Times*, February 27, 2020. https:// www.nst.com.my/news/politics/2020/02/569774/dr-m-does-notshare-muhy-iddins-views-umno-cooperation (accessed July 27, 2020).

Rahim, Rahimy. 2020. Bersatu to Join Muafakat Nasional, Says Muhyiddin. *The Star*, August 15, 2020. https://www.thestar.com.my/news/nation/2020/08/15/ bersatu-to-join-muafakat-nasional-says-muhyiddin (accessed August 5, 2020).

Robertson, May. 2018. Non-Muslims Have Right to Debate Shariah Bill Too, Says Anwar. *Malay Mail*, June 10, 2018. https://www.malaymail.com/news/ malaysia/2018/06/10/non-muslims-have-right-to-debate-shariah-billtoo-says-anwar/1640379 (accessed July 29, 2020).

Standard and Poor's. 2020. S&P Revises Malaysia's Outlook to Negative on Risks to Fiscal Metrics. S&P Global Market Intelligence Website. Last modified June 26, 2020. https://www.spglobal.com/marketintelligence/en/ news-insights/latest-news-headlines/s-p-revises-malaysia-s-outlook-to-negative-on-risks-to-fiscal-metrics-59214999 (accessed August 1, 2020).

Shankar, Arjuna Chandran. 2020. 59 Chambers of Commerce and Industry Associations Call for All States to Restart Economic Activities. *The Edge Markets*, May 5, 2020. https://www.theedgemarkets.com/article/59-cham-bers-commerce-and-industry-associations-call-all-states-restarteconomic-activities (accessed August 4, 2020).

Sipalan, Joseph and Rozanna Latiff. 2019. Malaysia's Hopes of Economic Revival under Mahathir Fade. *Reuters*, May 10, 2019. https://www.reuters. com/article/us-malaysia-politics-analysis/malaysias-hopes-ofeconomic-revival-under-mahathir-fade-idUSKCN1SG08R (accessed July 31, 2020).

Suhaimi, Nazmi. 2020. 'Alcohol Ban' Sign of Things to Come. *New Sarawak Tribune*, May 28, 2020. https://www.newsarawaktribune.com.my/alcoholban-sign-of-things-to-come/ (accessed July 28, 2020).

Tan, Arial. 2020c. Why Pakatan Harapan Fell, *Today Online*, March 3, 2020, https://www.todayonline.com/commentary/why-pakatan-harapan-fell-mahathir-anwar-muhiyiddin-malaysia (accessed July 27, 2020).

Tan, Tarrence. 2020a. FT Minister: Stop Issuing Liquor Licenses Until New Guidelines in Place, Laws Revised. *The Star*, June 1, 2020. https://www. thestar.com.my/news/nation/2020/06/01/ft-minister-stop-issuingliquor-licences-until-new-guidelines-in-place-laws-revised (accessed July 28, 2020).

Tan, Tarrence. 2020b. Zahid: Umno Will Not Formally Join Perikatan, To Continue Alliance with Muafakat (Updated). *The Star*, July 30, 2020. https://www. thestar.com.my/news/nation/2020/07/30/zahid-umno-will-not-formallyjoin-perikatan-to-continue-alliance-with-muafakat (accessed August 5, 2020).

The Edge Markets. 2020. Party Leaders Leaving without Holding Press Conference. *The Edge Markets*, February 23, 2020. https://www.theedge-markets.com/article/more-20-vip-carsseen-entering-istana-negara-follow-ing-flurry-meetings-among-political (accessed July 27, 2020).

The Malaysian Insight. 2020a. 'Fei musilin sui you he jiu quan', lu zhaofu: jiu hou kaiche jue bu kuanrong (Non-Muslims Have the Right to Drink, Loke Siew Fook: No Tolerance on Drunk Driving). *The Malaysian Insight*, May 27, 2020. https://www.themalaysianinsight.com/chinese/s/248680 (accessed July 28, 2020).

The Malaysian Insight. 2020b. RUU355 to Take a Backseat, Says PAS Veep. *The Malaysian Insight*, July 28, 2020. https://www.themalaysianinsight. com/s/263556 (accessed July 29, 2020).

The Star. 2018. UMNO Claims UEC Recognition is a Conspiracy to Erode Bumi Right. *The Star*, July 13, 2018. https://www.thestar.com.my/news/ nation/2018/07/13/umno-claims-uec-recognition-is-a-conspiracy-to-erode-bumi-rights/ (accessed July 29, 2020).

The Star. 2020a. Selangor MB: We Need Not Fully Comply with Govt's CMCO Requisites. *The Star*, May 6, 2020. https://www.thestar.com.my/news/ nation/2020/05/06/selangor-mb-we-need-not-fully-comply-with-govtscmco-requisites (accessed August 2, 2020).

The Star. 2020b. Six Party Leaders Granted Audience with King. *The Star*, February 23, 2020. https://www.thestar.com.my/news/nation/2020/02/23/ six-party-leadersgranted-audience-with-king (accessed July 27, 2020).

Trisha, N. 2020. CMCO: We're Ready to Face Any Legal Suits for Protecting 1.8 Million Penangites, Says State CM. *The Star*, May 5, 2020. https://www. thestar.com.my/news/nation/2020/05/05/conditional-mco-we039reready-to-face-any-legal-suits-for-protecting-18mil-penangites-says-state-cm (accessed August 2, 2020).

Wahid, Ramieza and Xiang Yi Ng. 2020. Fishermen are Dumping their Catch as Well. *Malaysiakini*, March 26, 2020. https://www.malaysiakini.com/news/516942 (accessed August 4, 2020).

Welsh, Bridget. 2020a. Muhyiddin's 100 Days. Bridget Welsh Website. Last modified June 9, 2020. https://bridgetwelsh.com/articles/muhyiddins-100-days/ (accessed July 30, 2020).

Welsh, Bridget. 2020b. The Day the Harapan Government Died. Bridget Welsh Website. Last modified February 24, 2020. https://bridgetwelsh.com/articles/the-day-theharapan-government-died/ (accessed July 28, 2020).

Welsh, Bridget. 2020c. The Sabah Political Crisis: What It Means for Pakatan, Perikatan and Malaysia. Bridget Welsh Website. Last modified August 8, 2020. https://bridgetwelsh.com/articles/the-sabah-political-crisis-what-it-means-for-pakatanperikatan-and-malaysia/ (accessed August 9, 2020).

Woo, Wing Thye. 2019. Decentralisation the Best Bet for Malaysia's Growth. *East Asia Forum*, March 24, 2019. https://www.eastasiaforum.org/2019/03/24/decentralisation-the-best-bet-for-malaysiasgrowth/ (accessed July 26, 2020).

World Bank. 2020. Malaysia's Economy Expected to Contract Sharply Due to COVID-19 in 2020; Growth to Rebound in 2021: World Bank. World Bank Website. Last modified June 24, 2020. https://www.worldbank.org/en/news/press-release/2020/06/24/malaysias-economy-expected-to-contractsharply-due-to-covid-19-in-2020-growth-to-rebound-in-2021-world-bank (accessed August 1, 2020).

Yeoh, Tricia. April 2019. Reviving the Spirit of Federalism: Decentralisation Policy Options for a New Malaysia. *Policy Ideas* 59: 1–26.

Zain, Haspaizi. 2018. Ummah: Permit or No Permit, Anti-Icerd Rally will Go on. *Malaysiakini*, November 22, 2018. https://www.malaysiakini.com/news/452860 (accessed July 31, 2020).

Zainuddin, Dania. 2017. RUU 355 — Will It Affect the Non-Muslims? *Astro Awani*, March 18, 2017. http://english.astroawani.com/malaysia-news/ruu-355-will-it-affect-non-muslims-135896 (accessed August 1, 2020).

Chapter 12

Conclusion: Prospect for a More Resilient Southeast Asia Embedded in the Major Power Politics

Masahiro Matsumura and Alan Hao Yang

Introduction

This book is aimed at highlighting many ASEAN factors and echoes the importance of ASEAN in the fields of geopolitics, economic and trade and traditional security cooperation, and major/middle powers' regional strategies. However, the authors of this book are not overoptimistic ASEAN idealists. Instead, the authors all embraced a pragmatic idea that ASEAN has been regarded as an intervening variable in the study of political economy in Southeast Asia as well as a core platform for regional interaction and a facilitator. Although ASEAN is situated in and constrained by the competition and cooperation of power politics, ASEAN-led regionalism cannot be overlooked.

In this concluding chapter, discussion will begin with the recent U.S.-led engagement in Southeast Asia since the summer of 2021, echoing the U.S.–Indonesia maritime cooperation analysis of the introduction chapter to unpack how the United States, an important global power. The discussion will prioritize Southeast Asia on its geo-political and economic agenda with the purpose of illustrating our research findings and highlight the future direction of navigating the evolving regional political economy in Southeast Asia.

Vice U.S. President Harris' Asia Trip in the Summer of 2021

After taking office, U.S. President Joe Biden has repeatedly highlighted the importance of internationalism, rule-based international order, and Indo-Pacific cooperation in his foreign policy. Since the summer of 2021, Biden's security and diplomatic hands have actively visited Europe and the Indo-Pacific region to gain the trust and support of its allies.

In addition to his own trip to Europe in June 2021 to participate in several summits, President Biden reached with his counterparts many value-based high-level consensus (which had specific implications on the security of the Taiwan Strait and the wider Indo-Pacific region). Furthermore, he tried to strengthen the ties with Europe by strengthening the strategic partnerships for shaping the liberal international order; then, the Deputy Secretary of State Wendy Sherman visited Indonesia, Cambodia, and Thailand in May and June; Secretary of State Antony Blinken visited India in July and participated in Japan and South Korea Foreign Ministers Dialogue, and also attended the virtual meeting of ASEAN foreign ministers, while Defense Secretary Lloyd Austin visited Singapore, the Philippines, and Vietnam at the end of July. These high-level visits did increase U.S. engagement in Southeast Asia.

Notably, Vice President Kamala Harris made her first official trip to the Indo-Pacific region in August 2021, and visited Singapore and Vietnam. Following the Biden doctrine in defense and diplomacy, Harris' interviews and remarks during her Asian visit have demonstrated that some new features in the U.S. Indo-Pacific strategy and regional architecture are emerging in a more pragmatic manner. As for Southeast Asia, Harris' visit in August 2021 arguably has at least three strategic implications as "one reinforcement," "two reaffirmations," and "three priorities".

A reinforcement

Harris' visit coincided with the hasty withdrawal of U.S. armed forces from Afghanistan. Amid surprise and skepticism thereof across Asia, Harris' public speeches in Singapore and Vietnam repeatedly referred to the importance of Singapore and Vietnam, two important members of ASEAN. This affirmation also clearly indicates U.S. support for the important role of Southeast Asia in achieving a peaceful, stable, and prosperous Indo-Pacific region, as well as its long-term commitment to strengthening partnerships with regional countries. Harris' trip to Asia also highlights different approaches to Southeast Asia between the Biden and Trump administration.

In the first year of the Biden administration, its several high-level officials visited Asia one after another to exchange views with leaders of various countries, plausibly with intention to continue and strengthen former U.S. President Obama's commitment to strengthening the cooperation with ASEAN in the first U.S.–ASEAN Summit of 2016.

More recently, in May 2022, the U.S.–ASEAN special summit held in Washington D.C., demonstrated the Biden administration's emphasis on the importance of Southeast Asia, its support for the overall recovery structure of the ASEAN, and U.S. multifaceted cooperation with Southeast Asia, and also revealed that the advancement of the ASEAN–U.S. comprehensive strategic partnership to be realized by the end of 2022.

Two reaffirmations

The unity of ASEAN countries and the partnership of a more integrated ASEAN community with the United States will contribute significantly to the peace and stability of the Indo-Pacific mega-region. In addition to countering China's stronger regional hegemonic ambition, more urgently in the face of the raging COVID-19 pandemic today, Southeast Asia has continued to fight against the pandemic, and is committed to the recovery of economic and social resilience. ASEAN countries are in great need of gaining external support and seeking for closer partnerships with major powers in the process of pandemic control and post pandemic recovery.

This clearly reflects the two reaffirmations of Harris' Asia trip. The first is on the importance of a free and open Indo-Pacific region, especially freedom of navigation in the South China Sea. In this regard, during Harris' visit to Singapore, she articulated that the U.S. will maintain freedom of navigation in the region through effective partnerships. During her visit to Vietnam, she further expressed that the U.S. would continue to assist Vietnam in maintaining maritime security, and, in the future, more U.S. warships would visit Vietnam and defend freedom of navigation in the South China Sea. It is worth noting that the approach is not designed for the use of armed force against China, but to apply various "rule-based" pressures onto China, in order to compel it to abide by international law, including the Convention on the Law of the Sea and reduce Beijing's hegemony-seeking behavior.

The second reaffirmation refers to the U.S. commitment to actively strengthening its partnership with Indo-Pacific (especially ASEAN) countries, through which to work with regional partners in coping with the ongoing tensions with China and the "new normal" as set by the global COVID-19 pandemic.

Three priority

In coping with the new normal, the U.S. and ASEAN partners will surely focus on three priority issues, namely peace and security, economy and growth, and global health. First, their cooperation on peace and security issues will respond to China's regional hegemony-seeking behavior, in particular to its military threat in the South China Sea, and will demonstrate the willingness and commitment of Washington in partnering with ASEAN countries to maintain the rule-based international order for the purpose of strengthening freedom of navigation in a free and open Indo-Pacific region and the South China Sea. Second, given the U.S.–China trade war, economic security, with a focus on resilient supply chain restructuring, is on priority, in the context of the economic recession worsened by the COVID-19 pandemic. Clearly, the state of affairs requires more effective cooperation for recovery.

Third, Southeast Asian countries and Indo-Pacific stakeholders should be most concerned about how to implement effective pandemic control and post-pandemic recovery. Global health cooperation, especially in effective vaccination, is imperative for these countries that prioritize popular livelihood and welfare. During her visit to Vietnam, Harris also announced that she would provide another 1 million supplementary doses of the Moderna vaccine to Vietnam, in addition to previous 5 million doses of it. While Vietnam is developing an indigenous vaccine, the move was timely given a resurgence of the endemic.

Evidently, the above characteristics of Harris' Asia trip highlight that the United States is willing to be a prime partner of ASEAN and its member states, while they are unwilling to take a side between the United States and China. Washington understands this dilemma. Therefore, Washington will keep working on strengthening the partnership with specific demands and actions and then winning the trust and support of Southeast Asian partners.

ASEAN's Take in Post-Pandemic Recovery

ASEAN took the lead in 2020 in charting the framework of regional collaboration during and after the COVID-19 pandemic, that is, the ASEAN Comprehensive Recovery Framework (ACRF). ASEAN has approved and implemented a comprehensive recovery framework under the pandemic toward the steady post-pandemic recovery. This is a strategic reference for ASEAN collaboration for re-building economic and social resilience. The ACRF, on the one hand, unites the ASEAN countries to jointly respond to the challenges imposed by the pandemic, and at the same time focuses on specific cooperation plans (ASEAN 2020). Thus, the United States can contribute to stability and growth of the Indo-Pacific through security and economic engagement, particularly in the post pandemic era.

According to ACRF, ASEAN will work together on five dimensions to lead the region toward a full recovery, including five broad strategic goals: (1) strengthening the health systems; (2) strengthening human security including social security and food safety; (3) maximizing the potential of Intra-ASEAN market and broader economic integration; (4) accelerating inclusive digital transformation; and (5) creating a more sustainable and resilient future (see Table 1).

The strategic goals and priorities outlined in the framework and the approach to implementation are the head and tail. Of course, they also show that ASEAN attaches great importance to the connectivity and facilitation of the supply chain. But, great attention has been directed to the active response and collective actions to the existing or emerging threats imposed by the COVID-19 pandemic and U.S.–China rivalry, to social stability and common challenges of the regional community. They, to some extent, present a rough reference for policy action to craft a "survival chain" as the key drive for the survival and resilience of one country (Yang 2022), rather than a supply chain of certain component for some specific manufacture industry. In other words, while the cooperation of ASEAN countries as highlighted in the ACRF focuses on economic recovery, smoother development of the ASEAN community will be made feasible through adequate social recovery and resilience,

Table 1:   ACRF Broader Strategies and Key Priorities

Broad strategy (1): *Enhancing health systems*	1-a. Building and sustaining current health gains and measures. 1-b. Maintaining and strengthening essential health services. 1-c. Strengthening vaccine security and self-reliance including its equitable access, affordability, safety, and quality. 1-d. Enhancing capacity of human resources for health. 1-e. Strengthening prevention and preparedness detection, and response and resilience to emerging/re-emerging infectious diseases, public health emergencies and pandemics; and strengthening relevant regional coordination mechanisms including development of health protocols or frameworks during recovery phase. 1-f. Enhancing capacity of public health services to enable health emergency response including ensuring food safety and nutrition in emergencies.
Broader Strategy (2): *Strengthening human security*	2-a. further strengthening and broadening of social protection and social welfare, especially for vulnerable groups. 2-b. Ensuring food security, food safety, and nutrition. 2-c. Promoting human capital development, including: (i) promoting digital skills and literacy, and 21st-century skills in basic education, TVET, and higher education, through Human Resource Development Roadmap for Changing World of Work; (ii) reskilling and upskilling for employment, including digital skills and creating job opportunities; (iii) capacity building program of women and youth development; (iv) more contribution of rural area production by promoting digital skills of MSMEs; and (v) promoting eco-technology. 2-d. Ensuring responsive labor Policies for the new normal through social dialogue (cross-border labor movement, WFH, occupational health, and safety). 2-e. Mainstreaming gender equality throughout recovery scheme and actions of ASEAN.

Table 1: (*Continued*)

Broader Strategy (3): *Maximizing the potential of the intra-ASEAN market and broader economic integration*	3-a. Keeping markets open for trade and investment.
	3-b. Strengthening supply chain connectivity and resilience.
	3-c. Enabling trade facilitation in the new normal.
	3-d. Elimination of Non-Tariff Barriers (NTBs) and cutting down market-distorting policies.
	3-e. Setting up travel bubble/corridor framework. (*Note*: ASEAN Travel Corridor Arrangement is now being discussed at SOM. As agreed by the SOM on September 7, 2020, the Concept Note would be consulted with other sectoral bodies. The Concept Note has since been circulated to SOMHD, STOM, and DGICM for comments/inputs.)
	3-f. Strengthening transport facilitation/connectivity.
	3-g. Accelerating sectoral recovery (tourism, MSMEs), and safeguarding employment in most affected sectors.
	3-h. Streamlining and expediting investment process and facilitation and joint promotion initiatives.
	3-i. Enhancing Public and Private Partnership (PPP) for regional connectivity.
	3-j. Signing and early entry into force of RCEP.
Broader Strategy (4): *Accelerating inclusive digital transformation*	4-a. Preparing for the Fourth Industrial Revolution.
	4-b. Promoting e-commerce and the digital economy.
	4-c. Promoting e-government and e-services.
	4-d. Promoting financial inclusion including through digital financial services and regional payment connectivity.
	4-e. Providing a digital platform and related policy for promoting MSME digital upskilling and providing digital technology and fin-tech to access markets.
	4-f. Enhancing connectivity.
	4-g. Promoting ICT in education.
	4-h. Improving digital legal framework and institutional capacity.
	4-i. Strengthening data governance and cybersecurity.
	4-j. Strengthening consumer protection.
	4-k. Promoting the adoption of digital technologies in ASEAN businesses.

(*Continued*)

Table 1:   (*Continued*)

Broader Strategy (5):	5-a. Promoting sustainable development in all dimensions.
Advancing toward a more sustainable and resilient future	5-b. Facilitating the transition to sustainable energy.
	5-c. Building green infrastructure and addressing basic infrastructure gaps.
	5-d. Promoting sustainable and responsible investment.
	5-e. Promoting high-value industries, sustainability, and productivity.
	5-f. Managing disaster risks and strengthening disaster management.
	5-g. Promoting sustainable financing [these are the efforts undertaken by the WC-CMD and ACMF via the capital markets. These are the outcomes of engagements with the private sectors via round table discussions and comprise actionable recommendations that focus on the private sector, and broad recommendations that are to be implemented by AMS individually based on their respective timelines, and others by ASEAN as a region].

Source: Summarized from the ACRF: Implementation Plans (ASEAN 2020).

where the basic significance of the comprehensive recovery framework lies (Yang 2022). Evidently, this ACRF is also prioritized in the U.S.–ASEAN Special Summit held in Washington D.C. in the mid May.

New Directions for Navigating New Political Economy in the Region

The new political economy in Southeast Asia should highlight the complex regional issues. To sum up the entire analysis and discussion of this book, the last section will unpack essential directions for building a more resilient region in the near future:

(1) Great power struggle is still important. With the strengthening of U.S. engagement in Southeast Asia, China will counter the move by reinforcing its cooperation with Southeast Asian countries and support for ASEAN during a third term of Xi Jinping.

(2) The institutional architecture for international cooperation needs to pivot on strengthening ASEAN, both its institution and community.

(3) ASEAN's comprehensive recovery plan (ACRF) aimed at strengthening public health system, steady development of regional trade and investment, ensuring human security and promoting a collective action plan that can meet future challenges will all be more welcomed by regional countries and major powers in the Indo-Pacific region.

(4) Finally, the people-centered agenda and approach for regional cooperation and strategies will be deemed necessary so that the social resilience of regional and respective societies will be seriously taken into consideration for post-pandemic recovery.

As for the prospect of the research finding of this book, the following scenarios are to be highlighted.

(1) Although the U.S.–China rivalry continues, the role of other major and middle powers in the Indo-Pacific will be highlighted. They may be more proactive in facilitating partnership with ASEAN partners. Among them, the collaboration between Japan and Taiwan in particular will make a distinct contribution to the prosperity and stability of Southeast Asia.

(2) Post-pandemic recovery and reconstruction is the focus of collaboration among ASEAN countries and Indo-Pacific stakeholders. The process will not be in a short term, and will involve great demand of resources and financing over next 3–5 years. Also, the process does not simply aim at the *status quo ante* in political economy at the national and regional levels, but at a higher level of resiliency in order and governance that is built on the experience and lesson regarding the recent 2-year battle against the pandemic. The ACRF will definitely be a major reference for regional stakeholders and major powers, individually or jointly, in search of their strategy and priority.

(3) Finally, although the Russo-Ukrainian war will cast a profound impact on the liberal international liberal order, it has also consolidated the consensus and unity of democratic countries to a certain extent. Regardless of the final outcome, hopefully, the post-war international order will make an authoritarian regime to take unilateral aggressive behavior more difficult.

References

ASEAN. 2020. *The ASEAN Comprehensive Recovery Framework.* Jakarta: ASEAN Secretariat.

Yang, Alan H. 2022. From Supply Chain to Survival Chain? Strategizing ASEAN–Taiwan Collaboration in the Post-Pandemic Recovery. *AEI Insights,* 8: Forthcoming.

Index

Printed in the United States
by Baker & Taylor Publisher Services